WITH DIGNITY

Recent Titles in
Contributions in Political Science
Series Editor: Bernard K. Johnpoll

The Liberal Future in America: Essays in Renewal
Philip Abbott and Michael B. Levy, editors

A Change of Course: The West German Social Democrats and NATO,
1957-1961
Stephen J. Artner

Power and Policy in Transition: Essays Presented on the Tenth Anniversary of
the National Committee on American Foreign Policy in Honor of Its Founder,
Hans J. Morgenthau
Vojtech Mastny, editor

Ideology and Soviet Industrialization
Timothy W. Luke

Administrative Rulemaking: Politics and Processes
William F. West

Recovering from Catastrophes: Federal Disaster Relief Policy and Politics
Peter J. May

Judges, Bureaucrats, and the Question of Independence: A Study of the Social
Security Administration Hearing Process
Donna Price Cofer

Party Identification, Political Behavior, and the American Electorate
Sheldon Kamieniecki

Without Justice for All: The Constitutional Rights of Aliens
Elizabeth Hull

Neighborhood Organizations: Seeds of a New Urban Life
Michael R. Williams

The State Politics of Judicial and Congressional Reform: Legitimizing Criminal
Justice Policies
Thomas Carlyle Dalton

WITH DIGNITY

The Search for Medicare and Medicaid

Sheri I. David

CONTRIBUTIONS IN POLITICAL SCIENCE,
NUMBER 132

GREENWOOD PRESS
WESTPORT, CONNECTICUT • LONDON, ENGLAND

Library of Congress Cataloging in Publication Data

David, Sheri I.
  With dignity.

  (Contributions in political science, ISSN 0147-1066;
no. 132)
    Bibliography: p.
    Includes index.
    1. Medicare—History.   2. Medicaid—History.
I. Title.   II. Series.
HD7102.U4D275   1985   362.1'04252'0973   84-27941
ISBN 0-313-24720-X (lib. bdg.)

Library of Congress Catalog Card Number: 84-27941
ISBN: 0-313-24720-X
ISSN: 0147-1066

First published in 1985

Greenwood Press
A division of Congressional Information Service, Inc.
88 Post Road West
Westport, Connecticut 06881

Printed in the United States of America

10 9 8 7 6 5 4 3 2 1

FOR IDA FELDMAN,
on her eightieth birthday

Contents

Acknowledgments

Since the events of the book are barely twenty-five years old, I owe many debts to people who were willing to search their memories in order to aid me. Primarily I would like to thank Wilbur J. Cohen for extending an hour interview well beyond and for allowing me access to lengthy and excellent Oral Histories. I would like to thank Nelson Cruikshank and Elizabeth Wickenden for sharing with me their thoughts on the events of Medicare. Thanks also to Wilbur Mills, whose genius one can't help but admire after researching such a topic as this. I am appreciative of the most helpful staff at the Library of Congress, the John F. Kennedy Library, the Lyndon Baines Johnson Library, and the excellent Oral History project on Social Security at Columbia University.

Any historian incurs professional debts. I owe an enormous one to Arthur M. Schlesinger, Jr. I am grateful not only for his excellent editing, but also for his patient confidence that sustained me through numerous delays in finishing the first draft of this book. Two other professors helped by reading this work in its entirety: Richard Gerber and Richard Wade.

I would like to thank my typists, Mary Chiffriller and Leni Kecher, for their assistance.

To my parents, Rosanne and Jack Lichtenstein, who helped in so many ways, and who waited so long for this book to be a reality, I owe a very special debt.

To my sons, Matthew Todd David and Ryan Douglas David, whose births and childhood frequently took precedence over my writing and research, I acknowledge a debt of another kind.

My husband, Edward Daniel David, has lived with this work as long as I have. My gratitude for his being there is overwhelming.

Introduction

The Medicare bill of 1965 reflects a deep ambivalence that Americans have long felt about poverty. The traditional idea was that poverty was caused by personal moral delinquency. In the early twentieth century some social thinkers argued that poverty could result from other factors: ill health, unemployment, old age, widowhood, and disability. Judging from the tumultuous history of legislation when state and federal government tried to ameliorate those factors, it seems that many Americans were never completely convinced that poverty was not the fault of the individual.

It took a major Depression to pass the Social Security Act, which at least provided protection from poverty in old age and widowhood. It took twenty more years of argument to get a disability bill passed by Congress. Ill health took even longer. The majority of Americans still wait for a solution to the unaffordable costs of sickness and hospitals.

It was ironic that reform leaders in the 1920s predicted that health insurance would be among the first items of progressive legislation to be part of the Social Security Act. However, it was dropped by President Franklin D. Roosevelt and his advisors because they were afraid that it would hold back the rest of the bill—so great was American reluctance to interfere in the medical field.

Thirty years later Medicare required a bitter fight in Congress after a tremendous expenditure of money by lobbying groups such as the American Medical Association and the American Federation of Labor-Congress of Industrial Organizations (AFL-CIO). Medicare copies the already successful Social Security program in using the social insurance principle as its method of finance. The advocates of Medicare narrowed its goals to cover hospital insurance only for the elderly.

Therein lay the problem. The Social Security approach meant that services were distributed to rich and poor alike—all who paid in to the system. The alternative was a charity or welfare approach, where services were distributed to those who could prove their need. What constituted proof was a means test. Such a test, popular in the United States for years, was a carry-over from the English Poor Law tradition.

While the means test was an important method to determine who "deserved" help, the popular abhorrence of such a test was equally important. To have to prove poverty before a judge was so awful an experience that many risked starvation or lengthy sickness before seeking help. Liberals sought a better way to dispense funds.

That better way was the method employed by Social Security: social insurance—a contributory payment system administered by the Federal Government. It had several advantages. Help was a matter of earned right. One contributed to a trust fund when one was employed, on a pay-as-you-go basis. The money was available when it was needed. There was no proof of need required, no relinquishing of life savings or house in order to receive Public Aid, and no embarrassing search into personal financial affairs.

Since 1935 the Social Security system has been enlarged to include a broader base of people—even those who did not pay into the Fund. The ability to do so is considered one of the benefits of the insurance part of the law. The insurance principle enabled the Social Security Administration to spread the risk. State unemployment programs also use the insurance method of payment.

Part of the debate over Medicare was whether the insurance method of payment would work in the case of ill health. Social insurance advocates from the early part of the twentieth century such as I. M. Rubinow, and later ones such as Wilbur Cohen, I. S. Falk, Arthur Altmeyer, Nelson Cruikshank, and Robert Ball, believed that social insurance was the best method of providing protection against ill health. Many doctors thought otherwise. They argued that the inability of the poor and the elderly to meet the rising costs of health care could best be handled in other ways. Those ways were reflected in a long assortment of bills offered as alternatives to Medicare. They generally incorporated some definition of need or means test to prove indigency. The Kerr-Mills program, passed in 1960 and establishing the blueprint for the

Medicaid system for poor people, even tried to define "medical" indigency.

Since the subject involved medicine, the issue was far more complex than whether to use a charity/welfare approach or a social insurance method to aid those who could not afford medical care. Medicine has always been an individualized business in this country. Doctors' privacy was sacrosanct. Government medicine on the European model was misunderstood and feared. For many Americans it sounded like one more step toward socialism. It threatened to entangle people's lives in bureaucratic red tape. It meant a free vacation in the hospital for those patients who abused the system. It meant, pessimists cried, the downfall of American medicine.[1]

Because of the private nature of American medicine, ill health was the last frontier to be explored in mitigating poverty. Before that territory was conquered finally, albeit for the elderly only, almost every conceivable alternative was debated: Federal subsidies to private insurance carriers; state grants to those in need; an insurance system limited to long-term illness; a call to the medical profession to donate hours to charity; a government co-insurance plan for those who could not afford to purchase health insurance; tax rebates for the same purpose; Social Security rebates; etc. In 1965, after 30 years of Social Security, many Americans were still not convinced of the benefits of Social Insurance. The means test-charity approach was very much present as an alternative to Medicare.

The Medicare Act, as passed in 1965, did not end the debate by any means. The act was a master stroke of political compromise, designed to please all sides. Representative Wilbur Mills (D-Arkansas), architect of the final bill, incorporated three different health care plans into a single law; a "three layered cake" it was called. Each plan, however, was based on a different philosophy. Put together, they did not solve the dilemma of the charity or social insurance debate. They postponed it for later discussion. The Medicare part of the bill, incorporating the social insurance method, appears to be working well. The only problem with the law has been the government's inability to control skyrocketing costs. Medicaid, the charity part, is in a terrible mess of misuse of funds and scandals.

This is not to say that the whole history of Medicare legislation was always one of conscious choice. More had to do with emotions, values, political give-and-take, and to an even greater extent, personalities. If what Wilbur Cohen said was true, it was a very Hegelian debate right from the start. The thesis was the compulsory health insurance bills proposed by liberals and labor. The AMA's violent opposition in conjunction with Congressional conservative leaders provided the antithesis. The combination of Medicare with Medicaid was the synthesis.[2]

Health insurance will continue to generate debate, with new antithesis and synthesis. The rising costs of health care make that inevitable. Senator Edward Kennedy's legislative proposals for national health insurance require Americans to make a comprehensive commitment to the social insurance principle. In order to make some sense out of the current legislative proposals it is important to look back at the events leading up to 1965. By recalling the history of Medicare, we can learn what was done or not done and why. We can then examine present and future possibilities more intelligently.

WITH DIGNITY

1

Focus on the Elderly

Representative Jere Cooper of Tennessee, Democratic chairman of the House Ways and Means Committee in 1957, was not interested in any new version of a national health insurance bill that, in one form or another, had been offered to Congress every year since 1943. Wilbur Mills, soon to be Cooper's successor as chairman, rejected the new bill without even looking at it. The third Democrat in seniority on Ways and Means was Noble Gregory of Kentucky, and he too declined sponsorship. Next in line was Aime Forand, Democrat from Rhode Island. He at least agreed to think about it.[1]

It was the end of the 85th Congress. A small group of national health insurance advocates, I. S. Falk, Wilbur Cohen, Robert Ball, and Nelson Cruikshank, decided that it was time to try a successor to the Wagner-Murray-Dingell bills. The Wagner-Murray-Dingell bills proposed a system of contributory health insurance for the entire population. Despite President Harry Truman's warm support, the bills floundered. Failing in a broad-scale approach, Falk, Cohen, Ball, and Cruikshank created a new limited bill, applying only to those over 65 years of age and only to those participating in the Social Security system. To that special segment of the population the bill offered 60 days of hospitalization, 60 days of nursing home coverage and some surgical benefits.

There were several reasons why a new focus on the elderly was appropriate in 1957. The number of persons over 65 was increasing. As against 3 million American citizens over 65 in 1900, there were 14 million in 1957. That represented a growth rate of approximately three times that of the rest of the population.[2] The trend of the 1950s was toward a lowering of the retirement age and formalizing it to 65.

Older people were visibly left out of advances made for the rest of the population. During the 1950s, labor unions made significant gains at the collective bargaining table in including health insurance for their workers. Retired employees, however, were usually not included in the new contracts. Employees found that on retirement their policies were automatically cancelled, or cancelled at their first illness. If by some chance they could keep their insurance, they found their premiums unaffordable. Given their age, they could not qualify for a new policy. The problems of those retiring on a pension were more apparent in the light of the new benefits won by younger workers.[3]

Nor did the elderly benefit very much from the tremendous growth, in the 1940s and 1950s, in Blue Cross and Blue Shield coverage. The Blues were non-profit organizations. At first, Blue Cross allowed its holders to keep their policies after retirement at the same premium but for greatly reduced coverage. Any worker who expected to do this had to make such a choice early in his career. He could not suddenly decide to keep his health insurance the day he retired. Moreover, if he failed to make a payment, his policy was permanently cancelled.[4]

As more companies went to other private insurance firms to negotiate for union health plans, those private carriers were able to move further in the health fields and lower their premiums for group coverage. By 1957, corporations purchased about one-half of all health insurance policies from commercial carriers.[5] Blue Cross was left with a larger share of high risk clients. Blue Cross was eventually forced to raise its premiums for senior citizens in order to stay in business. By 1958, it too was out of the price range of those living on a pension or Social Security checks.[6]

Employers were loath to include retired workers in union health programs. The expense was too great. Private insurance carriers were not anxious to get into the field. There was a growing gap in the new field of health insurance. Only 22 percent of all labor contracts provided medical benefits for retired workers. Only 1.8 million persons over 65 were so covered. In such contracts, only the retired worker and not his spouse was covered. Also the worker had to be with the company at least 20 years to gain medical benefits.[7]

It was estimated that the average elderly couple had to spend more than 15 percent of their income for a health insurance policy that covered little. In a study made by the Bureau of Old-Age and Survivors Insurance, only 430 out of every 1,000 senior citizens had any hospital or health policy. Of that 430, 285 had hospital benefits with some surgical reimbursement, and 145 persons had hospital coverage only. The study found that very few persons over 73 had any coverage.[8] Also, those not eligible for a union pension or Social Security check were even worse off. They could ill afford to purchase a health plan.

In the field of education a cultural revolution was underway that also affected the plight of the elderly. More young people went to college. Their parents were hard pressed to purchase their children's education and at the same time meet the bills for aging parents' health care.[9] The economic squeeze strengthened the case for Medicare. The government needed to save its citizens from having to choose between their children's education and their parents' health.[10]

Finally, the architects of health insurance for the elderly saw it as a promising issue for Democrats seeking to combat the popularity of the Eisenhower Administration. As a political issue, it had both substance and appeal.[11]

The two men who handed the bill to Forand, Nelson Cruikshank and Andrew Biemiller, both from the American Federation of Labor, knew that Forand was not entirely committed to the bill as written. Still, they had found someone on the right committee to submit their bill.

Forand was near the end of his political career (he retired in 1960) when he received the health insurance bill that quickly became known as the Forand Bill.

He did not spend too much time thinking about the bill. A few days before the close of the 85th session, he quietly dropped the bill into the hopper. It was a shock to all supporters, Forand recalled. "They didn't think I was going to do it."[12]

Throughout his Congressional career Forand had been interested in easing the burden of retirement for workers. After being elected to Congress in 1949, he joined the Ways and Means Committee where he immediately gravitated into the welfare fields.[13] He saw the bill as his chance to help the "old folks."[14]

Personally, Forand had not made up his mind yet about the compulsory insurance approach. He privately doubted that any action would take place for at least ten years. Without press or publicity, he asked his Congressional colleagues to schedule hearings for the following year. By introducing the bill he hoped to stimulate discussion. Hearings might lead to a second and better piece of legislation.[15]

What happened to the Forand Bill after it was introduced was a complete surprise to its sponsor. Aime Forand, "a slightly bald, round, cigar-smoking man of medium size and somewhat lackluster manner,"[16] was catapulted into the center of publicity and controversy.

He learned of the bill's enthusiastic reception by Rhode Island workers, a factor which caused him to make a more personal commitment to the bill.[17] However, it shocked him that his bill generated such angry reaction from the American Medical Association. After a few months Forand decided to take advantage of the controversy and "keep fuel on the fire."[18] In fact, he thanked the AMA for advertising his bill so well.[19]

In 1958, Forand was almost alone in his support of health insurance for the elderly. Other liberal Congressmen had seen Wagner-Murray-Dingell bills introduced regularly since 1943. Nothing positive ever happened to them. Few thought that Forand's bill would have any different fate. None of the House leaders expressed an interest in the legislation and only a small handful of Forand's colleagues on Ways and Means offered support. (They were Democrats Cecil King of California, Eugene Keogh of New York, Tom O'Brien of Illinois, and Frank M. Karston of Mississippi.)

Jere Cooper died in 1957. The new Chairman of the Ways and Means Committee, Wilbur Mills, was so opposed to the Forand Bill that he refused to even schedule hearings. Forand's Bill and other bills extending Social Security benefits were discussed briefly in hearings on June 24, 1958. The Committee concluded that they needed more information.

The following year, 1959, Forand introduced HR4700 to the 86th Congress. His bill was "to provide hospital, surgical and nursing home benefits for old-age and survivor's insurance beneficiaries using the Social Security Administration mechanism; the program was to be financed by an increase in the Social Security tax." Forand was anxious to hold new hearings. After several frustrating attempts to persuade Mills to change his mind, Forand threatened to say publicly that Mills was personally holding up the hearings. Mills finally relented and scheduled hearings on HR4700 immediately after the July 4 Congressional break, a traditionally poor time to gain public attention. Even then, Mills would not participate and Forand had to chair the Hearings himself.[20]

The first, June 24, 1958, and the second, July 13–17, 1959, Ways and Means Committee Hearings on the Forand Bill accomplished two things: They set a pattern for subsequent hearings in terms of witnesses and their arguments, and they started a vast accumulation of materials "for the record." Accumulation of "the record" was psychologically important. It probably changed no one's mind. Nevertheless, it was necessary, almost as a ritual, for eventual passage. A record seemed especially important in 1958 because little data was available on the medical and financial capabilities of older people. Whatever paltry information collected by Forand and his committee colleagues was obtained with the indirect cooperation of the Social Security Administration.[21] A Department of Health, Education and Welfare study on the feasibility of using the Social Security System to pay out hospital benefits was completed the Friday before the 1959 hearings. It had been due three months earlier.[22] The hearings called attention to the fact that both proponents and opponents needed more statistics to support their cases.

In addition to establishing a written record, these first hearings introduced the arguments in the Medicare debate. Congressmen (and to some extent the public) became familiar with the people and organizations that would testify in future hearings. Later changes were mostly on details: how much and how long. The Forand Bill, with its simple 60 days of hospitalization and 60 days of nursing home coverage, became the original script from which each side opened its dialogue. The pros regarded the Forand Bill as a minimum; the cons rejected it as too much and on the wrong track.

The primary witnesses on behalf of health insurance for the elderly using the social security approach were men from the Social Security Administration itself, such as Wilbur Cohen, Arthur Altmeyer and Charles Schottland, or labor officials such as Nelson Cruikshank who helped write the Forand Bill, George Meany, and Walter Reuther who had tried for years to get a more radical bill passed.

When Cohen appeared as witness before the first Ways and Means Committee hearings on Medicare, he told the congressmen that he was responding to the same arguments against health insurance that he had heard in 1945. Cohen observed that public opinion had changed little on the subject. The number one fear of those opposing health insurance was the use of compulsory contributions and participation.[23]

Cohen, like other advocates of social insurance, believed that without compulsory taxation many people will not voluntarily protect themselves, whether for ill health, old age, or unemployment. Years before, I. M. Rubinow, one of the early advocates of social insurance, had insisted that a voluntary insurance system presupposed the existence of a budget surplus and a cultural appreciation of the benefits of an insurance program. These presuppositions, Rubinow said, were least present in the lower sector of the population that needed the most protection.[24] Cohen explained that citizens faced with a disastrous economic situation, having no savings or other resources, would seek public assistance paid out of general taxes. In the end, the taxpayer would pay a greater bill because of those who did not or could not take adequate insurance against emergencies. "Compulsion," Cohen added, was only an emotionally charged word that made little sense when accepting one kind of taxation while rejecting another.

Cohen pointed out to the Ways and Means Committee that even a voluntary insurance system was not really voluntary at all. If an employer takes a contribution on an insurance policy for his employees, he will also take a tax deduction from the U.S. Treasury. The average taxpayer would not voluntarily agree to that deduction.[25] Social insurance, while it involved compulsion, is best defined as a policy of organized society which deals with a social problem through the use of insurance.[26]

As a bonus, Cohen told the Committee, the Forand Bill would remove the high risk group from private insurance rolls so that the insurance companies could do a better job with other age groups. This argument that Medicare was actually helping the private companies was used frequently throughout the debate. The logic, however, failed to impress the insurance industry.[27]

Local and state governments could not be expected to handle the problems of the aged, Cohen argued. United States citizens were too mobile. They worked and paid taxes in one state and then retired in another. There would be the difficult question of which state was responsible for their aid. For practical reasons, a national solution was called for. From Cohen's vantage point the logical solution lay in applying Social Security methods toward health care.[28]

Wilbur Cohen's former boss, Arthur Altmeyer, who had served 18 years as chairman of the Social Security Board from 1935 to 1953, was not able to attend the hearings. He sent a telegram, read the first day by Forand. Altmeyer was widely respected by politicians and labor alike. He stated in his telegram that he had no reservations about the feasibility of the program called for in Forand's Bill.[29]

Returning to Washington to testify on behalf of the Bill was another social security expert, Dr. Charles Schottland. Schottland had served the Social Security Administration between 1954 and 1958 as an Eisenhower appointee. He retired from that position in 1958 to serve as Dean of the Florence Heller School of Social Work at Brandeis University.

Schottland, who had a long background in social work, came to the dismal conclusion, which he shared with the committee, that medical care in the United States was "like any other commodity," available for those who had the purchase price.[30] He thought that there were five ways of buying medical care: an individual paid for his own care; a voluntary (charity) organization paid; an individual had private insurance; he went on public assistance and the government paid; or this country legislated social insurance for health.

Charity organizations, Dr. Schottland added, would be the first to admit that they could not handle the medical costs of the elderly. If the individual got by on the first four ways for most of his life, in his upper years his choices diminished. They were most often limited to two: public assistance or Social Insurance. The latter was a *uniquely American* method of insuring against social risk. Clearly it was a better alternative than public assistance with its degrading means tests. As for the possible administrative difficulties, Schottland personally doubted they would cause problems as great as those faced by the Social Security planners.[31]

A fourth member of the Social Security team who testified for the Forand Bill was J. Douglas Brown, Dean of Faculty and Professor of Economics at Princeton University. Brown had helped to write the original Social Security Act and served as Chairman to the Advisory Council between 1937 and 1938. After that he held numerous posts in the Social Security Administration. Like the others, Brown thought that the Social Insurance method was the best payment mechanism to help the elderly with their health bills.[32] Brown believed that people would be willing to pay the costs of such a program and that they would not object to extending the Social Security system for such a purpose. He also believed that Social Security could be safely enlarged to incorporate medical payments and that only the Federal Government could handle the job.[33]

During the first hearings, attendance by members of the Ways and Means Committee was not great, but those who attended and disliked the Forand Bill did not sit back passively. Cohen, Altmeyer, and Brown were critically attacked by Representative Bruce Alger. Only Schottland escaped controversy, perhaps because of his association with the Eisenhower Administration. Alger asked about the ideas of the contributory method which Forand's Bill employed: specifically, where would the money come from for the 13 million people who would be covered, but who had not contributed into the system. Brown answered Alger by analyzing the nature of the Social Insurance concept. It planned to make up the difference from future contributions. The same was true of Social Security. Whenever Old Age Survivor and Disability Insurance benefits were increased people were not asked to go back and contribute more. Those who were eligible received the increase immediately. The whole system always relied on future contributions.[34]

When Walter Reuther came before the Committee, representing one and a half million workers as President of the United Auto Workers, he contended that the Forand Bill was a very modest yet practical attempt to deal with the "most glaring deficiency in health security today."[35] Reuther attempted to talk in non-ideological terms and stressed the practical aspects of using the Social Security system for health coverage. In trying to minimize the purpose of Forand's Bill, he unintentionally struck a match under the opposition. Declaring the Bill a modest step, he honestly stated that he would like to see the benefits go further. The Forand Bill was a first step that would not solve all of the health problems of the elderly. That was exactly what all of the opponents were afraid of: Forand's Bill was a foot in the door. Reuther had lost his efficacy as a supporter.

The fear of the "first step" or the "opening wedge" was so pronounced in the minds of doctors, Republicans, conservative Democrats, and probably a good part of the American public that the liberals actually won an ideological point. Instead of having to establish *that* the elderly needed health insurance, they had to spend their time convincing everyone that *only* the elderly needed coverage.

As soon as Reuther completed his statement, Bruce Alger opened a verbal attack against him. The rotund and idiosyncratic Congressman from Texas had been angry at Reuther even before the hearings began.

Alger's congressional district in Dallas included a large union population and Reuther had given the Texan a score of zero for his congressional votes on labor issues. As a result Alger almost lost his renomination in 1958.[36]

Alger called the Forand Bill un-American. Government regulation of medicine means government control of medicine. When combined with compulsory taxation, the result was socialized medicine. Reuther replied by defining un-American as something that would be contrary to our concept of human freedom and the values and rights of the human individual. Alger replied tartly, "Your definition of words is positively amazing."[37]

Another labor leader, Nelson Cruikshank, took the stand on the second day of hearings. One of the architects of the Forand Bill, Cruikshank became the American Federation of Labor spokesman for Medicare. Accepting the politics of the possible, and sharing Wilbur Cohen's philosophy of gradualism, Cruikshank was a more credible representative of labor than Reuther.

Labor, Cruikshank said, supported the "earned right" principle upon which Social Security was based: by virtue of a person paying into the system he or she established a right to the benefits that he or she could claim at some point in the future.[38] This arrangement was also called a contributory system.

Cruikshank mentioned precedents that already established the Federal Government in the health field: aid to hospitals; Veterans Hospitals; military health benefits; and public assistance. His was not a radical argument. Nevertheless, opponents on the Ways and Means Committee again raised the objection of compulsion. What about those who did not want to contribute? Why have a mandatory program in a free society? The objection to compulsion was not so much intellectual as emotional. The response was obvious: Even in a free society there exist forms of compulsion such as education, taxes, tolls, etc. Compulsion can mean nothing more than the laws that a group of people make in a democracy that all are forced to obey. Only the word sounded ominous.[39]

During these first hearings on the Forand Bill, negative responses came from four main sources: the American Medical Association, the Eisenhower Administration, the insurance industry, and the individual congressmen on the Ways and Means Committee.

The AMA had been vigilant against any hint of government interference in its domain since 1943. In 1957, they were still expecting a broad attack, like the Wagner-Murray-Dingell national health insurance program. Health insurance for just the elderly almost slipped their attention.

The President of the AMA, Dr. David Allman, announced to the December 1957 meeting of the delegates that the Forand Bill was "at least nine parts evil and one part sincerity."[40] After realizing the depth of Forand's new threat, the AMA dropped its conviction about the one part sincerity and directed its resources toward the new legislative battle. Over the course of the next seven years, they operated a "War Chest," spent millions of dollars, and hired a public relations firm to fight Medicare.

At the hearings in 1959, Dr. Leonard Larson, Chairman of the Board of Trustees of the AMA, argued that the unhappy situation of the elderly could best be handled by the medical profession—privately and voluntarily. The AMA viewed the medical problem of the aged as more of a social problem. Chronic illness, such as diabetes or hearing loss, was not disabling and required no government legislation. What the elderly needed was a place in society—a role as well as a place to live where medical care was available. Larson argued that any Federal legislation would "undermine or destroy" the progress of the medical profession.[41]

Larson raised the problem of need. Not only would Forand's program cover at least a million people who did not need aid, but it would *not* cover about 3 million people who needed it most. In fact, this group of indigent elderly was outside of the Social Security system, depending on Old-Age assistance programs run by the states. Forand and the proponents of his Bill had wanted to stick to the Social Security recipients for simplicity and reasons of principle.[42]

Dr. Frederick Swartz told the Committee that if Forand's Bill passed, the Federal Government would find itself in the disbursement of money, determining benefits, and setting rates of compensation. The government would get into the business of auditing the records of health facilities and find itself trying to enforce standards of care. When the government guarantees services "which it cannot itself provide, it inevitably tends to control the purveyors of these services."[43] The President of the American Society of Internal Medicine put the matter in more national terms. "Does it not seem inconsistent that we should be fighting Communism in Geneva while introducing legislation supporting it in Washington?"[44]

President Dwight Eisenhower had made commitments to the AMA during his first term of office. The Republican President had promised Administration opposition to National Health Insurance in exchange for AMA support of the proposed Department of HEW. The American Medical Association had prevented Truman from establishing the new department. The medical organization kept its part of the bargain and HEW was established in 1955.[45]

Eisenhower was against health insurance anyway. His personal feelings were on record. "If all that Americans want is security, they can go to prison. They'll have enough to eat, a bed, and a roof over their heads."[46] Eisenhower never liked to be reminded that as an Army officer he had always been the recipient of government medicine.

Arthur Flemming, Secretary of HEW, was the lead witness for the 1959 hearings. For the record he told the Committee exactly what his predecessor, Marion Folsom, told the Committee in 1958: that the objective of adequate medical care could be achieved through individual and organized voluntary action. A health insurance program "would become frozen in a vast and unfair government system, foreclosing future opportunity for private groups, non-profit and commercial, to demonstrate their capacity to deal with the problem."[47]

Flemming was following the Republican line of letting the the private insurance industry have a chance to develop positive programs.[48] Six months later, the President sent Congress a warning. "The Social Security System," he said, "is not intended as a substitute for private savings, pension plans, and insurance protection. It is rather intended as a foundation upon which other forms of protection can be built."[49] The President was buying time for the private sector.

Blue Cross and Blue Shield, as well as private insurance companies represented nationally by the Health Insurance Association, responded quickly to Eisenhower's embryo programs. The private companies flooded the press with statistics about their ability to handle the problem, given sufficient time. They assured the public that "a great many people are working on the problem." Only one or two of the programs ever materialized but the Eisenhower Administration kept their "we can do it privately" argument. Continental Casualty Company of Chicago and Mutual of Omaha Company initiated limited state drives to cover the elderly for up to 31 days in the hospital and between $5 and $200 of surgical benefits at a cost of $6.50 a month. James Stuart, an associate of Blue Cross, labeled the Forand Bill as a "frightening nightmare."

Stuart said, "Just think of all the families that will rush aged relatives into nursing homes at the government's expense."[50]

Actually, the Eisenhower-Nixon team did not have to work very hard to convince Congress of the evils of Forand's Bill. Opposition within the Ways and Means Committee was more than enough. Of the 25 Committee members, 15 were Democrats and ten were Republicans. Besides Forand, only four Democrats on the Committee supported the Bill. Outside of Ways and Means, members of the House of Representatives who either co-sponsored Forand's Bill or offered similar bills were equally few: James Roosevelt, Seymour Halpern, John Dingell, Isodore Dollinger, Charles O'Porter, Lee Metcalf, and Joseph Karth. Forand's Bill would have to go a long way before it received the support of the majority of the Ways and Means Committee members and the majority of the House.

In 1958, the leading opponents of the Forand Bill on the Ways and Means Committee were Chairman Wilbur Mills who did not even want to schedule hearings on the subject, John Byrnes, Thomas Curtis, and Bruce Alger. Of the four, Alger was most outspoken at the 1958 hearings. His philosophy was simple. "You are not going to change human nature by passing another law." Alger was a maverick from Texas, "a down home on the ranch boy," self-conscious about his law degree from Princeton. His guiding force was a moral antipathy toward politicians who meddled in business affairs and toward people who wanted something for nothing. He harassed and criticized liberal witnesses before the committee, but died before Medicare was passed in 1965.[51]

On the Republican side, John Byrnes and Thomas Curtis kept quiet during the initial hearings. Curtis was waiting to see what Byrnes would do and Byrnes was waiting for Mills to act. Neither Byrnes nor Curtis attended the sessions with any frequency. Only Representative Noah Mason joined Alger in questioning the witnesses. Mason, a retired school teacher past 75 years old, had little sympathy for his fellow senior citizens. He was a hard-bitten, self-made man, who frequently announced that he could always make his own way and pay his own medical expenses. Mason retired in 1962.[52]

The most impressive opposition, the single main force in preventing any Medicare-type legislation from passing the House, was Chairman Wilbur Mills. Neither Forand nor the American Federation of Labor people anticipated the depth of his opposition. The only thing that was known was the extent of his knowledge. Of the 535 members of Congress, Mills was the only man who thoroughly understood the Social Security System and the complicated actuarial basis of making estimates of financing needs for the future.[53]

Mills's opposition was based mostly on a personal commitment never to endorse a bill that lacked majority support in the Congress and in the nation. He also jealously guarded the financial soundness of Social Security and was loath to expand it.[54] "Wilbur always had been very jealous of guarding the Social Security Trust Fund without imposing additional taxes on anybody."[55]

All of the main issues of the Ways and Means Committee were decided upon by Mills. He built an alliance with senior ranking Republican John Byrnes to their mutual benefit. They rarely crossed each other on a key vote.[56] As a Congressional leader, he enjoyed almost total political independence. Rarely did a candidate oppose him for re-election. Perhaps because of that, he could be depended upon to think in national levels more than in local terms.

If a vote were taken in 1959, the results would have been eight yeas and 13 nays. Forand did not want a negative vote. What he had hoped for was accomplished. Discussion was underway and 720 pages were contributed to the record. It seemed clear to the advocates that either the Ways and Means Committee and Chairman Mills would have to change dramatically—or the Senate would have to carry the ball.

2

The Senate Debate Begins

The Senate was slower than the House to recognize and respond to the health needs of the elderly. In 1958, few Senators had identified the Forand Bill as a major piece of social legislation. Representative Aime Forand had not sought a Senate sponsor for his bill, nor had the group of AFL-CIO leaders from whom Forand got the bill, notably Nelson Cruikshank and Andrew Biemiller, selected a Senate sponsor.[1] Even so informed a liberal as Senator Paul Douglas (D-Illinois) first learned about the Forand Bill in the Fall of 1958 from a constituent. Said Douglas,

I shall never forget my surprise when at a scantily attended meeting at McLeansboro . . . deep in southern Illinois, a bedraggled oldster with many missing teeth asked me about the chances of passing the Forand bill. . . . Then he said, "I need it badly . . ." I immediately telephoned my Washington office. . . .[2]

Senator Wayne Morse (D-Oregon) was the first in the Senate to discover the new idea of using the Social Security system to finance hospital care for the elderly. Convinced of its moral rightness, Morse offered the Forand Bill in the Senate as S881 on February 2, 1959.[3] Morse had never met Forand personally and was not approached by any of the bill's supporters. He was acting entirely on his own.[4] Testifying before the House Ways and Means Committee Hearings on July 15, 1959, Morse explained his immediate and positive reaction by stressing the "social responsibility which we bear toward the elderly of our population."[5]

Morse's efforts, though, had little immediate impact. Because he was regarded as a maverick, his positions did not greatly influence his fellow Senators. Other leadership was required to win the legislation a serious hearing.[6]

The Senate members of the 86th Congress were generally conservative, content to follow President Eisenhower's non-innovative leadership. The Senate was ruled by a small clique popularly referred to as the "inner circle."[7] Republicans frequently formed a coalition with Southern Democrats, many of whom held key positions on the most important Senate committees.[8] A small minority of outspoken liberals, however, were potential sponsors of a health insurance program for the elderly—Hubert Humphrey (D-Minnesota), Vance Hartke (D-Indiana), Philip Hart (D-Michigan), Pat McNamara (D-Michigan), and Paul Douglas (D-Illinois). A bastion of liberalism resided in the Committee on Labor and Public Welfare ("Labor" for short). The Labor Committee, in fact, had kept the national health insurance movement alive throughout the 1940s and 1950s.

The Chairman of the Labor Committee, Senator Lister Hill, a moderate Democrat from Alabama, was much interested in health matters. Born in 1894, he was the son of a nationally prominent surgeon. He came to the Senate in 1938 as an active supporter of the New Deal. He sponsored the Hill-Burton Act of 1946 which established a national system of Federal subsidization of hospital construction, a measure unpopular with organized medicine. The American Medical Association agreed with Secretary of HEW Olvetta Culp Hobby when she labeled Hill-Burton as "Socialized Medicine by the back door."[9] Hill became chairman of the Labor Committee in 1955. The first major bill that he endorsed as chairman was a program to provide free distribution of the Salk polio vaccine to children in the United States—a program which won him the further enmity of the AMA.[10]

Hill had taken over as Chairman of Labor when Senator James E. Murray (D-Montana) became Chairman of the Interior Committee in 1955. Murray, sponsor of the numerous Wagner-Murray-Dingell national health insurance bills, had left a strong mark on the Labor Committee, building an excellent staff committed to the concept of social insurance.

One staff member, William Reidy, had worked on an idea to develop a Subcommittee on Aging and then hold hearings around the country. The purpose was to highlight local problems of the aged.[11] With a presidential election approaching, Reidy thought that the time was right for such action. He was politically astute and he was committed to reform. The problems of the elderly, ignored by the Eisenhower Administration, Reidy thought, were dynamic political issues. "We were surrounded by Democratic candidates who needed issues to go against Eisenhower's popularity."[12]

Reidy was well-schooled in reform movements. He graduated from the University of Wisconsin in 1934, along with Wilbur Cohen, when the University was a seedbed of progressive politics. Reidy eventually became an associate of Dr. Michael Davis, a New York physician and sociologist who headed the Committee for the Nation's Health—a volunteer organization dedicated to keeping alive the idea of national health insurance throughout the 1940s and 1950s.[13] (Its members included such luminaries as Eleanor Roosevelt, Mrs. Albert Lasker, Chester Bowles, Abe Fortas, Robert F. Wagner, Jr., Mrs. Leon Keyserling, and the presidents of the AFL and the CIO, William Green and Philip Murray.) Davis, an expert in medical economics, had worked with Murray on the series of Wagner-Murray-Dingell bills. When Murray needed staff assistance, he naturally turned to Davis for recommendations. Davis sent Reidy to Washington.[14]

The rest of the Labor staff, including Sid Spector and Hal Sheppard, were pleased with the idea of a new subcommittee. Reidy and his colleagues wanted to give it to the man who they thought could carry it furthest in terms of political mileage. It was their intention to sell the idea of the subcommittee to the youngest committee member, Senator John F. Kennedy (D-Massachusetts). They were aware of the Senator's presidential ambitions and thought that the relatively unknown Kennedy, in the ring with better known aspirants like Hubert Humphrey, Lyndon Johnson, Robert Kerr, Adlai Stevenson, and Stuart Symington, might profit from the exposure of chairing a subcommittee.[15]

Kennedy had already heard about the Forand Bill and had sent to Forand's office in the House for copies of the legislation as well as available supporting information.[16] He was interested, but unlike Wayne Morse had not had the opportunity to do anything about it. In addition to his Senatorial race in 1958, Kennedy was on the select committee investigating labor racketeering (the McClellan Committee) and was managing a labor reform bill. When Reidy went to Senator Kennedy's office, he got no further than his assistant Theodore Sorensen. After hearing Reidy out, Sorensen's response was negative.[17]

Reidy was disappointed but still thought Kennedy the best choice and did not give up. With persistence, he eventually got through to another Kennedy aide, Myer Feldman, who, unlike Sorensen, liked the idea very much. Feldman promised to take up the matter with his boss.

Feldman's enthusiasm was shared by Wilbur Cohen. Cohen, now a professor at the University of Michigan, was a frequent visitor to Washington. He first came to work with Senator Walter George (D-Georgia) on the disability insurance program. In 1956 he became special consultant on aging to the Labor Committee. He frequently stopped by the Kennedy office to talk to Sorensen and Feldman and help in drafting bills on aid to dependent children and unemployment insurance amendments. He also worked on Kennedy's Ten Point Program for the Aged. Cohen was in favor of having Kennedy lead a subcommittee for the aged, and joined Feldman in the effort to get Kennedy's approval.[18]

While Reidy was waiting to hear from the Kennedy people, another member of the Labor Committee, Pat McNamara, heard about the subcommittee idea and was immediately interested. McNamara had no presidential ambition, but he desperately needed a good political issue for his Senate race in 1960.[19]

McNamara had worked hard to win the support of Michigan's Democratic machine. He supported labor issues, such as an increase in minimum wage, and civil rights issues, such as a guarantee of equal voting and educational rights for blacks. His efforts were not unnoticed. He earned a rating from the Americans for Democratic Action of 100 percent for his liberal voting record.[20]

McNamara was also one of six liberal Senators who in 1957 issued a 16 point Democratic Declaration. One of the outstanding features of that Declaration was its call for a replacement of Senate Rule 22—the one that permitted long filibusters. Yet, despite his liberal credentials, he was running a very tight race for re-election. The subcommittee idea, particularly the part about holding regional hearings, was exactly what McNamara needed for his career. He was generally uncomfortable in the spotlight of major Congressional hearings. Once he heard about Reidy's plan, McNamara immediately expressed an interest to his Chairman Lister Hill.

Normally, a request for establishing a subcommittee is put forth during an executive session of the parent committee. The parent committee in this case had no such sessions scheduled. Rather than wait, Hill, who had the power to do so, decided to make the decision himself.

He asked both McNamara's staff and Kennedy's staff to get something in writing to his office.[21]

Both senatorial staffs rushed to draft a resolution and get it to Hill. Each was aware of the need for haste. McNamara's staff, however, had the advantage of having power of attorney for the Senator, and so with a valid signature their resolution arrived in Hill's office.[22] In 1958 Lister Hill arranged for the creation of the new Subcommittee on Aging and appointed McNamara its chairman. John Kennedy was named a member along with two other Democrats, Joseph Clark of Pennsylvania and Jennings Randolph of West Virginia. The two Republican members were Everett McKinley Dirksen of Illinois and Barry Goldwater of Arizona.

The first hearings of the new Subcommittee on Aging were held in 1959 in six different cities: Washington, D.C., Boston, Pittsburgh, San Francisco, Charleston, Grand Rapids, Miami, and Detroit. In each city McNamara shared the spotlight with the congressmen from that state. The goal was to hold informal hearings and then open up the floor for discussion so that the older people could discuss what they themselves considered their most pressing problem.[23]

Attendance at each hearing was overwhelming. Sid Spector, McNamara's chief legislative assistant, made certain of adequate press and television coverage. The hearings were a great success on all accounts. Pat McNamara won acclaim for his role as presiding Chairman. Individual congressmen were happy to participate in the publicity. Older persons were especially pleased by the opportunity to speak out in a national forum.

The McNamara Subcommittee found a profound grass-roots interest in health matters. The elderly talked mostly about their inability to afford proper health care. Personal experiences, emotionally recounted before Congressmen and press, were heart-rending. The whole atmosphere provided an effective boost for the advocates of a health insurance program. In an editorial entitled "Wave of the Future" the *Nation* suggested that the appeal of such a program was "not sectional, narrow, or remote; it is nearly universal . . . the aged are everywhere, and most of them need help."[24]

McNamara delivered his formal report on the regional hearings to the Senate on February 15, 1960. The hearings, he said, showed that first priority must be given to the difficulties the elderly had in financing their medical bills. "There is simply no human justification," Mc-

Namara wrote, "for any American to have to suffer unnecessarily a prolonged illness or put off a medical check-up because of his fear of hospital bills and of the exorbitant prices of medicine."[25] Having delivered his report, McNamara immediately requested that a second set of hearings be scheduled for the spring of 1960.

However, not everyone on the Subcommittee was as impressed by the problems of the elderly as was McNamara. The two Republican members, Senators Everett Dirksen (Illinois) and Barry Goldwater (Arizona) dissented and delivered their own minority report. Their report said, in effect, that the problems of older Americans were basically no different from those of other citizens.[26]

In order to keep the Forand Bill before the public eye, labor leaders held regional rallies and demonstrations of retired workers. On March 15, 1960, the United Auto Workers (UAW) organized a special rally at the State Fair Coliseum in Detroit. Over 13,000 retired UAW people attended to hear three Democratic candidates, John Kennedy, Hubert Humphrey, and Stuart Symington, address issues relevant to older people. The topic that won the most significant response was Medicare. Shortly after Detroit, Kennedy, along with Forand, addressed a retired union crowd in Buffalo. This time health insurance was the main topic. On March 24 in New York City, the AFL-CIO sponsored a rally at City Central Labor Council in Manhattan Center to demonstrate support for the Forand Bill. Mayor Richard Wagner was on hand to express his approval of the legislative proposal. The Mayor said that the Forand Bill "is in every way a logical and necessary extension of the Social Security program."[27] George Meany added that the issue "has never been more alive as it has these last few weeks."[28]

That spring, Older Workers Committees were established in many unions to increase pressure for a Forand-type bill. James O'Brien set up such a committee for the steel workers, and Charles Odell organized one for the UAW.[29] Labor leaders such as O'Brien and Odell wanted to create an effective retired workers lobby to support Medicare. They were not satisfied with the grass-roots support organization given to the McNamara hearings. However, AFL-CIO national leaders such as George Meany and Nelson Cruikshank were not convinced of the wisdom of a grass-roots movement. They were reluctant to create another "old folks" power base such as the Townsend movement or the Technocrats of the 1930s.[30]

Amidst a climate of rallies and letter-writing campaigns, McNamara held his second set of hearings on April 4, 5, 6, and 11, 12, 13 in Washington. Except for the change of one Republican member, from Goldwater to Norman Brundale of North Dakota, the members of the Subcommittee remained the same. Taking the lead from the regional hearings, the Senators focused on health problems of the aged. While the Subcommittee was not considering specific legislation, and indeed was not empowered to do so, it investigated various possibilities that might aid the elderly in solving their health financing problems. The results were similar in terms of the ideas generated from testimony to the 1958 and 1959 House Ways and Means Committee hearings on the Forand Bill. McNamara and the other Democrats on the Committee favored using the social security method of financing to pay for a broad range of health benefits to the elderly.[31]

The only new element was a political attack on the Eisenhower Administration for coming up with no viable alternative to the Forand Bill. The *New York Times* also criticized the Administration for endorsing no positive programs and no new ideas. Eisenhower seemed to be stalling, while requesting more exploration and study.[32]

One of the first witnesses was Leonard Lesser, speaking on behalf of Walter Reuther of the UAW. As Reuther would have done, Lesser gave an emotional critique of Republican "do-nothingism."[33] As soon as Lesser finished, he was challenged by Senator Dirksen who resented the "insidious slurs on the President." Dirksen claimed to have spoken with President Eisenhower only two weeks before at a leadership conference during which Eisenhower said that he was not opposed to action on the subject of health care of the elderly. Dirksen contended that there was merely a difference of opinion in approach and not on the objectives.[34]

When Lesser insisted that labor did not like the continual demands by Republicans for more study, Dirksen responded with what was to become the standard conservative response: That the current Forand Bill would do nothing for the 2 million or more senior citizens receiving old-age assistance but not Social Security. Dirksen asked Lesser if he was not in fact supporting a partial approach. Lesser responded that he was in favor of a total approach but did not want to hold up legislation for the 13 million who would benefit by passing the Forand Bill.[35] Dirksen then sarcastically summarized his position by stating that the Republicans "are as interested in doing something for the aged as Walter Reuther, or Victor Reuther, or Emil E. Mazey . . ."[36] (All three were liberal UAW leaders anathema to conservative members of the Senate.)

All semblance of professional decorum broke down when union leader James B. Carey took the stand. Carey was General Secretary of the CIO, as well as President of the International Union of Electricians, Radio, and Machine Workers. His mere presence seemed to offend Everett Dirksen. Dirksen spent a good deal of time at the hearings shouting at witnesses and calling those who supported the Forand Bill "insane" and "stinking."[37] Carey commented that the Eisenhower people seemed intent on studying the problem to death. Carey and Dirksen launched into an argument about the recently passed Landrum-Griffin law.[38] This polarization between conservative congressmen and many labor leaders was to continue throughout the Medicare debate, making the roles of those more "moderate" advocates like Nelson Cruikshank and Wilbur Cohen even more significant. At least they were able to sit down and talk with both sides.

By the time that Dr. James Appel, Chairman of the Board of Trustees of the American Medical Association, took the stand, it was apparent that the AMA leaders had made some advance from their earlier 1958–1959 negative position. The AMA spent the 1959–1960 year putting their members on a "legislative alert." That meant a warning to doctors of the dangers of the Forand Bill. While the negativism continued, the AMA emphasized that doctors never turned down charity cases (a disputed issue).[39] They still saw no need for national legislation. Instead, they were now interested in a campaign to correct difficulties in state and local assistance programs for the needy. Their priorities were similar to the recommendations read by the Surgeon-General, Dr. John Porterfield, who had already testified. Those priorities were basically two: training programs, and research into health problems and community health services which emphasized preventative techniques. In other words, the AMA's goal was to expand the voluntary welfare services and charity-oriented programs.[40]

When the second round of McNamara hearings ended, more material was added to the record. Liberal Democrats called for action, conservative Democrats opposed action, and Republicans claimed to be taking action by exploring various proposals.

This time McNamara's report to the Senate went beyond a statement of the problems. His findings first defined health insurance as a system of prepaid coverage to finance certain services. Then McNamara detailed specific recommendations: an emphasis on prevention and early diagnosis of disease; adequate coverage of hospital costs; treatment of a person who has been in a hospital in a skilled nursing home or in a supervised program of home nursing care; help in meeting costs of very expensive drugs; coverage of older persons who were presently retired but who did not qualify for Social Security yet who urgently needed health insurance; and lastly, stimulation of research and experiments for community health centers. McNamara's recommendations were more extensive than the simple 60 day hospital and 60 day nursing home coverage for Social Security recipients that the Forand Bill offered. Partly, he was attempting to meet the early criticism incurred by Forand for leaving out those older persons outside of the Social Security system.[41]

The next step for McNamara was to translate the subcommittee's recommendations into legislation. The Subcommittee on Aging was empowered *only* to investigate and recommend legislation. It could not report out or vote on specific bills. McNamara would have to go through the parent committee: Labor and Public Welfare.

With respect to committee choice, the Medicare advocates disagreed on strategy. Wilbur Cohen, Nelson Cruikshank, and Andrew Biemiller thought that the Senate Labor Committee was not the best vehicle for Medicare. It did not have enough influence in the generally conservative Senate. The several Wagner-Murray-Dingell bills, sponsored in the Labor Committee throughout the Truman Administration, had failed even to come to a vote.[42]

The Finance Committee had more suasion within the Senate. If Medicare could pass the Finance Committee, it could easily pass the Senate.[43] In addition, if Medicare was tied to the Social Security system, it had to pass the Finance Committee at some point, if only for its funding. Having one bill go through Labor, and a separate tax bill go through Finance, would decrease the likelihood of a Senate bill. Taking all things into consideration, Cohen believed that Finance offered the only logical route.[44]

On the other hand, the Labor Committee had established precedents with the Wagner-Murray-Dingell bills and other health legislation. Its members had a declared interest in Medicare. A new subcommittee had already held two public hearings. It had an earnest and committed staff. Bill Reidy and others on the staff thought that to make a stand in Finance was politically naive.

The ultimate decision to go through the Finance Committee created a bitter rift within the ranks of the Medicare advocates. McNamara continued to hold exploratory hearings within his Subcommittee and was always included in top level policy decisions affecting Medicare. He remained convinced that he should have managed the legislation.[45]

Meanwhile, John Kennedy remained aloof from the quarrel. His Ten Point Program on Old Age, delivered to the Senate on August 19, 1958, had already established him as vitally interested in the problems of the elderly. Popularly known as a Bill of Rights for the Elderly, it was written by a group from Kennedy's staff, particularly Myer Feldman, with the outside help of Wilbur Cohen. This program laid the foundation for Kennedy's later New Frontier goals for senior citizens.[46]

Although jobs and housing were the top two priorities in Kennedy's program, medical insurance was the third.[47] Kennedy had followed the McNamara Subcommittee hearings with interest. In 1959, Kennedy requested that Nelson Cruikshank and Leonard Lesser join Myer Feldman in drafting a bill similar to the Forand Bill for the Senator to sponsor. The result was S2915, sponsored by Kennedy and his friend, Senator Philip Hart. The Kennedy-Hart Bill followed the Forand Bill in using the Social Security principle, but it extended the number of days of benefits.[48] Cruikshank, working with Kennedy on S2915, was impressed with Kennedy's interest and knowledge. "He knew every detail of it intimately and sweated over and knew the reasons why he didn't want this or that. He was very well informed."[49]

Kennedy had become so well-informed by absorbing material prepared by a member of the Labor Committee staff, Ralph Dungan. In 1959 Kennedy directed Dungan to learn as much as he could about the health problems of the elderly. Dungan sent to the Library of Congress for all of the books available on the subject. After six months of intensive study, Dungan emerged as a self-educated "expert."[50] Dungan became a speech writer for Kennedy's 1960 campaign for the Presidency. In 1961, he joined the White House staff, with liaison responsibilities toward labor.

The Kennedy-Hart Bill, on the advice of Cohen and Cruikshank, went to the Finance Committee. The Senate now had two bills calling for a national health insurance program for those receiving Social Security benefits. One was sponsored by Morse, the other by Kennedy and Hart.

The Finance Committee was far more conservative than the Labor Committee. The Chairman, Harry F. Byrd, a Southern gentleman from Virginia, was totally opposed to national health insurance in any form. So too were the next three ranking Democrats, Russell Long of Louisiana, George A. Smathers of Florida, and Robert Kerr of Oklahoma. Long, son of Huey Long, thought that the Forand Bill was a terrible idea. He complained that it would make hospitals into free vacation spots for the elderly.[51] Smathers had made an alliance with the Florida doctors to win the Democratic nomination for the Senator over Claude Pepper, a strong supporter of national health insurance in the 1940s, and owed the doctors a considerable debt.[52] Robert Kerr had planned to make a one man crusade out of defeating any national health insurance program for the elderly that might come up in the Senate.[53]

Next were the fourth and fifth ranking Democrats, Clinton Anderson of New Mexico and Paul Douglas of Illinois. Douglas was well known as a friend to liberal and labor causes. Before coming to the Senate in 1948, Douglas had been a professor of economics at the University of Chicago. With a Senate image as an intellectual and liberal, Douglas feared that his sponsorship would jeopardize the bill. Douglas always remained an interested partisan in the Medicare debate but for political reasons kept his distance.[54]

That left Clinton Anderson. At first glance, Anderson was an unlikely sponsor for so controversial a piece of legislation. He devoted much of his time to the two committee assignments that interested him most: Agriculture and the Joint Committee on Atomic Energy of which he was Chairman. Yet, his credentials in the insurance business were excellent. Even while a Senator he remained President of his firm, the Mountain Life Insurance Company. He knew first hand what previous insurance companies were capable of doing or not doing. He understood the language of the industry.

Like his two closest friends in the Senate, Lyndon Johnson and Robert Kerr, Anderson was not born to wealth or power. He acquired both. Less of a wheeler-dealer type than either Johnson or Kerr, and plagued by poor health that limited his working day, Anderson was still not a bad choice for sponsoring Medicare. While he could never be mistaken for a crusading liberal, he was a popular Senator and one who, at least, could not be accused of having socialist connections (although he later was so accused).

Biemiller, Cohen, Cruikshank, and Lesser discussed the Forand Bill with Senator Anderson, who immediately agreed to sponsor a similar bill in the Senate. Anderson liked the idea of using the Social Security system to provide health benefits to the elderly. Elements in his background and personality made him amenable to a major liberal issue. He committed himself to making Medicare a priority in his legislative goals. In some ways, his fight to win health benefits for the elderly paralleled his own struggle to remain in good health. Anderson was successful in both. He died in 1975 at the age of 80.[55]

Shortly after McNamara's Subcommittee held its Spring 1960 hearings, Finance began its own hearings on the Social Security Amendments of 1960: HR12580, passed by the House by 381–23 on July 13, 1960. This bill contained no amendment for a social insurance approach to health care: the Ways and Means Committee had turned down the Forand Bill 17–8. It did have one new element. Its new Title XVI provided Federal grants to states to help pay costs of medical care for those elderly not on Old Age Assistance but yet unable to meet medical costs. This new title was written into the House bill, with no hearings, by Chairman Mills who thought it a satisfactory alternative to Forand's Bill.[56]

The 1960 hearings were the first opportunity for Clinton Anderson to test the Forand legislation in the Finance Committee. Anderson knew that he was working against tough odds. He estimated that of the 17 members of Finance (11 Democrats and six Republicans) only four or five would vote for a Forand-type bill. He counted only the votes of Democratic Senators Paul Douglas, Albert Gore (Tennessee), Eugene McCarthy (Minnesota), and Vance Hartke (Indiana) as favorable.[57]

The Finance Committee had a complicated task ahead and not very much time. It scheduled only two days of hearings, June 29 and June 30, hurrying to break for the Democratic and Republican conventions. As in the House, no public hearings had ever been held in the Senate for the new Title XVI.

Also, a plethora of recent bills were before the Finance Committee covering the whole range of approaches to health problems for the elderly. *The New Republic* referred to the bills as a "disorderly collection of jerry-built substitutes and compromises."[58] After the 1959 and 1960 McNamara hearings, Senate interest in the subject was at a high point. Letters from constituents were becoming irresistible. Not all of them were from AMA or Labor.[59] An editorial in *The Nation* declared, "Not in years had Congress been subjected to so much pressure as is currently applied for and against health insurance for the aged."[60] The *New York Times* reported that the "question of medical insurance for persons 65 years of age has become one of the hottest political issues in the nation."[61]

The Morse Bill and the Kennedy-Hart Bill were merely the first in the Senate to propose a payroll tax deduction approach to financing health care for the aged. On May 6 McNamara, along with 23 Democrats, including Morse, Kennedy, and Hart, sponsored a more inclusive bill, S3503, covering all the retired aged population, including those outside the Social Security system. It provided 90 days of hospital coverage (an increase from 60 day coverage of the Forand Bill), 180 days in a skilled nursing home (up from 60 days) or 240 days of home health care. The bill was estimated to cover about 14.8 million people. Of that number, 11.3 were already receiving OASDI (Social Security) benefits, 1.7 million on Old Age Assistance rolls, and 1.8 outside of both systems.[62]

With the upcoming election and Medicare the "Number One domestic issue" the Republicans felt public pressure to offer a positive program to go against the Democratic bills. Vice President Richard Nixon was reportedly anxious for Eisenhower to support a plan, but did not want to take the initiative to endorse something without Eisenhower. Eisenhower refused to endorse any plan. Secretary of HEW Arthur Flemming worked out a list of five possibilities from which the Administration could choose, but the President remained silent. Edward Chase, a well-known writer on medical subjects, explained that the President for "some inexplicable reason equates tax derived funds with socialized medicine."[63]

Nixon stuck by his favorite comment that he was "searching for an acceptable solution to the problem."[64] A letter, drafted April 5 by Nixon's administrative assistant Robert Fitch, and mailed to doctors around the country by the AMA, said that Nixon favored a program whereby those who desire to do so will be able to purchase health insurance from private companies on a voluntary basis. That meant that the Federal and state governments would subsidize the purchase of such policies—one of the five plans suggested by Flemming.[65]

Despite Flemming's efforts to get Eisenhower to make a commitment, the Administration remained silent, "talking through its leaks." Rumors that Nixon wanted a more positive program abounded. Nixon was satisfied with the rumors, but did not make a direct comment either way.[66]

At the end of June, on the second day of Finance Committee hearings, Eisenhower finally allowed Flemming to endorse a program. It was introduced as S3784 by Senator Leverett Saltonstall, Republican of Massachusetts, on June 30, 1960, and explained to the Finance Committee on June 29 by Arthur Flemming. The bill proposed Federal and state partnership on a program offering protection against long term (catastrophic) illness for low-income senior citizens. An income test would determine eligibility: $2,500 yearly income for a couple was the maximum earnings for eligibility. There was also a $24 a year enrollment fee; deductible of the first $250 of expenses; and the bill covered only 80 percent of costs after the deductible.

This program would be financed by the Federal Government out of general tax revenues and by state revenues on a special matching basis. If passed, the Administration's plan would do nothing more than expand the public assistance programs. Edward Chase wrote, "It is hard to escape the conclusion that the plan is strictly a political gesture, reluctantly taken to ease the politically untenable situation into which sheer negativism had placed the Party."[67]

Jacob Javits and other liberal Republicans, meanwhile, had refused to sit back and wait until the Administration broke its "log-jam." Javits and George Aiken (Vermont), Clifford Case (New Jersey), John Sherman Cooper (Kentucky), Hiram Fong (Hawaii), Kenneth Keating (New York), Hugh Scott, Jr. (Pennsylvania) and Winston Prouty (Vermont) sponsored their own bill, S3350. The Javits Bill was closer to the program that the AMA letter described as Nixon's favored approach. The bill offered matching grants to states to subsidize the purchase of private health insurance policies for low-income persons over 65. Like the Eisenhower Bill, there was an income test to determine eligibility. Another feature was a $75 deductible, which was necessary according to Javits to "de-emphasize institutional care." Supposedly, if a poor person knew he had to pay the first $75 of his bill, then he would not enter a health "institution" unless absolutely necessary. Javits estimated that his program would assist about 11 million older persons.[68]

The AFL-CIO called Javits's program "laudable" but said that it "cannot accomplish the fine things it aims to do." Labor spokesmen said that there was "virtually no possibility that each of the fifty states would raise the necessary funds for this program."[69] Javits, however, defended his bill before the Finance Committee. He said that his bill would provide the "most good in the shortest time." Javits criticized the Finance Committee for holding only two days of hearings with no further plans until after the break for the conventions. Javits said that what was needed was a good two or three day debate on the Senate floor for all of the amendments on health care of the aged. Then a decision could be reached. "I think," Javits told the Finance Committee, "if we really wanted to we could have this job done by the end of next week" (the first week of July).[70]

J. Linder, Chairman of the National Committee on Social Legislation of the National Lawyers Guild, reiterated the criticism that the AFL-CIO had made of the Javits Bill. The problem, Linder said, was that the Javits Bill—and the Eisenhower Bill—required a brand new administrative and bureaucratic structure. Each individual state had to enact legislation. That took time. Javits's Bill was also extremely costly. The states would have to put up about $640 million and the Federal Government about $400 million.[71]

Of all the Republican leaders, Governor Nelson Rockefeller of New York was the only one to endorse the Social Security method of financing as the most effective. At the 1960 Conference of Governors, held concurrently to the Finance Committee hearings, a majority of Governors submitted a resolution urging Congress to adopt "a health insurance plan for persons 65 years of age and over to be financed principally through the contributory plan and framework of the old-age, survivors, and disability insurance system."[72] Curiously, the Eisenhower Administration did not submit its own plan to the Governors for their approval. Senator George Smathers (D-Florida) commented during the Finance Committee hearings that, since the Eisenhower Bill would require the cooperation of the state governors, the Administration should at least have sent a representative to the governors' conference to explain the bill.[73]

After the July break for the conventions, the Finance Committee resumed its consideration. Kennedy, now his party's candidate for the Presidency, pledged that some version of his Bill S2915 would become a major legislative goal for the brief August Congressional session. The Kennedy staff joined efforts with Senator Clinton Anderson to propose a revised version of the Kennedy-Forand Bill as an amendment to HR12580. It was sponsored by Kennedy and Anderson, as well as by Hubert Humphrey, Paul Douglas, Albert Gore, Pat McNamara, Eugene McCarthy, Vance Hartke, and Jennings Randolph (D-West Virginia). However, the Finance Committee rejected it 12–5.

Javits's Bill as well as the Administration Bill were also rejected. Only Senator Robert Kerr's amendment, which he sponsored with J. Allen Frear, Jr. (D-Delaware), passed. This was the Senate version of Wilbur Mill's proposal to establish the new Title XVI in the Senate

1960 Social Security Amendments. The Finance Committee had, like the Ways and Means Committee, found its own hasty alternative to the Medicare debate. The Kerr Bill provided Federal grants to the states to help defray the costs of medical services for those among the elderly who were *not* on the Public Assistance rolls but yet who were unable to meet their medical expenses. Kerr-Frear passed 12–5 with Senators Kerr, Frear, Chairman Harry F. Byrd, Russell Long, George Smathers, Herman Talmadge (D-Georgia), John Williams (R-Delaware), Frank Carlson (R-Kansas), Wallace Bennett (R-Utah), John Marshall Butler (R-Maryland), Carl T. Curtis (R-Nebraska), and Thruston Morton voting yea. There had been no testimony or debate on the measure.[74]

When HR12580 went to the floor of the Senate, only three major medical care amendments were debated. Anderson, with Kennedy's strong backing, tried again, and offered the Forand Bill as a floor amendment. It was defeated 44–51 on a roll call vote. Javits tried again and offered his bill as a floor amendment. That too was defeated by roll call 28–67. A third amendment offered by Russell Long to allow the Social Security System to reimburse vendor payments to public mental and tuberculosis hospitals was adopted on the floor 51–38. It was, however, thrown out in Conference.

The Conference Committee reported out HR12580 on August 24, 1960. HR12580 was approved by the House on August 26, 368–17. After a drawn-out debate led by Russell Long who argued against passing the conference bill without his tuberculosis amendment, the bill passed the Senate 74–11 on August 29, 1960. It was signed into law by President Eisenhower on September 13. The law contained the new Title XVI commonly known as "Kerr-Mills" after its two sponsors, Senator Robert Kerr and Chairman Wilbur Mills. Eventually providing the basis for the 1965 Medicaid program, it was a significant and controversial idea favored by the two leading anti-social insurance Democrats. Within the House and the Senate, it introduced a whole new dimension to the Medicare fight.

3

The Kerr-Mills Program

In the summer of 1960, Congress had before it four options with regard to health assistance for the elderly: a contributory, Social Security type of program such as the one supported by Forand, Anderson, and Kennedy; a government-subsidized voluntary catastrophic program as proposed by the Eisenhower Administration with variations proposed by liberal Republicans; an expansion of the existing welfare system to cover those elderly unable to afford health care; or nothing. The first two choices were rejected by the Senate and the House in their respective hearings. Given the fact, as Tom Wicker noted in the *New York Times*, that the high cost of medical care for the elderly "was the most potent political issue in domestic politics,"[1] the last course, that is, no action, seemed unlikely that summer. That left only one route: an expansion of the existing welfare system.[2]

It was a choice that organized labor opposed. In early April, armed with lists of signatures, United Auto Workers President Walter Reuther met with House leaders Sam Rayburn and John McCormack. Up to that point, Rayburn had been neutral, thinking only that the Forand Bill went too far in its benefits.[3] Under pressure from Reuther, Rayburn and McCormack agreed to try to influence Mills to endorse a limited, contributory-type health bill, covering the minimum of hospital and nursing home care for Social Security recipients.[4] Odin Anderson reported in the *Times* that "this effort was an attempt on Rayburn's part to boost the chances of fellow Texan Johnson for the presidential nomination at the coming Democratic Convention."[5] Rayburn, along with Lyndon Johnson and Reuther, went to talk to Mills. Mills had assured Rayburn and Johnson that he would get a bill out of his committee during the hearing. He had specifically said a Social Security type bill to Rayburn in front of Reuther. Yet he felt that his welfare plan got him off the hook.[6]

Apparently, Mills told no one about his new bill. The *New York Times* reported the week after the Mills-Reuther-Rayburn confrontation that Mills was working on a Rayburn-Johnson Bill as well as an option plan where Social Security beneficiaries had a choice of an insurance program or a cash equivalent to buy their own private health insurance plan. Everyone in Congress knew that Eisenhower would veto either bill.[7]

Despite his commitments to the Democratic leaders, Mills felt a deeper obligation to what he believed was the congressional consensus. That consensus lay with the Southern conservatives, a group of which he was a member. He grew up with the traditional values celebrated by the American middle class: life was based on mutual respect and understanding. People took care of their own problems and families, including the elderly members.[8]

While his own career goals took him far from Kensitt, indeed as far as Harvard Law School, he never escaped the influence of his birthplace. His associate in Congress often remarked that he could turn off and on a Southern cracker voice like running water. During a conversation in which he was speaking as a knowledgeable Harvard-trained leader of Washington, he might answer a call from Little Rock as if he had never left Arkansas; then he would replace the receiver and resume his national accent and demeanor unperplexed.[9]

In Congress, Mills was a respected and powerful leader. He did his homework thoroughly and had a lawyer's interest in details. As Chairman of the Ways and Means, a position that he assumed in 1957, he had as his special charge the Social Security system. According to his peers, one of his most impressive abilities was his complete understanding of that system. Wilbur Cohen said that Mills was the *only* one out of 535 Congressmen who was able to master the actuarial basis of Social Security as well as its financial underpinnings. He was "completely conversant" with all the factors involved in making actuarial estimates of Social Security payments.[10]

Mills's plan to expand the welfare system to include health payments for impoverished elderly was not a novel idea. Although Mills was not aware of its antecedents, a similar program had been suggested as far back as 1947 by the Republican Senator from Ohio, Robert Taft. Taft, Chairman of the Senate Labor and Public Welfare Committee, had put together a package providing Federal matching funds to the states to be used for medical purposes for those welfare recipients who could prove their need via the traditional "means test." Taft's Bill, offered in 1947 and again in 1949, was never passed.[11] It would have applied to all ages. At the time no thought was given to limiting coverage to any one group in the population, such as the elderly. That idea did not appear until the late 1950s.

Taft had offered his bill, S545, as a Republican alternative to the Wagner-Murray-Dingell bills described in an earlier chapter. In the respective bills, the Democrats and the Republicans were expressing two entirely different philosophies of social welfare. The Democrats were assuming that health care was a necessity and a matter of right. The Republicans were assuming that it was a necessity also, but an abhorrent one.[12] Taft put it succinctly:

It has always been assumed in this country that those able to pay for medical care could buy their own medical service just as under any other system, except a socialistic system, they buy their own food, their own housing, their own clothing, and their own automobiles . . . undeniably, in that system there are gaps, particularly in rural districts and poorer districts in the cities, and we have a very definite interest in trying to fill those gaps.[13]

While Taft lost interest in "filling those gaps" after he was refused the Republican nomination in 1952, another significant event in welfare history contributed to the Mills Bill. The 1950 Social Security Amendments legislated a minor revolution in welfare payments. For the first time, Federal and state governments were authorized to pay money directly to the institutions that were providing the services. In the language of welfare, such direct payment is called vendor payment. The vendor is synonymous with all types of institutions providing services. This meant that the government could directly reimburse hospitals, nursing homes and doctors for their "charity" cases. The men responsible for this innovation were Oscar Ewing, the Truman appointed Director of the Social Security Administration, Arthur Altmeyer, I. S. Falk, and Wilbur Cohen, also from SSA.[14]

During the next ten years the vendor payment program continued to expand. In 1960, the total dollar outlay of the nation toward medical payments was 514 million dollars. This included all types of public assistance programs. More than half of that dollar amount was going for hospital and nursing home care.[15]

With the growth in dollars spent came a growth in inequity in the spending. Vendor payments depended upon state and even local qualifications for eligibility. By 1960, ten states, mostly in the South, had no legislation providing for vendor payments for medical purposes. The most comprehensive medical payment program was in Wisconsin. The least was in Montana.[16]

The whole welfare system was growing in a confusing fashion. In addition to many state public assistance programs, the national Social Security Administration provided the following programs:

OAA (Old Age Assistance) Title I, a non-contributory welfare program for elderly persons not entitled to a Social Security pension. The Federal Government contributed 60 percent in matched funds to the states. Each state had its own plan.

OASDI (Old age, survivors, and disability insurance) Title II, a contributory pension system. The OAI was the original Social Security program passed in 1935. The "survivors" was added in 1939, and the "disability" was added in 1956.

ADC (Aid to Dependent Children) Title IV.

AB (Aid to the Blind) Title X.[17]

Mills's Bill proposed to increase the money available for vendor payments for persons in the OAA program. An estimated 10 million people would be covered *if* all of the states participated fully. About 500,000 to 1 million would be expected to use medical services from the program each year.[18]

The attractive feature of the Mills plan was that it required no new financial structure for its application. It involved no new social philosophy. It simply built upon the existing system, putting the onus of the administration back on the states, Therefore, it had the backing of powerful conservatives in both the Democratic and Republican parties. It provided an invitation to the states to relax their eligibility requirements for public assistance for medical expenses. In short, it was a modest plan, less costly than even the Eisenhower Administration Bill, and it "rocked no boats." It was financed by general revenue, and did not involve any strain on the Social Security Trust Fund, the solvency of which Mills worried about a great deal.

Mills presented his plan during the Ways and Means hearings on the Social Security Amendments and the Forand Bill. Since it had not been available before the hearings, there was no testimony or discussion. The plan was simply presented, passed immediately by the Ways and Means Committee, and then by the House on June 3, 1960, under closed rule. The *Times* described the Mills Bill as a "hand washing performance."

Mills had indeed washed his hands, dried them, and walked away from the sink. To his satisfaction he discharged his obligations to the Democratic Party. The bill now went to the Senate Finance Committee for hearings. The liberals on the Ways and Means Committee privately hoped that the Senate would approve a health insurance amendment and then there would be a forced compromise in Conference.[19]

As the proponents of health insurance for the elderly found out, the main thing that the opposition had going was Wilbur Mills in the House and Robert Kerr in the Senate.[20] Like Mills, Kerr was opposed to expanding the Social Security system to finance health care. As a Democrat, he was also against the Republican ideas of subsidizing the private insurance industry.[21] He needed an alternative for very special political reasons. Kennedy had announced that he was in favor of a Social Security approach, and if his bill did not pass, he planned to make health insurance for the elderly a campaign issue.

Kennedy was also going to lose the state of Oklahoma on the religious issue. (Oklahoma was mostly Baptist.) Kerr, himself a Baptist, was up for re-election in 1960 and figured that he needed something to distinguish himself from the Kennedy program. He needed a significant idea that would appeal to Oklahomans and that might also satisfy the state's powerful medical association.[22]

Kerr lost no time in consulting the Washington expert on the subject of Social Security, Wilbur Cohen. "Any man who said that he was an expert on Social Security was a man with Cohen's name in his pocket."[23] After asking Cohen what he thought about the Mills Amendment, Kerr requested that Cohen develop a bill along the same lines, but one that would particularly benefit Oklahoma.[24]

With Wilbur Cohen's assistance, Kerr put together an amendment based on the same philosophy as the Mills Amendment, that of expanding the existing welfare structure. Cohen and Kerr added a second section that created a new category of welfare recipients. They called it MAA (similar to OAA) "medical aged assistance." It was based on a new classification of poverty, known as "medical indigency." The new Program assumed that old people receiving welfare might be pushed into their needy position by virtue of medical bills.

Cohen was the first to admit that the Kerr Amendment was written with a certain bias toward Oklahoma and Arkansas.[25] Kerr announced that his program was available to every citizen 65 and older if he or she came under a program adopted by his state. If the state chose to adopt the fullest program, the MAA could cover hospital, doctor, surgeon, and dental services.

For Oklahoma in particular, Kerr announced that his amendment would enable an additional 180,000 to 270,000 to receive benefits. There were only 90,000 persons receiving OAA aid in that state in 1960. Kerr-Mills promised to increase the recipient numbers by as much as four times in Oklahoma.[26] Since his election to the Senate in 1948, Kerr had always been generous to his home state. The Public Works Committee, his Senate power base, gave him ample opportunity to channel special programs toward Oklahoma.

The fact that Cohen was assisting the "opposition" was enough to raise some liberal eyebrows. Although Cohen was working with Sorensen and Feldman on the Kennedy team, he was also interested in developing the welfare approach not merely as an alternative to the Kennedy-Anderson Bill, but as an addition. Cohen recognized that Kerr needed a bill to come out politically as anti-Kennedy or anti-Catholic in order to be sure of his own reelection in Oklahoma. Cohen believed that a different approach to the health insurance issue would satisfactorily solve the political problem for Kerr, separating him from the Kennedy platform in the minds of his Baptist constituents, and at the same time advance the cause of Medicare.

Cohen was never one to quibble about playing both sides, as long as it fit into the larger scenario of passing Medicare. Cohen made Kerr-Mills fit. In his own words, the first target for developing a medical care program was to get the public used to the idea of assuming responsibility for financing medical care. Kerr-Mills could certainly be a step in that direction. If passed, the program would establish Public responsibility for financing medical care for the neediest of the elderly. Then, Cohen thought, once the idea was accepted, "then we can say— let's get a better way of carrying out the principles."[27]

Through the years Cohen became an expert on the political game of gradualism or incrementalism. His technique received the nickname of "salami slicing." This was Cohen's way of getting one slice of salami at a time until there was enough for a whole sandwich.[28] His brilliance was in his ability at all times to keep a clear view of that whole sandwich, i.e., the ultimate goal.

Kerr proposed his amendment during the Finance Committee hearings in July. J. Allen Frear, Jr. (D-Delaware) cosponsored the proposal. The bill caused little debate since the hearings were brief and most of the attention had gone to other bills. It passed 12–5. Chairman Harry F. Byrd, Russell Long, George Smathers, Herman Talmadge, John Williams (R-Delaware), Frank Carlson (R-Kansas), Wallace Bennett (R-Utah), John Marshall Butler (R-Maryland), Carl T. Curtis (R-Nebraska), Thruston Morton, Kerr, and Frear voting yea. Only five liberal Democrats, Anderson, Douglas, McCarthy, Hartke, and Gore, voted nay.[29]

When HR2580, which included Kerr-Mills (also known as Kerr-Eisenhower-Byrd Bill), went to the floor of the Senate, Kerr was well prepared for debate. Speaking eloquently in defense of his bill, he claimed that it was fair if everyone in the population contributed to health care of the elderly who needed it rather than take contributions only from those paying Social Security. Also, Kerr added that his plan would better safeguard freedom of choice for doctors and hospitals.[30]

Enough time had elapsed so that liberal Democrats were able to think through the implications of Kerr-Mills and ask pointed questions. Kerr, anticipating opposition, received special permission from Majority Leader Lyndon Johnson to have Robert Myers at his side during the debate. Myers provided on the spot cost estimates and technical advice. Kerr also had available, not on the floor, but standing by for quick phone calls, two research assistants from the Library of Congress, Fred Arner and Helen Livingston. According to Arner, both he and Livingston were providing assistance to all Congressional members as their jobs implied. It was just that Kerr requested their services more frequently.[31]

The problem for the pro-Medicare group was that they were not as well organized as Kerr. As Myers commented after the vote, "There was no match for Kerr." He was master of "resounding rebuttal."[32] Said Sam Rayburn, "Bob Kerr is the kind of man who would charge hell with a bucket of water and believe he could put it out."[33] Said Albert Gore, "The distinguished Senator from Oklahoma can take the least amount of information and look and act more authoritative than any man in the world.''[34] After Kerr's death, Carl Albert commented,

He was like a great engine powered by super fuel as he drove to every task. He never worried about finesse. He could accomplish almost any task he undertook by man strength—by sheer weight of his intellect, by his rock like determination, and his vast energy.... [35]

During the floor debate it almost appeared that the liberals had abandoned their cause. Kennedy came for a brief speech on the merits of health insurance, but left before the debate. Anderson remained as "somewhat" of a leader but was not very forceful. The Kennedy-Anderson floor amendment was defeated 44–51 on a roll call vote.

Appearances to the contrary, the liberals had not, in fact, retreated. What had actually happened was a change in strategy, due to the influence of Wilbur Cohen. Cohen had persuaded Walter Reuther, Sorensen, Feldman, and finally Kennedy that Kerr-Mills could be considered as a necessary step toward getting Medicare passed at another date. Anderson and Gore went along. Douglas was reluctant, believing that Kerr-Mills went against the Democratic platform. This was so because a person had to profess he is a pauper in order to receive aid. However, he agreed to go along with the other Medicare advocates.

Cohen managed to convince the Senators that they could be for Medicare plus something else. That something else could be what Medicare left out: the indigent elderly.[36] Cohen's philosophy of always working for the possible, even when it involved great compromise, cost him support among no-compromise liberals.

The one Senator that Cohen never managed to convince was Pat McNamara, further broadening the rift within the pro-Medicare group between the McNamara camp and the Kennedy-Anderson camp. McNamara thought in terms of one strategy only and wanted to stick to it. He believed that alternative bills or compromises, no matter how appealing, would only dilute the chances for Medicare. (Nelson Cruikshank, who did not openly dispute the Kerr-Mills legislation, privately concurred with McNamara. He believed that the efforts on behalf of Kerr-Mills would slow up Medicare passage.)[37]

Kerr's Bill passed the Senate 91–2. The two nays were Goldwater and Strom Thurmond (D-South Carolina). In addition to Kennedy and Anderson, both Javits and Long used the floor amendment approach to try for the last time to get their respective bills passed. Javits's voluntary option plan was defeated 28–67, after Republicans found that they had more in common with the philosophy of Kerr-Mills. Russell Long was more successful. His amendment to allow the Social Security system to reimburse vendor payments to public mental and tuberculosis hospitals passed on a roll call vote of 51–38.

The Social Security Amendments of 1960, including Kerr-Mills, was reported out of conference August 24, 1960. The Conference Committee had acted quickly. It left the bill primarily intact, throwing out only the Long Amendment to which Mills was personally opposed because of the cost. The House approved HR12580 on August 26, by a margin of 368–17. The Senate voted out the bill 74–11, three days later. (Only Long engaged in angry debate because the final bill was without his amendment.) President Eisenhower signed the bill into law on September 13.[38]

Response to the new Kerr-Mills program was mixed. Initially the medical profession did not appreciate Kerr's efforts on their behalf. They had opposed it when it was first suggested as a further extension of the government into the health field. Kerr actually traveled to Chicago in early August to win the approval of AMA leaders, but got nowhere. Gradually, the AMA changed its mind. The organization members became convinced the Kerr-Mills had at least one benefit. It would forestall any future discussion of health insurance should Kennedy win the election.[39]

On August 15, AMA President-elect Dr. Leonard Larson (of Bismark, North Dakota) announced the results of a survey that found, contrary to popular opinion, most persons over 65 did *not* want a government program of health care. Only ten percent of those polled favored a compulsory plan. The survey was conducted by Emory University sociologists, James W, Wiggins and Helmut Schoeck, and funded by the William Volker Fund. The professors interviewed 1,500 "representative persons" selected by scientific survey techniques. The survey reported little reason to believe that the elderly were suffering from medical hardship. Of those polled, 60 percent said that, if they sold all they owned and paid all their bills, they would still have more than $7,500 in the bank.[40]

At the same time that Larson announced the results of the survey, the AMA took out a full-page ad in major newspapers around the country supporting Kerr-Mills. The ad said that Title XVI (Kerr-Mills) was the "answer to problems" for the minority of the aged who needed help with their medical bills. The "other approach," the broader Kennedy-Anderson Bill, "would be just the beginning of compulsory, government-run medical care for every man, woman and child in the U.S." The ad warned ominously: "For it wouldn't be long before the Federal Government would be lowering the age of which people would be eligible, and adding one costly service after another to a program that would place the health care under the Federal Government's thumb."[41]

Throughout the rest of August the AMA advertised its support of Kerr-Mills. The proper role of government, the advertisements said, should be to make grants-in-aid to the states; the OAA was a beneficial welfare program; that whatever changes were needed could be made at the local level. In other words, most doctors were supporting the status quo state administered welfare systems, where they had a direct input at the state and community level. The Chamber of Commerce had another idea. It called upon employers to voluntarily cover retired workers in order to "head off" the government. Cruikshank responded, "as usual the Chamber would cover a national need with a postage stamp."[42]

At least one significant group of doctors, the Physicians Forum, took exception to the policy of the AMA. Dr. Allen M. Butler, Chairman of the Physicians Forum, reported in a letter to the editor of the *New York Times* that Kerr-Mills is "an unsound extension of charity medicine—and is no solution to the health needs of the aged. . . . Quality of care can be protected only if benefits are in the form of services, not cash indemnities."[43] The Physicians Forum was an association of about 1,000 doctors who disagreed with the goals and methods of the more establishment AMA. Because of their connection with the large teaching universities of the East their opinions were usually accorded a measure of respect, although since its formation in the early 1940s the Forum never had the lobbying power of the AMA.

Kerr-Mills was never hailed as a major breakthrough in social policy by the AMA or anyone else. While Congressmen were glad to have the matter resolved and leave Washington before September 1, sentiment around the country was mostly negative.[44] Aime Forand spoke for many fellow liberals when he said that, while the new legislation would "not do any harm it would not do any good. Personally, I think it's a shame, I think it's a mirage that we are holding up to the old folks to look at and think they are going to get something."[45]

The *Saturday Evening Post* published an editorial arguing that Kerr-

Mills put too much emphasis on welfare, and "a race in welfare programs is just what we don't need."[46] As Tom Wicker observed in the
Times, the plan appealed only to poor states with big relief rolls.[47]
Wicker's associate on the *Times*, Joseph Loftus, wrote that Kerr-Mills
"does greater violence to some of the basic principles" than the Kennedy-Anderson Bill. Kerr-Mills is "government medicine controlled by
politicians."[48] Another critic charged that the new law would do less
to help the health of the elderly and more to help county hospitals relieve
themselves of their charity cases."[49] A survey taken in St. Petersburg,
Florida, by the *New York Times* showed that the elderly had a low
opinion of Kerr-Mills.[50]

During the annual meeting of the National Conference on Social
Welfare, Kerr-Mills was a main topic of discussion. The group met in
July in Atlantic City. New Jersey Governor Robert Meyner, a guest
speaker, attacked the Kerr-Mills proposal as "just another relief program." The keynote speaker, Charles Schottland, agreed; Title XVI
"would merely set up another group on relief . . . the wealthier states
would be obliged to add a new category to public assistance while the
poorer states could continue their negligence."[51] Meyner and Schottland
set the tone for the consensus of the welfare personnel at the meeting:
Kerr-Mills was a disappointing new law that added further confusion
to the welfare situation. Its benefits were too few to make up for the
complications in application.

Kerr-Mills *implied* great things. It offered the states generous Federal
grants for medical care for their welfare recipients. This was an expense
that in the past had either been ignored or totally paid for by county
and state revenues. Also, the new program had no dollar limits. This
unusual feature meant that there was no dollar total on how much the
states could get so long as they were willing to match the amount
requested. It also meant that there was no Federal ceiling on individual
payments, It was left to the states to decide the limits.

The Federal Government was empowered to provide between 50
percent to 80 percent of the costs on a matching basis. That 50 percent
to 80 percent was based on a very complicated formula using national
and state per capita incomes. According to Robert J, Myers, who was
Deputy Commissioner of the Bureau of Labor Statistics, the only state
actually qualifying for the full 80 percent funding was Mississippi. On
the other hand, 18 states were allowed only the minimum 50 percent.
The rest fell somewhere in between.[52]

Federal guidelines for applying Kerr-Mills were minimal. The states were not allowed to charge an "enrollment fee" for a recipient; that is, the states could not require their poor elderly to pay dollars in order to receive benefits when needed such as might be done in a private insurance plan. Secondly, the states had to offer institutional and non-institutional care for any service that they wanted covered by Kerr-Mills. This meant, for example, that if the state were covering nursing care, it had to reimburse private, home-visiting nurses as well as nursing care in a nursing home or hospital. Thirdly, any program that the states offered had to be in effect in all parts of the state. In other words, if the state allowed one county to reimburse for dental payments, then it had to make sure that all of the counties in that state had the same coverage.

There were no medical services that were mandatory. Under the new law, a state could reimburse for hospital stays, nursing homes, physicians, dentists, private duty nurses, physical therapists, osteopaths, chiropractors, optometrists, home health care, lab work, X-rays, prescribed drugs, eyeglasses, dentures, or anything else. Only mental hospitals were specifically excluded.[53]

The law went into effect on October 1, 1960. HEW was responsible for approving the state plans. Like OAA, the new MAA was to be administered by the Bureau of Public Assistance, a division of SSA. Arthur Flemming, Secretary of HEW, asked all state governors to initiate the necessary legislative action to get the new law started. The Bureau of Public Assistance also sent out letters to the states summarizing the provisions of the new law.[54]

The bill that "could do no harm" had difficulty proving that it could do any good. The effectiveness of Kerr-Mills depended on state action. The states did not rush to take advantage of the new law. Forand expressed the problem to his Congressional colleagues, "I am sure all of you know enough about legislative bodies to realize that the list of items the states could provide under the plan would never be realized." Even the states which stood to get reimbursed for over 70 percent of their dollars spent could not or would not budget funds for the remainder.[55]

By the time Eisenhower left office, only five states had passed legislation providing for at least some of the benefits under Kerr-Mills: Michigan, Oklahoma, Massachusetts, West Virginia, Kentucky. The Massachusetts program was more apparent than real. Instead of instituting new medical coverage for a wider group of persons over 65,

Massachusetts transferred 14,000 persons from other Public assistance programs to the new MAA program. The Federal dollar share was higher for MAA recipients. Over the next five years other states did the same: transferred names from older welfare programs to the new program in order to get back more Federal money. This meant that Kerr-Mills was not benefiting as many new older persons as was possible.[56]

Other states created different impediments to the success of Kerr-Mills. New Mexico, Tennessee, and Oregon required a deductible which lessened the very purpose of Kerr-Mills: to reach the very poor. Nine other states enacted laws which allowed the state to take a lien after death on the property of the MAA recipient.[57] New York decided not to join in. Governor Rockefeller preferred to wait and see if the Social Security approach would pass in 1961.[58]

The elderly, who needed and expected help in financing their health bills, were the losers with Kerr-Mills. With the inequities existing among the states, location had more to do with a poor senior citizen's health care than need. As with other welfare programs, the means test was a deterrent. In order to qualify as "medically indigent" an older person had to attest to the fact that he or she had exhausted all resources and was thus unable to pay large medical bills. The criticism of this aspect of the MAA program was similar to criticisms of other welfare programs: the law did not help prevent illness; it took care of the results after illness occurred.[59]

Only four months after Kerr-Mills became law it was spoken of as a failure at the White House Conference on Aging. The Conference, one of the last major events in Eisenhower's Administration, was scheduled for four days beginning January 8, 1961.[60]

Twenty-seven thousand delegates attended about 20 paneled sessions. The group was composed of a broad distribution: 267 business executives, 353 educators, 219 clergymen, 132 labor representatives, 283 physicians and dentists, and 368 social welfare personnel.[61] Although the discussions were scheduled to cover all issues affecting the elderly, including income, housing, employment, leisure, religion, and health, the subject that received most publicity was financing health care.[62] Edward Chase wrote:

No speaker seemed both willing and able to make a persuasive case for the Kerr-Mills bill. . . . Aside from any objections on social or philosophical grounds, the bill has exhibited this further defect: it doesn't work. Most states simply lack the funds to match the proposed Federal grants.[63]

The doctors had planned to dominate the discussion of medical care financing. Much to their annoyance they were out-maneuvered by the combined efforts of Arthur Flemming and labor leaders George Meany and Nelson Cruikshank. Flemming quietly informed Meany and Cruikshank that the financing of health care was scheduled for a panel heavily stacked by the medical profession. The three men arranged for the agenda to be changed and health care financing rescheduled for another panel, the income maintenance group. This gave Cruikshank a chance to stack that group with pro-Medicare panelists. The AMA tried to have the topic changed again but were ruled out of order by the Chairman of the Conference, former Republican Representative from New Jersey, R. W. Kean.[64] The AMA then charged Soviet dictation by "inner-circles" during the planning for the conference.[65]

Liberals and labor claimed that the conference was "rigged" by the AMA.[66] George Meany told the press that the AMA "was conducting a reckless campaign of rule or ruin and the public be damned."[67] Labor complained that the conference was stacked with wealthy doctors. Wilbur Cohen announced that the "huge parley had been captured by the AMA, private insurance, and industrial interests." Cohen even went so far as to inform the President that he could not accept an invitation to the conference because it was stacked in favor of organized medicine.[68] The AMA countered that the Democratic governors in at least two states, New Jersey and Florida, weighted their delegations with members strongly favoring the Social Security approach and slighted representatives of the medical profession.[69] Eisenhower staunchly defended the conference. He told reporters, "I thought the purpose of a conference . . . was to get opposing sides, to see whether there is a platform that can satisfy the sound . . . logic of people of good will."[70]

Though both sides charged that the other had more influence within the conference, two speeches delivered by former Eisenhower staff members had more to do with the outcome on medical care financing than the panel stacking or agenda manipulations. Those speeches were made by Marion Folsom, a director of Eastman-Kodak Company and former head of HEW, and Arthur Larson, currently director of the World Rule of Law Center at Duke University and former Assistant Secretary of Labor. Folsom announced his support of the Kennedy Medicare plan, and gave a "formidable factual analysis establishing the superiority of the Social Security mechanism over public assistance or charity for elderly citizens in need of health care." Folsom assured his fellow delegates that the Kennedy plan was the "logical plan for medical care of the aged, and in no sense a form of socialized medicine." Larson also added his weight to the Kennedy cause. He told the Conference that "it is the proper function of Social Security to provide medical care for the aged." Larson and Folsom created a considerable stir among Republicans. A rumor spread that Flemming too was going to come out for Medicare once he left the Eisenhower Cabinet.[71]

The vote for Social Security financing was 170–99. When Wilbur Cohen made an unexpected appearance on the third day of meetings, he was greeted by a standing ovation. The White House Conference gave the incoming Kennedy Administration an endorsement of experts in favor of Medicare. The AMA had "failed to offer anything like an effective rebuttal, let alone a persuasive program."[72]

As the Eisenhower Administration ended, Kerr-Mills had not won the approval of any group beyond the AMA. Still, if the new law lacked popularity, it was on the books. What McNamara and Cruikshank had feared did in part come true. Kerr-Mills was now used as an argument against Medicare if only because of a philosophy of "let's perfect what we have rather than establish something new." On the other hand, because of Kerr-Mills, the states themselves added their voice to the demand for a national Social Security financed program. The states could not bear the monetary burden that Kerr-Mills required. State governments, anxious for a way out of their dilemma, pressured their own Congressmen to find an alternative.[73] *The New Republic* warned: "It so happens that the present plan is going to cost the states some money; when the states begin to implement this program, they are going to cast longing eyes at the Social Security approach."[74] Ultimately, however, Wilbur Cohen's approach proved itself. His idea that the country needed Medicare plus something else that could take care of the elderly poor became the final choice. Kerr-Mills was eventually translated into the Medicaid program.

4

Medicare and the New Frontier

The outgoing Eisenhower Administration was most likely satisfied with its handling of the national health insurance for the elderly issue. Eisenhower had honored his commitment to the AMA to pass no Social Security-based health legislation. He had also managed to keep his top officials from publicly supporting health insurance legislation until the final few days of his term of office when Arthur Flemming announced his true position in favor of health insurance for the aged. On the positive side, the President signed the Kerr-Mills into law and held a White House Conference on Aging. Also he approved Republican alternatives to the Forand Bill which were satisfactory to all members of his party except the liberal wing. Yet, as Eisenhower left office, few people in the U.S. felt that the health needs of the elderly had been solved. Health insurance remained very much a major political issue; the country was waiting to see how the new President would handle it.

John Kennedy had made many promises during his 1960 campaign. In order to translate those promises into specific legislative proposals, Kennedy and his advisors appointed a number of task force to work out programs and guidelines. Social Security expert Wilbur Cohen was named Chairman of the task force on Health and Social Security.[1] Details of the task force were worked out with Kennedy's two top aides, Myer Feldman and Theodore Sorensen. Cohen was given great latitude in choosing his committee and in arranging the structure of the task force.[2] Without delay, Cohen appointed Dr. Dean Clark, general director of Massachusetts General Hospital in Boston; Dr. James Dixon, President of Antioch College; Herman S. Somers, Chairman of the

Department of Political Science at Haverford College; and Elizabeth Wickenden, a consultant on health and welfare matters and a good friend.[3] Feldman told Cohen that in addition to those four, Kennedy wanted to add two more names: Dr. Robert E. Cooke, a professor of pediatrics at Johns Hopkins University; and Dr. Joshua Lederberg, a Nobel prize winner and professor of pediatrics at Stanford University. These two men were primarily interested in setting up a Child Health Institute that would have some impact on the problem of mental retardation, a concern very much in the hearts of the Kennedy family.[4]

On January 10, 1961 (ironically the same day that the White House Conference on Aging opened), Cohen traveled to the Hotel Carlyle in New York to deliver his completed task force report. Cohen met with the President-elect. Present also were Sorensen; Abraham Ribicoff, the new Secretary of Health, Education and Welfare; and Pierre Salinger, the President's press secretary. Cohen noted: "The President looked at my report briefly. He suggested that for publication we omit the last three recommendations in the report so that the newspapers would concentrate on the health and recommendations relating to Medicare."[5] Cohen, Salinger, and Sorensen tore off the last pages and handed the rest of the copy to the press waiting in the hotel lobby.

At a later point Cohen commented that "the work of that task force was exceedingly interesting and significant because it resulted in establishing a framework of much of what President Kennedy tried to do." In fact, even though Medicare was given highest priority, other task force recommendations were passed into law first: the National Institute of Child Health and Human Development; the Aid to Dependent Children of Unemployed Parents; and government scholarships to medical students.[6]

On January 11 the press reported that the Kennedy task force had recommended a health insurance package tied to the Social Security System that would cover 14.5 million people. The new benefits would be financed by payroll tax increases of one fourth of one percent up to a base salary of $4,800. This was an expansion of the 1960 Kennedy-Anderson Bill that covered only 9.5 million people. A reduction in the eligibility age from 68 to 65 or 62 accounted for the increase in number of persons covered. Also, the press noted that the task force suggested inclusion of widows, orphans, and disabled in the health benefits.[7]

While the task forces were working out legislative programs, Kennedy was busy assembling a Cabinet. He had three top positions to fill in

HEW: Ribicoff's selection as Secretary was one of the first Cabinet positions that Kennedy decided upon.[8] In 1960, while Governor of Connecticut, Ribicoff played an instrumental role in the Kennedy campaign, particularly in its earlier stages. When Kennedy needed an experienced, non-controversial senior figure to help guide major programs, he turned to Ribicoff. Ribicoff seemed to fit the job better perhaps than Governor Mennen Williams of Michigan, a more controversial figure who wanted the chief position in HEW.[9]

During the Senate hearing for his nomination Ribicoff assured his friends on the Finance Committee that, while he supported Medicare, he did not feel committed to the task force report. Ribicoff took the opportunity to remind the Committee that he had voted against the establishment of HEW in 1955. Chairman Harry F. Byrd, delighted by Ribicoff's reassurances, called the nomination to HEW one of the best Cabinet appointments made in recent years by any President.[10]

Wilbur Cohen had already been approached by Ribicoff and Sorensen about joining the new Administration in some capacity relating to Social Security, but nothing definite was concluded. A week after Cohen had delivered his task force report in New York, Andrew Hatcher, an assistant press secretary, called Cohen at his home in Ann Arbor to tell him the news: Kennedy was going to announce Cohen's appointment as Assistant Secretary of HEW.[11] Assistant Secretary was a good Position for Cohen, The job involved policy and substance as well as legislative tactics. These were normally two different functions in other departments. The new position would give Cohen a chance to do what he liked best; write bills and formulate legislation.[12]

Yet Cohen knew that his nomination would not go easily. He informed Ribicoff that he was considered a very controversial figure "in the field of health and social security because of my strong views on the expansion of the programs." Ribicoff liked Cohen's frankness, Sorensen told Cohen that the President would stand by him.[13]

Cohen left nothing to chance. He went himself to talk to the individual members of the Finance Committee. Kerr, Douglas, and Anderson supported him. Even Byrd, whom Cohen approached directly, said that he would do nothing to block the nomination. Meanwhile, a storm of protest was working through George Smathers. Dr. Edward Annis of Miami, Florida, an influential member of the AMA, put pressure on Smathers to oppose Cohen's appointment. Smathers suggested to Byrd that Cohen withdraw his name and save everyone a fight.

As friendly as Smathers was with Dr, Annis, to whom he owed a major political debt, Smathers was equally close to Kennedy. They were old friends from Kennedy's Senate days. Kennedy personally intervened on behalf of Cohen. The President asked Smathers by phone to drop the whole idea of Cohen's withdrawal and see to it that Cohen was confirmed.

That settled, only Carl Curtis (R-Nebraska) was left to stage a fight against Cohen's appointment. Curtis tried to discredit Cohen by using material supplied by Margery Shearon, radical right lobbyist whose self-appointed job it was to keep tabs on important people's suspected Communist affiliations. Curtis lost. Wilbur Cohen was confirmed as Assistant Secretary of HEW in April by a vote of 13–1.[14]

The position of Under Secretary of HEW was filled by Ivan Nestingen, Mayor of Madison, Wisconsin. Nestengen's appointment was a non-controversial, mostly political appointment. Nestingen had been the only Protestant politician in Wisconsin to support Kennedy. Moreover, the Mayor had connections with Kenneth O'Donnell, another aid to the President.

The combination of the three personalities—Ribicoff, Nestingen, and Cohen—dashed hopes of a cooperative division of labor. The Kennedy team assumed that Cohen would take charge of the legislative fight for Medicare. He was supposed to report to Sorensen and Feldman in the White House for policy decisions and to Lawrence O'Brien for legislative tactics. Nestingen, as Under Secretary, was not supposed to get involved in tactics or policy. However, Nestingen had a direct line of contact with Walter Reuther, Charles Odell, and Ray Henry from the UAW. Cohen and Nestingen had entirely different approaches to getting Medicare passed. Moreover, Nestingen took on tactical responsibilities and arranged for meetings without consulting either Ribicoff or Cohen.

Cohen's approach was to gradually win over Wilbur Mills and the Ways and Means Committee by political compromise and a changing composition of Congress. Nestingen wanted to organize senior citizen groups and put direct political pressure on individual Congressmen to challenge Mills's authority. The two men ran a running battle up to 1964, and frequently worked against each other when dealing with Congress, especially with Mills.[15]

In 1964 Cohen said:

I am sure that Mr, Nestingen still harbors a violent grudge against me for not having supported his point of view and for not having cooperated in working with him. . . . Quite frankly I considered all of these other people as interlopers and interferers into the process for which I was being held responsible. . . . Nestingen and his group thought that they were a lot smarter than Ted Sorensen and myself.[16]

Ribicoff, in his role as Chairman, refused to get involved in the details of HEW. He considered the department an administrative monstrosity. Privately, however, he had a working respect for Cohen and an earnest dislike for Nestingen.[17]

In his State of the Union address, Kennedy made it clear that national health insurance for the elderly was going to be a priority issue. Delivered January 30, 1961, the President included the following words:

Medical research has achieved new wonders—but these wonders are too often beyond the reach of too many people owing to a lack of income (particularly among the elderly), a lack of hospital beds, a lack of nursing homes and a lack of doctors and dentists. Measures to provide health care for the aged under social security and to increase the supply of both facilities and personnel must be undertaken this year.[18]

On February 9, barely ten days later, Kennedy sent a special message to Congress on "Health and Hospital Care." It was the first message ever to be devoted entirely to the need of a health care program. In this speech Kennedy focused exclusively on the Administration's objectives for health.

In our social security and Railroad Retirement Systems we have the instruments which can spread the cost of health services in old age over the working years— effectively and in a manner consistent with the dignity of the individual. Those among us who are 65—16 million elderly in the U.S.—go to the hospital more often and stay longer than their younger neighbors. Their physical activity is limited by six times as much disability as the rest of the population. Their annual medical bill is twice that of persons under 65—their annual income is only half as high.[19]

Kennedy emphasized that his bill was not socialized medicine, "every person will choose his own doctor and hospital."

To remedy the medical problems of the elderly Kennedy recommended legislation very similar to the Kennedy-Anderson Bill that he had sponsored while still a Senator. The 1961 version included 90 days of hospital care (with a $10 deductible for the first nine days), 180 days of skilled nursing home care after discharge from a hospital, 240 days of home health visits a year, and outpatient diagnostic coverage from a hospital (with a $20 deductible per study). In all it was a 1.1 billion dollar program. The 1961 bill, as in the 1960 bill, left out surgeon's fees in the belief that the payment of surgical fees would be most anathema to the medical profession.

Medicare was only a part of the total package. Kennedy also called for nursing home construction grants, hospital research and development, training programs for more health personnel, increases in appropriations for maternal and child health, and the establishment of a National Institute of Child Health and Development—all programs recommended by the Cohen task force. Also, in his February 9 message, Kennedy designated Ribicoff as head of the President's Council on Youth Fitness.[20]

Congressional reaction was mixed. Speaker Sam Rayburn called it "a mighty fine thing" while Senate and House Republican leaders, Everett Dirksen and Charles Hallack, were indignant. Nine liberal Republican senators called the bill "inadequate" (Prouty, Aiken, Javits, Keating, Cooper, Scott, Fong, Cotton, and Saltonstall).[21]

On February 13, Clinton Anderson introduced the Administration Bill on Medicare as S909 in the Senate. Medicare, though, had no sponsor in the Ways and Means Committee. Aime Forand retired at the end of the 1960 legislative session, At the suggestion of Wilbur Mills, the Kennedy people turned to Cecil King, a Democrat from California who replaced Forand in seniority.[22] Representing a heavily industrialized district that included Los Angeles, King was known as an aloof, quiet, undynamic but reliable party man. He gladly took up the cudgels for Medicare. King introduced the Administration Bill, designated as HR4222, in the House.[23]

Kennedy sent letters to Vice President Lyndon Johnson and Speaker of the House Sam Rayburn urging Congress to enact the King-Anderson Bill as quickly as possible.

Enactment of the legislation would not relieve its beneficiaries of their entire responsibility for the costs incurred by their medical needs but it would enable them to meet most of their medical costs without any humiliating means test. The financing is based upon the sound and proven social security principles.[24]

Both the Vice President and the Speaker supported Medicare. A friend of Rayburn's said, "One of the stupidist mistakes the medical profession ever made was to charge Rayburn's brother in his last illness with enormous bills. This amounted to about $7,000 and Sam had to help pay them. He thought poorly of the medical profession ever since."[25]

The next step for Medicare was to schedule hearings in the Ways and Means Committee. Medicare, though, was only a part of the "thousand day" blitz of New Frontier legislation. Mills's Committee had to deal with even higher priority legislation, such as tax revision, anti-recession measures and a billion dollar Federal aid to education bill.[26] This other legislation was so important, and so dependent on Mills's total cooperation, that nobody in HEW and the Kennedy staff was willing to push him to schedule hearings for health insurance. According to Cohen, Mills had his own way of doing things and the best that Medicare supporters could do was follow his lead. Cohen made himself available as a general assistant and refrained from active lobbying.[27] As Mills himself remembers, he was at the White House almost daily to discuss the tax bill and Kennedy never mentioned Medicare to him.[28]

Meanwhile, public sentiment was being mobilized both for and against Medicare by the media and private lobby groups. In early February, Howard K. Smith in "CBS Reports" viewed a presentation on the pros and cons of medical insurance. It was entitled "The Business of Health, Medicine, Money and Politics." Its purpose was to examine various kinds of prepaid medical insurance in this country and elsewhere. It also took a look at the Kennedy proposals, the AMA's position, the ideas of labor and of liberal MD's, the opinions of health plan experts, and the high costs of medical care.

On this popular and controversial show, Dr. Ralph S. Emerson, of New York's Nassau County Medical Society, told the American public that "all America will topple into socialism or communism once American doctors topple the political control." Two other AMA representatives, E. Vincent Askey, the outgoing President of the AMA, and Leonard Larson, the President-elect, directed their comments to a discourse for free enterprise. According to press comments, the AMA paled in comparison with the other side.[29]

CBS showed a hospital in Harlan, Kentucky, operated by the UMW with physicians on salary, that illustrated expert care and modern facilities. Advocates of using the Social Security system to provide medical insurance, as well as liberal doctors, and even witnesses from Britain and Canada came out as more reasonable representatives than the AMA. In a column for *Commonweal* called "Adam Smith, M.D." Edward Chase castigated doctors for their "guileless use of the businessman's Babbitt-like rhetoric about free enterprise to defend the status quo."[30]

One major fact that surfaced from the show was that despite the fears of government control of medicine, 44 percent of all hospital care as of 1961 was already being financed by government: (14 percent by the Federal Government and 30 percent by local and state governments).

The AMA criticized the show as a monumental travesty on the medical profession. They called the CBS program a misrepresentation, bias, and distortion of the viewpoints of their representatives. AMA doctors claimed that CBS had cut about 40,000 feet of tape including their crucial arguments. Howard K. Smith responded to the clamor by spending an unprecedented six minutes during another show reading out loud pro and con mail from viewers.[31]

The AMA was the major lobby opposing the King-Anderson Bill. They were the most in earnest and had the biggest budget. After the CBS show, the AMA announced an "all-out effort" to fight the Kennedy health insurance program. The AMA doctors regarded Medicare as the "greatest deadly challenge" ever faced by the medical profession.[32]

As part of a multi-media publicity campaign, posters were distributed to AMA members entitled "Socialized Medicine and You." Along with the posters went a note suggesting that doctors hang the posters in their offices and discuss the topic with their patients. The note reminded the doctors, "Your freedom is at stake." Simultaneously, the AMA sponsored a series of ads on radio and television. These ads, aired four to five times a day, five days a week for five weeks, aimed to hit the average citizen, perhaps the wife and mother, to the point where he or she will say, "I can't bear the thought of socialized medicine!"[33]

Leading this effort was the AMA Board of Directors with headquarters on North Dearborn Street in Chicago. In 1961, the Board included the President, Dr. E. Vincent Askey; Leo Brown, the director of Communications; Dr, Francis James Blasingame, Executive Vice President; Dr. Ernest B. Howard, Assistant Vice President; and Dr. C. Joseph Stetler, director of the AMA scientific publications. In Washington, D.C. the AMA maintained an office with 12 rooms on L Street. Dr. Roy Lester, a Texas chest surgeon frequently described as "a popular member of the cocktail circuit," was director of the Washington lobby.[34]

Although by April the Ways and Means Committee had still not scheduled hearings, the AMA increased its publicity campaign. On April 19, it ran a full-page ad in 29 major newspapers across the country. The ad was called "Health Insurance and You" and listed all of the dangers of the King-Anderson Bill. Ribicoff promptly accused the AMA of false advertising, saying that the doctors were crying "wolf" to the American people. At that point the Board of Directors of the AMA challenged Ribicoff to a national debate on the subject of Medicare. From Chicago headquarters, Dr. Blasingame explained that the purpose of the debate would be to "end the continuous round of claims and counter-claims surrounding the Administration's programs.... The people are entitled to know whether the program is in fact socialized medicine for a segment of the population now and a foot in the door toward complete socialized medicine for everyone." The debate was never scheduled. Instead, Ribicoff and the doctors embarked on a cross-country exchange of invectives on the subject of Medicare. Ribicoff proved that he was equal to any verbal challenge that the AMA issued.[35]

Thaddeus Machrowicz (D-Michigan), member of the Ways and Means, commented that the AMA had the "most ruthless, powerful and thorough lobby in Washington."[36] Probably every member of Congress could attest to the power of the AMA's Washington lobby. Even so, in that Spring of 1961, the doctors felt that their existing organization was insufficient for the cause. A new entity was founded: American Medical Political Action Committee. AMPAC, as it was known, had the sole purpose of waging war on the Medicare Bill.

Presented as an independent organization, AMPAC was allowed by law to receive contributions for "educational purposes." As one of the directors nicely put it, "We are out to elect conservatives." Of course, the AMA is a collection of state societies, and not all states contributed equally to the new political action group. Three states that were the most earnest in their support were Texas, Iowa, and Indiana.[37]

The AMA and AMPAC concentrated on personalizing their campaign. In May, *Look* magazine published a moving account of a "family doctor's fight against socialized medicine." Dr. Joseph Ross Mallory, of Mattou, Illinois, told *Look* readers that the problems of older people were exaggerated. The King-Anderson Bill, he said, was founded on two erroneous assertions: the aged were mostly in poor health; and most needed financial help to meet their medical bills. Dr. Mallory said that this was simply not true. Most of the older people he knew were in good health and financially capable—even millionaires. Some 70 year oldsters were playing 18 holes of golf regularly.[38]

Dr. Mallory explained that the reason that he called King-Anderson socialized medicine was because the Federal Government would make direct payments to hospitals and could therefore set its own standards. Mallory preferred Kerr-Mills because it was state operated. Each state would decide who needed help. He figured, "We know more about our problems in Mattou than some government employee way off in Washington, D.C. Can there be any doubt in anyone's mind that once medicine is socialized, socialism will spread to every other aspect of American life.''[39] If this were representative of a small-town practitioner, and multiplied across the country, then one can realize that Medicare was in need of a good public relations campaign. A 1961 Gallup poll showed that 81 percent of American doctors were against the King-Anderson Bill.

However, a small minority of doctors, disgusted with the publicity methods and misrepresentations of the AMA, formed two new groups to counter the negative stance of the AMA. In California, about 200 doctors organized the Bay Area Committee for Medical Aid to the Aged through Social Security. Other doctors formed a smaller, national group called The Physicians Committee for Health Care for the Aged through Social Security.[40]

This last group included many prominent physicians such as Caldwell B. Esselstyn, president of Group Health Association and physician to Lou Gehrig and Eleanor Roosevelt, whose Rip Van Winkle Clinic in New York was forced to close by the AMA because of Esselstyn's "independent politics.''[41] Also in the Physicians Committee were David F. Bauer, chief physician at New York Hospital; Leona Baumgartner, New York City Commission of Health; Arthur Kornberg and Dickenson Richards, both Nobel Laureates in Physiology; Benjamin Spock, pediatrician and author; Helen Taussig, one of the founders of the "blue baby" operation, and Michael E. DeBakey, the noted heart surgeon.[42]

The independent doctors were no political match for the AMA. The only possibility in terms of real power was the AFL-CIO. Nelson Cruikshank, Andrew Biemiller, and Leonard Lesser continued to push for health insurance, Cruikshank, from his office in the AFL-CIO Social Security department, supplied vital arguments and technical information to pro-Medicare legislators and did so more quickly and efficiently than the Department of HEW. Cruikshank, Biemiller, and Lesser were present at most Congressional strategy sessions on Medicare. According to the labor historian J. David Greenstone, many liberal Congressmen believed that "organized labor was by all odds the single most important lobbying group (within the Democratic) party's welfare-oriented constituency."[43]

In contrast to Greenstone, Bill Reidy complained of the absence of labor help in the McNamara Senate Subcommittee hearings. Partly because of the lack of labor support, the National Council of Senior Citizens was established in July, 1961.[44] The new group grew out of the Democratic Senior Citizens for Kennedy, organized in March, 1960. The Senior Citizens for Kennedy had been largely the work of two men: James Cuff O'Brien, who headed a retired workers committee for the Steel Workers; and Charles Odell, who did the same for UAW.[45]

After the 1960 election, O'Brien and Odell wanted to make the group into a permanent organization. Top AFL-CIO officials hesitated. Cruikshank was afraid of another Townsend Movement, the national organization of older people so popular in the thirties. Cruikshank called the Townsend goals "wildly irresponsible."[46]

However, the need for organizing the elderly was there, and O'Brien and Odell had their way. The new Council while publicly advertising itself as bipartisan, drew support from three sources: the AFL-CIO; the Democratic National Committee (which, after analyzing the election returns for 1960, realized that the elderly played a significant role in getting Kennedy elected); and individual dues of one dollar.

Aime Forand was asked to become the first Chairman of the Council for Senior Citizens. He accepted, but with reluctance. Due to his poor health and age, his role was little more than that of a figurehead. James O'Brien, the real operating force, was described by Wilbur Cohen as a "very dedicated person," who in 1961 "could have had any government job he wanted—but he wanted only to work for the senior citizens." After O'Brien, William Hutton became another important force. Hutton, a New York public relations man, and former director of the British Information Service for Central Europe, was responsible for making the Council a first class social action lobby.[47]

While it never had the operating budget of the AMA and AMPAC, the National Council grew very quickly. Within six months it had a monthly newsletter and a membership of half a million. Eventually, all of the AFL-CIO, including Cruikshank, supported the Council, working with it to "keep it on the right track."[48]

In Congress, the chances of getting Medicare passed in 1961 were looking dim. Kennedy was asked at a press conference on April 22 if the Administration had reconciled itself to getting a "no" vote on medical care for the elderly that year. He answered that it was possible that someone might offer the King-Anderson Bill in the Senate as an amendment to another bill and Medicare could get a vote in the Senate that way—but the House was a different problem.[49]

As April ended, individual legislators were putting pressure on the President to do something about Medicare. Jacob Javits expressed dismay over the recurring rumors that the Administration had quietly decided to put off Medicare until the following year. Liberal Republicans in the Senate, led by Javits, were determined to accept the social security principle as a compromise and wanted to add their bill as an amendment to another bill—forcing the Democrats to do likewise.[50]

On April 28, Administration leaders sat down together for a strategy session on King-Anderson. At that session, attended by Wilbur Cohen, Clinton Anderson, Hubert Humphrey, and Wilbur Mills, Mills promised hearings on King-Anderson as soon as the tax revision bill was finished. Mills estimated that this would be sometime in late May.[51]

Hearings in the Ways and Means Committee were finally delayed until July 24. The Committee announced plans to investigate the following problems: the nature of medical care legislation for those over 65; whether the problems of those over 65 were unique; to what degree their health needs were already being met; to what extent this group could meet its own financial requirements; the impact of Medicare legislation on hospitals; and alternative means of financing health care.[52]

The Ways and Means Committee received over 400 requests to be heard. Opponents of the King-Anderson Bill were basically from two categories: either from doctors' groups or from conservative organizations coming to the support of "free enterprise." Those advocating the bill came from the government, labor organizations, or from various voluntary senior citizens clubs around the country. The Secretary of HEW was invited to speak first. Ribicoff, with Cohen by his side, told the Committee:

With lifespans lengthened, with medical science breaking into undreamed realms of discovery, the nation's aged now face another aspect of insecurity: how to meet the mounting costs of health care. The method of providing paid-up health insurance protection for retirement has not been followed on any large scale in private insurance, nor is it likely that it will be. The social insurance method, then, is the only practical way of enabling most people to pay during their working years towards meeting the health costs they will face in old age.[53]

In the questions and debate that followed, Ribicoff discussed his concern that there was a dollar limit to how far Social Security taxes could be raised within the realm of public tolerance. Ribicoff suggested the figure of ten percent of a wage-earner's salary as the limit that could go towards welfare and insurance programs. To keep costs down, Ribicoff recommended drawing the line as far as benefits go. This was his rationale for leaving out doctors' fees.

Representative Thomas Curtis was the first to inform the Ways and Means Committee of the ''foot in the door'' conservative position that the AMA had so ardently been advertising in the media. Curtis asked Ribicoff if ''the proponents of Medicare abandoned their original proposal to cover everyone''? Curtis announced to no one's surprise that the health needs of the elderly could best be solved by America's free enterprise system. This would happen if private industry worked out plans through collective bargaining. Then the consumer would pay the bill. Ribicoff replied that, if that were done, with whom you worked and where you lived would determine how much you enjoy good health.[54]

Ribicoff and Curtis engaged in a philosophical discussion over whether people were *entitled* to good health as a matter of right. This was a central argument in the welfare vs. insurance issue. Ribicoff argued that each person was indeed entitled to health care. Curtis disagreed. Society had a moral obligation to help only those who proved their need—the basic philosophy behind the Kerr-Mills Bill, which depended upon a state-run means test.[55]

George Meany and Walter Reuther testified on different days on behalf of King-Anderson. Meany, speaking for the AFL-CIO, and accompanied by Nelson Cruikshank and Andrew Biemiller, went right to the heart of the issue. ''Is there a problem? Are other effective remedies available? The health costs of the elderly are not and cannot be met by private insurance or Kerr-Mills. . . . In fact, HR4222 would make Kerr-Mills more effective by reducing the number of elderly who need help.''[56]

Walter Reuther was always a controversial figure when he appeared before a committee hearing. This time he was accompanied by James

Brindle, director of the Social Security Department of UAW and Leonard Lesser, who held a position in the Industrial Union Department of the AFL-CIO. Perhaps to appear less radical Reuther peppered his speech with numerous quotes from Abraham Lincoln on the importance of economic security. Representative John F. Byrnes asked Reuther if he was for covering medical costs of physicians. When Reuther answered yes, Byrnes wondered if people were behind the King Bill as a first step hoping to get broader coverage later. Reuther answered, "Obviously those who think the present bill is not adequate will want to continue their efforts to get unmet needs met in the future to make it more adequate . . . if we could get the principle established we want to build on that principle just as we built on Social Security."[57]

Reuther's statement of desired expansion was all that the conservatives needed to hear. They responded:

> Curtis: Don't you also advocate a complete program of health insurance for everyone. Isn't that your ultimate goal?
>
> Baker: If the rate of taxation is continually raised how high should taxes go to rendering all social security services?
>
> Alger: My closing remark is that I am just sorry you (Reuther) are as successful as you are.[58]

Despite the hostility, Reuther brought up another point in his testimony. He was disturbed, he said, about Dr. Annis's (of the AMA) claim that Medicare would destroy the Social Security system which is itself not on sound financial ground. Reuther told the Committee that there is an Advisory Council on Social Security Financing, not made up of agitators or socialists, but of responsible men like Elliott Bell, Malcolm Bragon, Carl Fisher, and Reinhard Attohauas.[59]

After Reuther, a third major labor spokesman, Joe Swire of the International Union of Electrical Workers, spoke for the bill. Swire was accorded the same contemptuous treatment that Reuther and Meany had received. In Swire's case, Baker was quiet and Curtis, Byrne, and Alger led the attack.[60]

Helen Hall, honorary President of the National Federation of Settlements and Neighborhood Associations, gave the next testimony endorsing the bill. Miss Hall had begun as a social worker in 1920, worked for the Red Cross during the First and Second World Wars, and served on Franklin Roosevelt's Presidential Advisory Council to the Committee on Economic Security. Miss Hall said that the "insurance principle is basic to American life, and we subscribe to it as the most self-respecting way of protecting ourselves against dependency and against disaster of all kinds." Moreover, she added, when the AMA talks about government destroying doctor-patient relationships, they are speaking of something that does not exist at least for the lower classes. Poor people in this country have no doctor-patient relationship—they go to clinics and hospitals to receive their basic care.[61]

The largest social group of senior citizens was the Council of Golden Ring Clubs that had branches in New York, New Jersey, Florida, California, Illinois, and Ohio. Their members were mostly middle class, and not eligible for Kerr-Mills benefits because they received Social Security checks and union pensions. The President of the Golden Rings, Adolph Held, testified that Kerr-Mills was so inadequate that it resulted in a change only in bookkeeping systems. The law shifted the source of support from the city and state governments to the Federal Government. There was really no increase in applications or eligibility. Held said that his organization favored Medicare because it got rid of the means test. Also, it was necessary because older people could not make payments on private policies after retirement.[62]

Other organizations that sent representatives to testify on behalf of Medicare were the National Association of Retired and Veteran Railway Employees with 800,000 members, the National Consumers League, the Council of Jewish Federation and Welfare Funds, and even the Socialist Party of the U.S., the SP-SDF. The Socialists, whose spokesman was Jean Donnelly, said that they were the experts on socialized medicine and HR4222 was clearly no socialized medicine. It was a watered down version of the conservative Forand Bill. If the country wanted socialized medicine then the Veteran's Administration Hospital system could be expanded to get a more complete socialization.[63] Others who spoke on behalf of HR4222 were Arthur Altmeyer, former head of the Social Security Administration; Dr. Evelyn M. Burns, professor at the New York School of Social Work at Columbia University and consultant to the Committee on Economic Security and the New York School of Social Work; Loula Dunn, director of the American Public Welfare Association; and Jane Hoey, director of the Bureau of Public Assistance.

Dr. Allen Butler, spokesman for the Physician's Forum, endorsed King-Anderson as "a major step toward filling the greatest gap in

American health insurance: inadequate coverage of the aged."[64] He commended the feature in the bill that provided benefits in the form of services instead of cash. As soon as Dr. Butler completed his testimony, Bruce Alger criticized the Physician's Forum's credentials, saying that the group published articles in the *Daily Worker* and the Communist press, and that members had been cited by the Attorney General in 1958 for joining the Joint Anti-Fascist Refugee Committee, a group on the list of subversion organizations. Dr. Butler, a professor at Harvard Medical School, a doctor at the Massachusetts General Hospital, and assistant editor of the *New England Journal of Medicine*, responded: "Representative Alger, I am shocked by what you just said. You did the same thing last year at these hearings.... Also, the John Birch Society included me along with President Eisenhower and Chief Justice Warren as communists."[65]

When Dr. Leonard Larson, President of the AMA, took the stand, Cecil King returned the invective. Dr. Larson came to the hearings with a 190–page statement. When asked to summarize the opposition of the AMA toward HR4222, Dr. Larson said that the bill would:

1. lower the quality of medical care
2. was unnecessary
3. unpredictably expensive
4. would endanger the whole social security system
5. undermine private insurance
6. lead to a decline in voluntary community efforts
7. cover millions who did not need help or who don't want it
8. has eligibility based on age instead of need
9. destroy the concept of family responsibility
10. eliminate the historical role of the states in health matters[66]

King responded:

It is an interesting statement from the standpoint of how far in my opinion desperate men will go to accomplish their purpose ... In all my legislative experience I have never heard a statement read or have to read a statement with respect to a legislative proposal more detailed with damning and criticism of features and substances not mentioned or provided in the language of the bill than your statement with respect to HR4222.[67]

Most state medical societies sent spokesmen to speak against King-Anderson. In addition, organizations of medical specialists testified against the bill, such as Dr. Stewart Seigle, President of the American Society of Internal Medicine; and Dr. L. Henry Garland, President of the American College of Radiology. Representatives from the dental profession, pharmacists, and ophthalmologists also expressed their disapproval. They all basically mentioned the same reasons as the AMA.

Only one doctor added something new. Representative Dale Alford (D-Arkansas) testified as both a doctor and a member of Congress. He raised the whole debate about King-Anderson to a philosophical metaphor. He stated, "In my view HR4222 is a measure cunningly devised for fishing in troubled waters. The bait is humanitarian; the hook is loss of freedom." Alford ended his testimony with a prayer. "Let us hope ... that we in America never set security over political freedom."[68]

The National Association of Manufacturers came to the assistance of the medical profession. Its chairman, John E. Carroll, said that he represented 19,000 members. Eighty percent of those members had less than 500 employees, and 50 percent had less than 100. Carroll expressed amazement that few witnesses had said anything about the cost of King-Anderson. Carroll figured that most of the witnesses in favor of the bill probably weren't concerned about the cost. The U.S., he told the Committee, was already paying higher salaries than foreign competitors and could not afford more payroll taxes.[69]

The American Hospital Association was slow to make up its mind about Medicare. It preferred a policy of "benevolent neutrality" but found that impossible, given the controversy over HR4222.[70] Senator Clinton Anderson and his administrative assistant Claude Wood were asked to lunch with Lacey Sharp and Kenneth Williamson, associate directors of the A.H.A., immediately prior to the July hearings. Williamson and Sharp said that they leaned toward supporting Medicare but others within their group weren't so sure. They were under tremendous pressure from the AMA to come out against King-Anderson.[71]

When it was their turn to testify, Sharp and Williamson, along with Dr. Frank S. Groner, president of the A.H.A., announced that they were against HR4222 for three reasons: 1. the government will exert too much power over the hospitals because it controlled the funds; 2. Medicare will lead to unnecessary utilization which will escalate costs; and 3. the bill would foster extension of the same services to everyone. The spokesman for the A.H.A. said that they were against deductibles and they favored state and local control of medical matters. However, the hospital group was not a united front. Two former officials of the A.H.A.—Dr. E. M. Bluestone, recipient of the 1961 distinguished service award of the A.H.A. and currently professor of Administration at New York University; and Dr. Basil McClean, former President of the A.H.A. and current President of the National Blue Cross Association—inserted statements into the record that they favored King-Anderson.[72]

The hearings ended after nine days and 1,850 pages of testimony. As Robert Myers, Director of the Bureau of Statistics for SSA, pointed out, the hearings were only to establish a record, they changed no one's mind.[73] They won no additional votes—to either side. Wilbur Mills was silent or absent during the entire hearings. The three outspoken Republican conservatives, Byrnes, Alger, and Curtis, remained convinced that HR4222 was "still a handout for those who have contributed nothing and are presently over 65."[74] The line-up of votes on the Ways and Means Committee remained heavily against King-Anderson. King and other Democratic and labor leaders preferred not to have a negative vote on the record.

In a letter to Senator Pat McNamara, President Kennedy pledged that Medicare would receive highest priority in next year's Congressional session. Kennedy promised a "great fight across that land" for enactment of a hospital insurance program for the aged in 1962.[75]

5

A Bipartisan Effort

As soon as the 87th Congress reconvened in January, 1962 for its second
session, Senator Clinton Anderson asked his Chairman of the Finance
Committee to hold immediate hearings on the King-Anderson (S909)
Bill. Anderson told Chairman Harry F. Byrd that the House Ways and
Means Committee had held its hearings on King-Anderson during the
first session, and that the Senate should not have to wait for further
action from the House before holding its own hearings. Byrd ignored
Anderson's request.[1]

Taking the initiative, Anderson introduced a motion to hold hearings
in the Finance Committee no later than April 1, 1952. The motion was
defeated 7–10. Including Anderson, only six of the 12 Democrats on
the Committee voted for hearings: Russell Long, Paul Douglas, Albert
Gore, Eugene McCarthy, Vance Hartke—along with a single Republican, Thruston Morton. The other five Democrats, Chairman Harry
Byrd, Robert Kerr, George Smathers, Herman Talmadge, and William
Fulbright, sided with the five Republicans, John J. Williams, Frank
Carlson, Carl T. Curtis, Wallace F. Bennett, and John Marshall Butler,
to defeat Anderson's motion. Kerr immediately offered another motion
to hold hearings in the Finance Committee as soon as the House passed
King-Anderson, an unlikely event that year. Kerr's motion carried 10–
7.[2]

Stalemated in the Finance Committee, the Kennedy Administration
pursued two different strategies simultaneously. Under Secretary of
HEW, Ivan Nestingen, working with labor leaders Walter Reuther and
Charles Odell, and the National Council for Senior Citizens, planned

a grass-roots campaign. Their goal was to go into Congressional districts and organize senior citizens and union people through meetings, rallies, and letter-writing campaigns aimed primarily at members of the Ways and Means Committee. Nestingen, Reuther, and Odell intended to "stir up" enough activity so that when Congressmen returned home for Easter recess they would find overwhelming public support for the King-Anderson Bill. Nestingen also wanted to put direct pressure on Wilbur Mills.[3]

The second approach, favored by HEW Secretary Abraham Ribicoff, Assistant Secretary Wilbur Cohen, labor representatives Nelson Cruikshank and Leonard Lesser, and White House staff members Theodore Sorensen and Myer Feldman, was to develop a compromise bill acceptable to the three or four indecisive members of the Ways and Means Committee which would allow Mills to have his majority and bring out the bill. Failing that, they were considering a floor amendment to get the bill through the Senate.[4]

On February 27, President Kennedy delivered a special message on health to Congress. The President had sent a similar message in 1961.

Whenever the miracles of modern medicine are beyond the reach of any group of Americans, for whatever reason—economic, geographic, occupational, or other—we must find a way to meet those needs. . . . Our social insurance system today guards against nearly every major financial setback: retirement, death, disability and unemployment. But it does not protect our older citizens against the hardships of prolonged and expensive illness.[5]

Two days after Kennedy's speech, the *Wall Street Journal* wrote in an editorial that the debate over health care for the aged was no longer a question of *whether*, but *how*.[6] "How" was a perplexing question for the administration, with no favorable action in either the Senate Finance Committee or the House Ways and Means Committee.

The Republicans provided a possible solution. Concerned over the prospects of the Democrats making Medicare an issue in the November 1962 Congressional elections, the Republicans felt that they should have something positive to offer. They developed three different legislative plans.[7] Representative Frank Bow (R-Ohio) introduced the first Republican bill, HR10755, on March 28. Bow's bill provided for a yearly income tax credit or a certificate for $125 to be used for purchasing a private health insurance policy. The certificate, financed out of general revenue, was for those who had no income or income tax to pay. The Bow Bill was wholeheartedly supported by Republican National Chairman and Representative William E. Miller (R-New York), who said that all Republicans should line up behind the Bow Bill. The Bow Bill had many co-sponsors. House Minority Leader Charles E. Halleck (Indiana) and House senior-ranking Republican John Byrnes (Wisconsin) did not agree. They preferred to offer no new legislation and to stay with the Kerr-Mills Bill.[8]

Representative John Lindsay (R-New York) sponsored the second Republican bill, HR11253, a bill that was developed in cooperation with New York Governor Nelson Rockefeller and his staff. The Lindsay Bill provided benefits that were identical to King-Anderson, but added an option for those over 65 who did not want to participate in the government's Medicare plan. The option was a cash increase to their Social Security checks with which the elderly could purchase their own private policy. The problem was that the participants had to decide on whether they wanted to exercise that cash option long before they turned 65. At the time of the decision they had to own a private policy that could convert on retirement.[9]

The third and most significant Republican bill came from Senator Jacob Javits (R-New York). Since 1960, Javits, a leading liberal Republican, had sought a major role in getting health insurance for senior citizens passed. Originally, he had been opposed to the Social Security approach for financing health care. He worried about the resentment of younger workers who would have to bear the greatest burden in contributions from their salaries. From his own surveys, he discovered that his concerns were ill-founded. The Social Security approach was the method that most workers actually preferred.[10]

Javits introduced S2664, which was co-sponsored by six other Republican liberals. The bill used Social Security financing to offer the retiree an option of two insurance plans: a short-term health policy with no deductible; or a simple cash payment for the retiree to purchase his or her own policy. Also, non-participants in the Social Security system were offered the same two choices, but their program was to be financed out of general tax revenue.[11]

Javits got his idea of voluntary options from two former Eisenhower people, Arthur Flemming and Marion Folsom. Winslow Carlton, Javits's administrative assistant, also favored the idea. Carlton played a major role in writing many of Javits's health bills. The free choice idea was proposed by yet another group that was close to Javits: American Association of Retired Persons.[12] The AARP was an association of mainly retired teachers, whose organization was partially funded by the Continental Casualty Insurance Company.[13]

Javits believed that a bipartisan approach was the only way to get Medicare passed in 1962. Toward that end in May, Wilbur Cohen joined Javits and his other administrative assistant, Allen Lesser, for lunch to explore a possible compromise between Javits and the other liberal Republicans and Clinton Anderson. Partly because of that lunch and partly because of the rumors around the Senate of a bipartisan bill, the *Wall Street Journal* reported that the backers of Medicare in the Kennedy Administration were willing to compromise. The *Journal* indicated that the compromise was aimed not only at the Senate Republican liberals but also at the four "fence-sitters" on the Ways and Means Committee: Burr Harrison (D-Virginia), Andrew Frazier (D-Tennessee), John Watts (D-Kentucky) and Howard H. Baker (R-Tennessee).[14]

After reading the article in the *Wall Street Journal*, Anderson noted that the Ways and Means Committee would more than likely resist all compromises. Possibly to halt speculation and further publicity, Anderson and King issued a press release saying that the Javits Bill was not in keeping with the principles of their bill and was not therefore a basis for compromise.[15]

Nevertheless, about a week after his luncheon meeting with Javits, Wilbur Cohen held an all day exploratory session with Nelson Cruikshank, Leonard Lesser, Winslow Carlton, and Steven Horn—Senator Kuchel's (R-California) administrative assistant. Robert Ball and his staff were also asked to attend. Ball was the Commissioner of Social Security and possessed and enviable amount of technical knowledge on the workings of the Social Security system.[16]

As one type of compromise, Anderson thought about the idea of revising S909 to permit higher income workers to use their share of money from Social Security benefits to buy a private health insurance policy. Anderson asked Ball if that type of arrangement would be feasible. Ball said no. SSA studies showed that that arrangement would not work. The workers who elected to participate in the government program would be those who anticipated being the highest users of the benefits. That would push up costs.

Ball explained in a memo to Anderson that the Social Security system

is financed by future contributions. Health insurance such as S909 would
be financed the same way. With any plan for voluntary "opting out"
of the system, it was always possible that the majority would choose
to opt out and the whole system would be thrown into insolvency. A
second reason that Ball was against any kind of voluntary arrangements
was that it negated the whole philosophy of social insurance: to protect
against future dependency. Practical administration made it necessary
for the worker to make his choice on health care at an early stage in
his working career. No worker could ever predict fully what his health
status and financial needs would be when he or she retired. "A younger
male worker who waives that protection could much later leave unprotected his widow. Also a commercial policy paid by a worker may be
inadequate by the time it is needed. Most commercial policies are based
on fixed dollars."[17]

Nothing definite came of the meeting between Cohen, Cruikshank,
Lesser and others. Javits suggested hearings in his own committee, the
Labor and Public Welfare Committee, as long as the Finance Committee
was doing nothing on King-Anderson. Cohen and Cruikshank were
strongly opposed to bypassing Finance, however long they had to wait
for action.[18] It was still early in May. The White House had made no
decision about bringing the King-Anderson to a vote in the Senate.
Mills was silent about the possibility of reporting King-Anderson out
of his committee.

While speculation increased about a Senate bipartisan Medicare bill,
the other White House group behind Nestingen was culminating its
grass-roots efforts on behalf of the Kennedy health insurance for senior
citizens plan. President Kennedy planned to address a crowd of about
20,000 senior citizens in Madison Square Garden on May 20, 1962. His
speech was broadcast over three television networks. The Garden rally
was organized by a joint effort between the AFL-CIO and the New
York Golden Rings clubs association. All persons paid one dollar ad-
mission to the Garden to hear the President.[19]

Kennedy spoke extemporaneously, aiming his speech for a political
rally, "I refuse to see us live on the accomplishments of another gen-
eration. I refuse to see this country and all of us shrink from the struggles
which we are responsible for in our time."[20] The President was effective
in the hall. The participants at the rally were already his supporters.
From the standpoint of television audience it was one of his least ef-

fective speeches. George Meany and Cruikshank believed that the speech was so inadequate that the President had killed the chance for Medicare's passage that year.[21]

The Madison Square Garden rally was only one of 33 rallies across the country to get support for health insurance for the elderly. Vice President Johnson addressed a crowd in St. Louis; Secretary of Labor Arthur Goldberg spoke in Miami Beach; Secretary of the Interior Stewart Udall spoke in Kansas City; Secretary of Commerce Luther Hodges in Boston; Wilbur Cohen in San Diego while Abraham Ribicoff stayed with the President. All the rallies were scheduled for the same week, May 20.[22]

The Administration did not have the last word. The American Medical Association had carefully planned a counter-event. Renting network time on 198 stations, Dr. Edward Annis, the Miami doctor who headed the AMA's Speakers Bureau and who had made a career out of fighting national health insurance, stood with the President of the AMA, Arthur Larson, on the podium of a totally empty Madison Square Garden. Speaking to an estimated nine million television viewers,[23] Annis said,

I'm not a cheerleader. I'm a physician.... These people [the Kennedy people] know how to rally votes, rally support, rally crowds and mass meetings. That's quite a lot of machinery to put behind something, isn't it? Who can match it? Certainly not your doctors.... We doctors fear that the American public is in danger of being blitzed, brainwashed, and bandwagoned into swallowing the idea that the King-Anderson bill is the only proposal—the only proposal that offers medical care for the aged.[24]

Most pro-Medicare supporters had to agree that the AMA had given the more effective speech.

The AMA had discovered that its most effective technique was to link King-Anderson with socialized medicine and link the latter with compulsion, poor quality, impersonal service, overcrowded hospital conditions, and the spectres of Kaiser Germany and Soviet Russia. "This campaign has been used by the AMA since the 1920s to fight Blue Cross, Social Security, workmen's compensation, disability," and the Salk vaccine. Some doctors even went beyond this "argument by association."[25] A group of doctors in Point Pleasant, New Jersey, proposed on May 19 (a day before Kennedy's Garden address) to boycott King-Anderson if it passed Congress. They vowed not to treat the recipients of "tainted" money. On that, the liberal magazine *Nation* made an interesting comment:

Assume it [King-Anderson] is passed—an elderly patient has a stroke or heart attack. The ambulance rushes him to the hospital. His family summons their regular physician, a passionate foe of anything that looks to him like socialized medicine. Discovering that the patient has passed the age of rugged individualism, the outraged healer refuses treatment. The first court test of this behavior will be fascinating indeed.[26]

Only a couple of days after announcing their initial intent to boycott, the Point Pleasant doctors issued a clarification of their position. They would not refuse treatment to their patients.

Many doctors did not go along with their peers. The Physicians Committee for Health Care of the Aged Through Social Security sent a full-page ad to the *Journal of the American Medical Association* [JAMA] and to the *A.M.A. News*. Their ad stated their position: "Only through Social Security can adequate health care be made available for American older citizens." The AMA rejected the ad as misleading and deceptive and refused to print it.[27] On the other hand, at the University of Chicago Medical School commencement, June 16, 1962, Dr. Lowell T. Coggeshall, Vice President of the University of Chicago, told the students to "recognize the role of government and help it take a fruitful direction."[28]

In early June *Nation's Business* published the results of a survey of medical students. The survey asked, "What is your opinion of the proposed legislation calling for Federal medical care for older citizens under social security?" Seventy percent of the students responding opposed the legislation; 30 percent were in favor. *Nation's Business* pointed out that the percentage of students in favor was much higher at two medical schools, Columbia University and New York University. The magazine also warned that greater Federal activity in health care would cause many Americans to abandon the study of medicine. Others would leave the U S. after graduation to practice in countries where the physician had more freedom.[29] (The article did not state which countries were possible places of relocation.)

Like the medical profession, the American Hospital Association was split in its attitude toward Medicare. In a special meeting called in the early part of 1962, A.H.A. and the Blue Cross Association tried to arrive at a joint policy decision. In an attempt to draw up a positive program, Walter J. McNerney, the new President of the Blue Cross Association, rallied 79 independent Blue Cross plans to get together and offer a uniform program for the elderly. The Blue Cross plan would provide 79 days of hospitalization for all subscribers over 65 at a cost of about $10 or $12 per month.

Some of the A.H.A. and Blue Cross resolutions were:

1. Recommend support for the Kerr-Mills act.
2. Develop new plans for the elderly with eligibility based on a simple income test.
3. Against King-Anderson.
4. Acknowledge that the private sector cannot meet the problem.
5. Need government assistance for voluntary plan of health insurance.
6. Method of financing not so important.[30]

It was the last resolution that really mattered to the Kennedy Administration. It was a subtle stamp of—if not approval—at least indifference, toward using the Social Security system to finance a health program. Yet there were so many contradictory resolutions that the meeting "provided all the main contestants in the national debate with the chance to read their own favorite interpretation into what took place."[31] The AFL-CIO and HEW called the meeting a victory for King-Anderson. The AMA said the A.H.A. stood solidly opposed to King-Anderson.[32]

As the summer of 1962 approached, *America*, a magazine that was keeping close watch on the progress of the Medicare debate, reported that King-Anderson belonged to the "seriously ill" if not "critical" list of pending legislation.[33] "The immediate danger was strangulation." Senator Harry F. Byrd, Chairman of the Finance Committee, was reported to have told the President that the White House could have its trade bill (for expanded trade and lower tariffs) or it could have Medicare, but not both.[34]

An editorial in *America* said,

the sheer volume of Congressional mail on the bill, the endless columns in newspapers and magazines, the unflagging series of radio and TV debates, round-tables, panels and documentaries, indicate the extent to which the question has gripped the nation ... unfortunately the debate now seems at the point where tempers flare, nerves fray, shows grow more guttural and accusations more wild. . . .[35]

Meanwhile, the line-up of votes on the Ways and Means Committee had not changed since the previous year's hearings. Mills did not have the clear majority in favor of King-Anderson necessary to report out the bill. Only 11 votes out of 25 favored the Administration's plan. One Republican, Burr Harrison of Virginia, said that he preferred King-Anderson to Kerr-Mills, but he wanted to see a higher deductible added to King-Anderson. He was listed as doubtful.[36]

On June 11, the Ways and Means Committee held executive hearings on HR10606, a general welfare bill. Adding King-Anderson as an amendment was a major topic of debate. The arguments for and against were identical to those in the 1961 hearings. Besides wanting a strong majority that he thought would carry in the House, Mills had two other considerations about reporting out a health insurance for the elderly bill. One was his own political future. As a result of the 1960 Census, Arkansas lost two representatives in the House. Mills's second district was redistributed in such a way that Mills would have to run against the very conservative Representative Dale Alford. Alford, a favorite of the Arkansas medical profession, remained a vigorous foe of King-Anderson.[37]

Secondly, Mills was under heavy personal pressure from individual congressmen not to report out a bill before the November elections. Many did not want to have to commit themselves either way. Mills, via Speaker of the House John McCormack, told the President that the best strategy would be to attach King-Anderson as a floor amendment to the welfare bill HR10606 that the House was sending over to the Senate. That way, the Ways and Means Committee would be circumvented and Mills would have to deal with the problem in conference with a mandate from the Senate. The Administration gave no answer.[38]

President Kennedy did not want to risk a defeat. In order for a floor amendment plan to work, the Administration had to have the necessary votes. There were not enough Democrats in the Senate in favor of the bill. The Administration could, however, win over the six or seven liberal Republican Senators behind Javits if a compromise could be drafted.

A team from the AFL-CIO, consisting of Nelson Cruikshank, Leonard Lesser, Andy Biemiller, and Jim Bindle, wrote out a compromise bill.

They modified King-Anderson to "let the private insurance companies handle out-of-pocket expenses on a reimbursement basis."[39] That is, they found a role for the privates but not in the traditional underwriting capacity. The privates would act as the administrators or "middlemen" between the hospitals and the government in reimbursing money. Another major change from the original King-Anderson Bill gave health insurance to those not eligible for Social Security. Those benefits would be financed out of general revenues. Javits later submitted an amendment to modify the Anderson Amendment to include an option for private coverage with a deductible or 45 day hospital coverage with no deductible. Anderson accepted the change.

The labor lobbyists did not know if their compromise would be acceptable to Javits because it limited his option idea and gave the privates a very restricted role. They also did not know if their compromise would be acceptable to George Meany because he was against giving the privates any role. Fortunately, within a couple of days, both Meany and Javits approved the new arrangement. Cohen agreed to the bill, as did Anderson. Anderson dropped the bill into the hopper on June 29. It was co-sponsored by 20 Democrats, including Anderson, and five Republicans, including Javits. The Senate was back in business.[40]

During the first two weeks of July, Javits and Anderson held a series of strategy meetings with their respective staffs. The personal styles of the two Senators were radically different. Javits was a brusque, "get down to business" person. Anderson was "laid back," jokes first and then on to business. It was not an easy relationship. Fortunately, the two had excellent staff members who carried out most of the work: Howard Bray for Anderson and Allen Lesser and Winslow Carlton for Javits. In addition, Nelson Cruikshank was usually at the meetings to act as labor and administration liaison.[41]

The Senate spent close to three weeks debating HR10606, the general welfare bill sent over from the House. Three alternatives to the revised King-Anderson Amendment were offered on the floor of the Senate. On July 5, Senator Thruston Morton proposed that the states who wanted to offer group policies to their aged be reimbursed by the Federal Government up to $125 per person. The group policy would have a choice between straight hospitalization or catastrophic insurance. Morton's amendment was defeated by a voice vote.[42] On July 9, Senator Leverett Saltonstall (R-Massachusetts) proposed that instead of Social Security financing, the Federal Government would give matching grants to the states to provide health insurance for the senior citizens. The states would have to offer three options to their seniors: short-term coverage, long-term coverage, or reimbursement for private purchase of insurance. Saltonstall's amendment was defeated 50–34.[43] Senator Prescott Bush (R-Connecticut) offered yet another variation, also on July 9. His idea was to take money out of the Social Security Trust fund and reimburse the Social Security beneficiaries up to $9 per month for the cost of buying their health insurance from private companies. The Bush Amendment was defeated 74–5.[44]

Most of the Senators had already made up their minds about the Javits-Anderson Amendment. Lawrence O'Brien, who headed the White House congressional liaison staff, counted about 48 votes—not enough to win. In addition, about four to six senators were listed as "maybes." Both Anderson and Majority Leader Mike Mansfield were making head counts of their own almost daily. It appeared to Anderson that they could count on about 50 votes, making the vote a tie. There were three main doubtfuls: Senator George Aiken (R-Vermont), Senator Mike Monroney (D-Oklahoma), and Senator Jennings Randolph (D-West Virginia).[45]

Senator Hugh Scott (R-Pennsylvania) had already changed his mind about going in with the Javits liberal group. He said that since the Kennedy speech at Madison Square Garden on May 20, his mail was running 2–1 against any administration health insurance bill. Senator Margaret Chase Smith (R-Maine) gave no reason for her decision not to support the amendment in 1962. She had supported Medicare in 1960, but apparently changed her mind this time.[46] Senator Aiken was another liberal Republican vote that Javits was supposed to "deliver." Aiken was the object of an intense letter-writing campaign by medical and nursing home constituents who informed him that, should the Javits-Anderson Amendment pass, only *three* out of 192 nursing homes in Vermont would qualify for new funds. Vermont had the largest number of senior citizens per capita in the nation. Aiken was in a tense position. It appeared to both Anderson and Larry O'Brien, who was keeping tabs on the votes for the White House, that Aiken would vote against the Javits-Anderson Bill.[47]

In the days before the Senate vote that was scheduled for July 17, Robert Kerr was a very busy man. With the help of the Legislative Reference Service, Kerr had prepared a breakdown of Kerr-Mills aid to states whose Senators remained doubtful. The list included Arizona

(Hayden); Alabama (Sparkman); Kentucky (Morton); Florida (Smath-ers); Kansas (Carlson); and Mississippi (Stennis). Kerr was keeping head counts of his own, but he did more than count votes. The quick-witted Senator from Oklahoma had drawn up an amendment to HR10606 that would allow persons past 65 to earn up to $50 a month in income and not be penalized in reduction of their Social Security benefits. This proposal, written by Wilbur Cohen and Robert Ball, had great popular appeal. On the face of it, it appeared to Cohen and others in HEW that it was a good thing. Any Senator who sponsored Kerr's proposal, regardless of his vote on Javits-Anderson, would return to their con-stituents with something concrete to help the elderly. Senator Douglas had already proposed an amendment to allow persons past 65 to earn as much as $25 a month if the states allowed. Douglas had been holding the amendment for some time, but all of a sudden Kerr urged him to offer it promptly before the votes on health care came up. Anderson was wondering why Kerr was so solicitous. He didn't have to wonder for long.

In a gesture of dubious good will, Kerr gave the amendment to Monroney, Aiken, and Randolph to sponsor. The three agreed. An-derson immediately grasped the significance of Kerr's action: it could be a basis for a trade of votes. Monroney, Aiken, and Randolph would be off the hook as far as their constituents go and free to vote with Kerr against the health insurance amendment. Anderson went immediately to Mike Mansfield and asked him to oppose the introduction of this new amendment that Kerr arranged. Apparently, Anderson was not fast enough. Mansfield had already seen the amendment, checked with the Social Security Administration and allowed it to be submitted. No one had viewed it as strange, because Douglas had offered it first.[48]

Mansfield and Anderson were still confident that they had at least 50 votes. The two Senators were relying on the usually very accurate vote-counting abilities of Mansfield's Assistant to the Majority Leader, Bobby Baker. Therein lay the cause for a critical discrepancy between estimates and reality.

Bobby Baker had been associated with the Senate since the 1950s. He had been an astute and able assistant to Lyndon Johnson when Johnson was the Senate Majority Leader. When Johnson became Vice President in 1960, Mike Mansfield took over as Majority Leader and inherited the services of Bobby Baker. With Johnson gone, Baker's allegiance was not to his new boss, but to the real power of the Senate, Robert Kerr.

Kerr and Baker did not want the White House worried. The two men knew that Aiken's vote was probably lost. So was Mike Monroney's. Monroney was considered doubtful because he was up for re-election that Fall. It was probably difficult for him to withstand the pressure of his fellow Oklahoman Kerr. To increase the pressure, Kerr sent a press release to his home state reporting that Oklahoma was in line for six or seven million dollars in Federal welfare assistance programs. In order to get that money, HR10606 had to pass. Furthermore, Kerr told his constituents, Oklahoma would benefit little from Javits-Anderson, which promised hospital and nursing home benefits. Only eight nursing homes in Oklahoma would meet the qualifications of Javits-Anderson. Therefore it was in Oklahoma's best interest for Monroney to defeat all controversial "riders" such as the Javits-Anderson Amendment. While knowing about Aiken and Monroney, Baker assured Mansfield that the Administration would have 50 votes. The Vice President could then break the tie in favor of Javits-Anderson.[49]

Carl Hayden was another problem. The 84–year-old senior Senator from Arizona had written privately to the President that he would vote for the health insurance amendment only if his vote were needed to win. Hayden was also up for reelection. His fellow Senator Barry Goldwater had made the issue of "socialized medicine" a central one in Arizona. That meant that there had to be at least 49 "yes" votes, and Hayden would be the 50th.[50]

According to Senate tallies, the 49th vote was Senator Jennings Randolph. Although Randolph was a former co-sponsor of the King-Anderson Bill, and usually a reliable party man, he was hesitant about his vote. His home state of West Virginia had overspent 21 million dollars in public welfare funds. According to the law, West Virginia could be subject to reprisals from the new welfare bill under discussion, HR10606. New appropriations that the state badly needed could be withheld.

In an act of beneficence and good timing, Kerr sponsored an amendment to HR10606 that would give West Virginia a 21 million dollar "kickback" and prevent the state from having future reductions in Federal aid for welfare. A "backroom manipulator of the first order," Kerr pointed out to Randolph that when HR10606 passed the Senate, and the bill went into conference, no one from the Administration would be there to protect West Virginia. The likely Senate conferees would be Harry Byrd, Kerr, and Russell Long. At the same time rumors were heard that Kerr, as Chairman of the Senate Appropriations Committee, had mentioned something to Randolph about coal research programs for West Virginia.[51]

For the Kennedy Administration the situation was very tense. On Friday, July 14, Mike Mansfield sent a telegram to Ribicoff in Hartford, Connecticut. Ribicoff had recently resigned his position as Secretary of HEW and returned to his home state to campaign for Senator. The telegram read, "Clint and I deeply appreciate if you could come to Washington to assist in health bill." Ribicoff came.[52] Anderson handed out folders of information about the amendment to all of its co-sponsors.

Twenty-four hours before the vote, Randolph was still listed as doubtful. Anderson did his best to allay Randolph's worries about his state's deficit. Anderson pointed out that the President could protect him as adequately as could Kerr on the final bill. The Kennedy Administration even flew the Governor of West Virginia to the capital to try to persuade Randolph that the money situation was not as bleak as Randolph thought and that he should vote with Anderson and support the President. Reassurances were not enough. Randolph was "in a sweat" and Kerr held the trump card.[53]

On Monday, July 17, the Senate remained in session until eight in the evening. Senate Minority Leader Everett McKinley Dirksen announced the schedule for the next day. There were to be two hours of formal debate under closed rule. The time would be divided equally between both sides. A vote would follow immediately.

Since it was still the day before the vote, Senators were under no time constraints for their remarks. Kerr opened discussion by mocking the numerous names for the Javits-Anderson Amendment. He kidded, "If I knew exactly how to identify it, I would do so; since I cannot do so exactly, I shall identify the proposal known before the Senate as the Anderson-Javits amendment."[54] Kerr proceeded to denounce the measure, using adjectives and homilies that ran from classical mythology to the Bible and all the way up to modern slang. Kerr, one of the smartest men in the Senate, was known as a "ruthless debator." His language was so fancy, and he spoke for so long that Senator Pat McNamara made a noticeable exit in disgust. Kerr was especially critical of the joint sponsorship between Anderson and Javits, between whose position there had been an insurmountable gulf such as would have dwarfed the gulf of burning fire between Dives, when he lifted up his eyes, being tormented, and looked yonder and saw Lazarus in Abraham's bosom. What a chasm was eliminated when these two men began to see the light.[55]

Senator Russell Long, son of the Kingfish, was more comfortable with folk metaphor. "Let us make no mistake about it. When we look at the Anderson-Javits amendment we are not staring at a sweet old lady in bed with her kimona and night cap. We are looking into the eyes of the wolf that ate Red Riding Hood's grandma."[56]

Long then treated his colleagues to one of his favorite arguments against a national health insurance bill. If the elderly are given hospitalization at government expense, many of them will make plans to spend their summer vacations in the hospitals. The medical resources of the country would become social clubs for the elderly. At that point, Senator Paul Douglas, who could stand no more of Long, remarked caustically, "The remarks of the Senator from Louisiana remind me of Stephen Leacock's story about the man who mounted his horse and rode off in all directions."[57]

Anderson spent an intensely debilitating day arguing for his amendment. Mostly, he defended the principle of the Social Security approach. As of 24 hours before the vote, Anderson still thought he had the 50 votes that Bobby Baker and Mansfield had counted.

On July 17, Anderson yielded most of the one hour debate to Mansfield and Javits. Some of the bill's other supporters, Douglas, Gore, McNamara, Humphrey, Cooper, and Kuchel, gave brief statements.

There were no surprises in the arguments. Javits addressed the fears of Senators that if the Medicare amendment passed, it would delay the parent bill HR10606 in conference. The parent bill brought immediate welfare funds to some states that needed money in a hurry. Javits said that Anderson had suggested that Congress grant a 60–day extension to the present welfare budget.

Javits spoke about the concern that the Javits-Anderson Bill had not gone through the Finance Committee with proper hearings. Javits reminded his colleagues that the Finance Committee had already held hearings on the subject in 1960. In addition, the Ways and Means Committee had held hearings on health insurance for the elderly in 1959, 1961, and 1962. The Special Senate Committee on the Aged—

McNamara's Committee—had held hearings during 1960 and 1961. There was already an enormous record on the topic, sufficient to support a positive vote.[58]

During the second hour, Dirksen yielded himself about half of his 60 minutes and gave most of the other half to his colleague, Carl Curtis of Nebraska. Dirksen was a flamboyant and powerful orator. He stood firmly opposed to any government tampering with the medical profession. In early 1960, Dirksen had been almost successful in wrecking Estes Kefauver's subcommittee investigation on drugs. For his efforts, Dirksen won the reputation of having "taken on himself the burden of defending American medical and pharmaceutical interests for the Republican Party." Also, Dirksen resented the manner in which the Javits-Anderson Amendment circumvented normal committee procedure. He had not forgiven the Kennedy Administration for pushing the Civil Rights Act of 1961 in the same way. In both cases Dirksen was on the committee that was circumvented.[59]

Dirksen was assisted by a conservative and long-time member of the Finance Committee, Carl Curtis of Nebraska. Between the two they covered the basic arguments of the opposition. Dirksen and Curtis did not want to see younger workers penalized by larger deductions from their paychecks. They did not want to endanger the Social Security system by adding the burden of health care and possibly throwing the whole system into bankruptcy. They did not want to ruin the quality of health care in America or open the door to socialism. Dirksen acknowledged a government responsibility for the elderly but not for those "who could afford to pay for themselves." To that Russell Long illustrated, "My mother's cook and yard boy would be asked to pay my mother's medical bill."[60]

After the debate, Kerr made a motion to table the Javits-Anderson Amendment. A vote was called at 6:15 p.m. All 100 Senators were present for the roll call. It was only the second time that year that so important a vote had brought all the Senators to the chamber. (The previous time was in February when the Senate rejected Kennedy's Department of Urban Affairs.) Kerr won. The vote was 52–48 in favor of tabling the amendment. Randolph had voted yea and Carl Hayden followed suit. The administration's bipartisan health insurance for the elderly bill was defeated by 31 Republicans and 21 Southern Democrats.

Anderson got up to leave as soon as the vote was over. He was surprised, disappointed, and very tired. On his way out, Robert Kerr

unexpectedly grabbed Anderson's hand in front of waiting photogra-
phers. A picture of the two opponents, shaking hands, appeared on the
front page of the next morning's papers.[61]

The White House was immediately informed of the defeat. The same
evening Kennedy made an unscheduled appearance before TV audiences
threatening to take the issue to the people in the November elections.
Health insurance, Kennedy said, was defeated by nearly all of the
Republicans and a handful of Democrats in the Senate. "It was a serious
defeat for every American family."[62]

The following day, Senator Thruston Morton pointed out that the
Democrats who voted to table Javits-Anderson were more than a "handful," and included ten major committee chairmen, the former Democratic candidate for Vice President, and the Secretary of the Democratic
National Committee. Morton added that "he for one was proud to be
associated with that group—many of whom had held office even before
the young President was born."[63] Also the next day, July 18, Bobby
Baker took out a large personal loan in an Oklahoma bank owned in
part by Robert Kerr.[64]

Clinton Anderson planned to leave Washington and return home to
New Mexico to restore his health. Before doing so, he and his assistant
Howard Bray sat down to analyze what went wrong with the vote. They
sent their conclusions in a long memo to the President. The main problem, in their minds, was "the constant claim, that given time, Kerr-
Mills will be expanded until it takes care of all the needy in every
state." Anderson urged the President not to sign any piece of welfare
legislation, including HR10606 when it came out of conference, until
an exhaustive study had been made of its future implications concerning
Medicare. For example, an enlargement of Federal grants to states for
welfare might be construed as money for health care for the elderly and
might well help defeat future Medicare bills.

In the same memo, Anderson also expressed his concern over the
power vacuum in HEW: no one was in charge of the Administration's
viewpoint during the July 17 vote and no one will be there when the
bill goes into conference. Ribicoff had left for Connecticut, and the
new Secretary of HEW, Anthony Celebrezze, was not ready to take
over. With the lack of HEW direction, Anderson complained about
Kerr's ability to convince Senate leaders of seemingly good intentions,
while his real motives were devious. Anderson cited the events con-

cerning the Aiken, Monroney, Randolph Amendment when Douglas was "duped." He mentioned the problem of Jennings Randolph and the legislative irregularity of Kerr's amendment to kick-back funds.[65] (At a later date Kennedy asked the Director of the Budget to cancel a public works project in West Virginia.)

Anderson spent the rest of the year in Albuquerque, New Mexico, resting. He stayed on top of new Medicare developments by frequent memos to his legislative assistant, Howard Bray. One such memo contained the advice from Bray that Senator Pat McNamara and his staff "should not be overlooked." McNamara felt out of the limelight during the July debate. Accordingly, Anderson drafted a letter to McNamara asking for his help in resuming the campaign in 1963 and suggesting that McNamara use his special committee on aging to study the nursing home situation and their affiliations with the hospitals. That issue was a sore spot during the recent Senate debates; that most nursing homes would not qualify for support was used by the opposition for at least two states, Vermont and Oklahoma.[66]

McNamara's staff had other plans. They were discussing the possibility of creating their own special subcommittee on health insurance for the aged. They reasoned that they could hold hearings quicker than the Finance Committee. Also, McNamara wanted his own bill in 1963. He believed that Wilbur Cohen and Clinton Anderson had compromised too much with Javits.[67]

Senator Javits was working on a different idea. In November he appointed his own task force called the National Committee on Health Care for the Aged. Its members included Dr. James Dixon, President of Antioch College; Marion Folsom; Dr. Dickenson Richards, associated with Columbia University Hospital and a member of the Physicians Committee for Health Care; John Tierney, an official with Blue Cross; Dr. Russell Lee, eminent member of the Physicians Committee for Health Care; and Herbert Yost, law professor at New York University.[68]

Anderson's staff was suspicious of the intentions of such a task force. Bray questioned Winslow Carlton, Javits's assistant, about the objectives of the new group. Bray was advised that the task force would not help or hurt the Kennedy Administration's position on Medicare. Javits wanted a report out by March 1963, but he lacked staff and money. Javits queried Mary Lasker as well as Governor Rockefeller about donations, but both parties refused. Only drug companies volunteered financial assistance.[69]

The November elections revealed that the American Medical Association, despite its huge political commitment that year, had very little sway over the electorate. The Senate picked up four new Democrats—all potential Medicare supporters; George McGovern of South Dakota, Abraham Ribicoff of Connecticut, Birch Bayh of Indiana, and Thomas McIntyre of New Hampshire. Tom Wicker in the *New York Times* added a warning that Bayh and McIntyre were "independents who would not rubber stamp the Kennedy legislative program." While not specifically endorsing Medicare, Bayh was quoted as saying that the Medicare bill should be broadened to encourage the use of private insurance companies.[70] Clinton Anderson immediately sent Bayh a note saying that, if the Social Security Administration assumed a large part of the insurance burden, then the private companies would be encouraged to fill in the gaps for services not provided by the government plan.[71]

As far as House seats were concerned, the AMA had tried very hard to keep Claude Pepper from being elected as a representative from Dade County, Florida. Pepper won. Senator Olin Johnston of South Carolina, another target of the AMA, also won re-election. The AMA made a powerful enemy of Senator Lister Hill. Hill had voted against the Anderson-Javits Bill, but he was usually a moderate. The AMA favored a more predictable conservative. Hill won by a narrow margin and never forgave the American Medical Association. On the other hand, Representative Andrew Frazier of Tennessee lost the election because of his anti-Medicare attitude. It was a major issue in his district.[72]

Wilbur Cohen once said, "One must work two steps ahead of the opposition with new programs and compromises."[73] Before 1962 was over, Cohen and Nelson Cruikshank were thinking about a new Kennedy health insurance bill for 1963. The most prevalent belief that the Medicare advocates needed to dispel was that only a small segment of the older population actually required additional government support in order to afford proper health care. Many people thought that the Kerr-Mills program, on top of an effort by private insurance companies, was solving the health problems of the elderly. As one reporter wrote in *Fortune*, the number of people who needed assistance from the government was diminishing. Only five out of 17 million older persons could not afford health insurance. Those 5 million would soon be taken care of by private group insurance policies. The article in *Fortune* concluded, "The fault with the Administration's program is that it has a remedy out of proportion to the problem.''[74] In 1963, the country had to be persuaded that a real problem existed and that Kerr-Mills and the private insurance companies were *not* meeting the financial health needs of the elderly.

6

Keeping Medicare Alive

After the close vote in the Senate in July 1962 on the Javits-Anderson Amendment, Medicare advocates needed to retrench in order to prepare a program with improved chances of clearing Congress. The year 1963 was one of planning. No one in the Kennedy Administration believed that a Medicare bill would come up for a vote in Congress that year. There were serious doubts that either the House Ways and Means Committee or the Senate Finance Committee would even hold hearings on a health insurance bill for the elderly. The Kennedy Administration's primary emphasis was on tax revision and inflation. The most optimistic members of the White House and HEW staff were predicting that a bill would come up for a vote in 1964.[1]

In the meantime, the campaign for Medicare had to be kept alive if only because the AMA was spending 2 million dollars a year on its crusade against "socialized medicine." Public support of Medicare was waning. The latest Gallup poll, taken in the Fall of 1962, showed public support of Medicare at only 43 percent. Interest peaked briefly in the Winter: On January 9, 1963, the public listed Medicare second on a list of issues that they were most concerned about. (Taxes were number one.) However, the resurgence was fleeting. By April, the public was concerned about Cuba and Berlin, and Medicare was not even mentioned. The same was true of another Gallup survey taken in October 1963. At that point the main issue on the public's mind was racial disturbances. Again, Medicare was not mentioned as a priority.[2]

The press interpreted the Congressional atmosphere in an altogether different way. The *Wall Street Journal* predicted that Medicare would sail through Congress in 1963, largely because of changes in the Ways and Means Committee.[3] Other newspaper editorials spoke similarly. This forecast was based in part on the analysis of the National Committee for an Effective Congress. This non-partisan (but liberal) committee believed that the 88th Congress should be more receptive to President Kennedy's legislative program. Because of shifts in population, the South had lost seats in the House. Those seats were taken by more liberal Westerners. Also, of four new Senators in 1963, three replaced conservative Republicans.[4]

Another factor was the death of that most articulate leader of the Medicare opposition, Robert Kerr, from a heart attack in January 1963. His position on the Finance Committee was taken by Abraham Ribicoff, who had recently been Secretary of Health, Education and Welfare. Yet the change in Congress had little effect on the status of Medicare. Even without Kerr, the Finance Committee was 10–7 against a Social Security-financed health insurance program for the elderly. Six Republicans joined four Democrats in opposition. These four Democrats were senior members: Chairman Harry F. Byrd, Russell Long, George Smathers, and Herman Talmadge.

The make-up of the Ways and Means Committee changed only slightly. Kennedy managed to get two probable supporters on the Committee, Birch Bayh (D-Indiana) and Pat Jennings (D-Virginia), but the pros still had only 11 votes as opposed to the 14 against.

The Kennedy Administration had a new Secretary of HEW to co-ordinate strategy on Medicare: Anthony Celebrezze, a five term mayor of Cleveland, Ohio.[5] The Kennedy people were impressed with Celebrezze's popularity and record. By his fifth term he received 75 percent of the popular vote and carried every ward in Cleveland. They also were glad to appoint an Italian American. Celebrezze, a self-made man whose main aspiration was to become a Federal judge, accepted the post.[6]

At the first Medicare strategy session in 1963, President Kennedy, Celebrezze, and Wilbur Cohen decided to initially follow the outline of the 1962 King-Anderson Bill, S909. Kennedy was working on a new program which was not yet ready and was to be delivered as a special message to Congress in February. Rather than start with nothing, the three decided to use the bill they had and make changes later.[7]

Soon after that meeting, Cohen held a more intensive strategy session with those who were working on the new bill: HEW officials Robert Ball, Arthur Hess, William Saperstein, William Stewart, and Irwin Wolkstein. While no legislators were present, a few key aides were: Howard Bray (for Senator Clinton Anderson), Allen Lesser (for Senator Jacob Javits), Stephen Horn (for Senator Thomas Kuchel), and Bailey Gerard (for Senator John Sherman Cooper). Their goal was to explore the possibility of a renewed bipartisan legislative effort.

At the meeting, however, it became apparent that such a bipartisan bill was going to be difficult. Allen Lesser said that Javits and the other Republicans wanted two changes. They wanted a simplification of the language used in writing the bill and they wanted broader home health services. The HEW people responded that the attempt to keep costs down would preclude any addition to home health services.

HEW also wanted two changes from the previous year. The deductible (that portion of the bill that the elderly would first have to pay before getting the rest of the charges reimbursed) on the 1962 bill was $20. HEW wanted it to be at least $40. HEW also wanted a stipulation in the part of the bill concerning nursing homes coverage that the nursing homes have an affiliation or relationship with a hospital in order to be qualified as a suitable institution for Medicare recipients.[8] Most Senators and Congressmen were under heavy pressure from their state nursing home associations to resist any writing of Federal standards into a bill.

Since Nelson Cruikshank had not been present at the strategy session, Cohen informed him of the details. Cruikshank believed that there was yet another source of trouble for a bipartisan bill that the meeting had not discussed. The Republicans, Cruikshank thought, might want to accommodate the private insurance companies by including an option package that allowed beneficiaries to "opt" out of the government system and purchase private coverage. The idea of options was not one of which labor was fond.[9] George Meany had always been opposed to including the private companies in any part of the Medicare program. Most labor officials concurred. In addition, Cruikshank and Meany disagreed with HEW over the deductible. Labor wanted as *low* a deductible as possible so that medical and hospital coverage would be easily accessible to everyone eligible from the first day services were needed.

Howard Bray, in reporting the discussion back to Anderson, was not encouraged. Bray said that the advocates could not agree on some issues like the deductible. There would be even more difficulty getting a resolution on the issues that separated the advocates from the five to seven liberal Republicans who wanted a bipartisan bill.[10]

Even without a bill in hand, Larry O'Brien and Nelson Cruikshank took a long look at the Congressional legislative schedule. There appeared to be no time available for Medicare legislation. President Kennedy's first priority for the Ways and Means Committee was tax revision. That tax bill was so important and so complicated that the White House could not predict how much time would elapse before Wilbur Mills was able to report it out. O'Brien and Cruikshank thought that the next item on the Mills agenda would be an unemployment benefits bill. Cruikshank conferred with Meany and other AFL-CIO leaders and decided that, in order to improve the prospects for Medicare hearings, labor might put off the unemployment compensation bill and settle for a simple extension of existing benefits. Because of the realignment of Mills's home district, Cruikshank added in a note to O'Brien, unions were gaining a foothold in Mills's home constituency.[11]

Without waiting for a specific bill, President Kennedy sent Congress an "across the board plan for improving American health" noting that the details of a health insurance program for the elderly would be forthcoming and it "should be at the top of the Congressional agenda on health."[12]

Finally, on February 21, 1963, Kennedy delivered his "Special Message on Aiding Our Senior Citizens." It was the first Presidential message to deal only with the problems of the elderly. The message contained 36 legislative recommendations. The key proposal was Medicare, which the President renamed, "The Hospital Insurance Act of 1963." Kennedy said that the program achieved two basic objectives: protection against the cost of serious illness, and a base of insurance protection upon which supplementary private programs could be added. The President commented: "It is based on the fundamental promise that contributions made during the working years, matched by employers contributions, should enable people to prepay and build earned rights and benefits to safeguard them in their old age."[13]

The new Hospital Act of 1963 was very different from the 1962 King-Anderson Bill. Some aspects came from the Javits-Anderson Amendment. Other ideas emerged out of the strategy sessions held between HEW people, Congressional assistants, and labor input. The new bill provided for three choices: a beneficiary could select a policy that covered 90 days of hospital care with a $10 a day deductible for the first nine days; or a policy that offered 180 days of hospitalization with a deductible that would equal two and a half days of average hospital costs; or hospital coverage for 45 days but with no deductible. Each potential beneficiary had to select the type of coverage before his or her 65th birthday. Kennedy said, "This new element of freedom of choice was a major improvement over past bills."[14]

Other parts of the bill remained the same as King-Anderson: after transference from a hospital the program covered 180 days of skilled nursing home care and 240 home health visits in a calendar year. Diagnostic services were also included with a $20 deductible.

To finance the new proposal, the earnings base on which Social Security taxes were paid was increased from $4,800 to $5,200. If the bill were passed in 1963, that increase was to take effect on January 1, 1965. In addition, Social Security taxes were to be increased a quarter of one percent on each of the employer-employee contributions.

Another new feature taken from the Javits-Anderson Amendment was a separate Federal Health Insurance Trust Fund. This was done primarily to keep the money separate from the Social Security Trust Fund and to allay the fears of more conservative members of Congress that Medicare would bankrupt the entire Social Security system. Also retained from the Javits-Anderson Amendment was the inclusion of 2.5 million elderly persons who were not eligible for Social Security benefits and therefore would not otherwise qualify for Medicare. The benefits for those persons were to be financed by general revenues. The private sector, such as Blue Cross, was assigned the role of reimbursor or "fiscal intermediary" for HEW and the hospitals. One major feature was absent. The new Kennedy program did *not* have the private option that Senator Javits wanted and had written into the 1962 amendment.[15]

In describing his program to Congress, Kennedy commented:

A proud and noble nation can no longer ask its older people to live in fear of serious illness for which adequate funds are not available. We owe the right of dignity in sickness as in health. We can achieve this by adding health insurance primarily hospital insurance to our successful Social Security System.

Further along in the address, Kennedy added: "It is not enough to a great nation merely to have added new years to life. Our objective must also be to add new life to those years."[16]

The day before the President's special message to Congress, Senator Clinton Anderson sent out a general letter to all Democrats in the Senate plus the five Republicans who worked with him in 1962:

Dear——————,
Tomorrow President Kennedy will send Congress his message on Medicare. Join us as a co-sponsor. This year the bill is better and less controversial than last year.

The replies to Anderson came in over the next few days. Senator Hubert Humphrey asked to be listed as the first co-sponsor. Senator Stuart Symington wrote that he was trying not to co-sponsor legislation although he was completely sympathetic to the bill, especially since his state would not even qualify for any Kerr-Mills funds. Carl Hayden, even though he had won in his 1962 election for another term in the Senate, declined sponsorship. Albert Gore said that it was his policy to refrain from co-sponsoring legislation but that he would be with Anderson when the bill came to the Senate floor.[17]

All five Republicans who received letters agreed to be listed as co-sponsors: Jacob Javits, Clifford Case, John Sherman Cooper, Thomas Kuchel, and Kenneth Keating. At a press conference the Republicans promised to cooperate in working for a passage of a law "which meets the pressing health needs of our aged citizens." Ultimately, there were 30 co-sponsors to Anderson's S880, which was the Senate version of the President's program.[18]

The American Medical Association was quick to publicize its own recommendations. The AMA, which claimed it spoke for 197,000 out of the country's 262,000 doctors, wanted to revise Kerr-Mills to provide aid for presently ineligible persons suffering from major illnesses, "if the extent of their illness would reduce their income for the year below the maximum specified."[19] Kerr-Mills, now in its third year, was operating in 25 states. The AMA adhered to the belief that, if only the Kerr-Mills program could be expanded, Medicare would be unnecessary.

To increase public confidence that the private insurance companies were capable of doing the job, the AMA claimed that 53 percent of the elderly already owned private insurance policies covering hospital and health care. In 1963, private companies were given state authorization to bank together to provide low-cost group coverage, commonly known as state "65" programs. For example, in New York, forty-nine insurance companies jointly sponsored a one month enrollment period for those over 65 to purchase a group medical plan. No medical exam was required. It was open to state residents only. The insurance group offered two plans: 31 days hospitalization at a cost of $10 per month; and 31 days plus major medical coverage beyond that for $19 per month.

During the first months' enrollment period a total of 107,600 persons signed up. The New York "65" group had a second enrollment period during which another 35,600 signed up. Altogether that represented about six percent of the eligible senior citizens in New York. The Connecticut "65" program, which was the first in the country to organize, had 30,000 members enrolled, or 12 percent of the eligible population. Massachusetts had a membership of 50,000 or nine percent of the eligible population. Only one other state, Texas, organized a state "65" program later on in 1963. The average age of all the enrollees for the "65" plan was 74. In total, the state "65" insurance programs signed up no more than 2 million persons in 1963. The costs of monthly premiums averaged $10 to $20 a month. Despite the myth that the private companies were gallantly responding to public need, only *two* insurance companies were actively enrolling the elderly: Mutual of Omaha and Continental Casualty of Chicago.[20]

In order to spur on the private insurance companies, the AMA proposed that the tax laws be revised to allow for liberal income tax deductions for medical premiums of the elderly. This was based on the understanding that families of older persons were buying health coverage for their senior relatives. The doctors said that Medicare isolated the elderly into a special category. The legislation treated the elderly as a "national problem." On the other hand, a change in the tax laws would affect the entire population. Then, the elderly would not be singled out and their individuality still preserved.[21]

Important members of Congress backed the AMA's campaign to strengthen Kerr-Mills. Both Chairman Wilbur Mills and Senator George Smathers believed in the Kerr-Mills approach, while the press was becoming more critical of the program. *Fortune* pointed to the basic problem with Kerr-Mills as "putting 50 fingers on 50 triggers."[22]

On April 25, 1963, Smathers and Mills introduced joint legislation to expand the Kerr-Mills Act. They asked Congress to provide better medical care for the aged under the Federal/State Old Age Assistance

Programs (OAA). The states would be required to provide medical care for the indigent equal to the protection afforded under the more comprehensive MAA programs.[23]

Because of his position as Chairman of the Senate Committee on Aging, Smathers was invited to speak at the Governors' Conference on Aging, held in New York in early May, 1963, at the request of Governor Rockefeller. Smathers gave an extemporaneous speech, criticizing the Administration's hospital insurance bill. Probably because of his rumored closeness with the President, his remarks were widely publicized.

Senator Anderson dashed off an angry letter to Wilbur Cohen wondering why Smathers was allowed to criticize the Administration's bill. Anderson asked if Kennedy had dropped support for Medicare that year.[24] Cohen responded calmly that no one could restrain the freedom of speech by a Senator, and no one could predict the extent to which the press "played up" Smather's comments.[25]

To reaffirm his support for Medicare, the President met with the leaders of the National Council of Senior Citizens in the White House Rose Garden. The President assured his supporters of his full intention to press for health insurance for the elderly. The timely occasion for the meeting came because the President was presented with an award of merit for the "hope and leadership he has given American senior citizens."[26]

In order to "increase community awareness of problems" of older people, the President designated the month of May as Senior Citizen's Month.[27] To commemorate the occasion, the President appointed a Cabinet Council on Aging: Anthony Celebrezze, Secretary of HEW; Douglas Dillon, Secretary of the Treasury; Orville Freeman, Secretary of Agriculture; Luther Hodges, Secretary of Commerce; W. Willard Wirtz, Secretary of Labor; John W. Macy, Jr., chairman of the Civil Service Commission; and J. J. Gleason, Jr., Administration of Housing and Home Financing Agency.[28]

On May 18, the Council issued a report entitled "The Older American" arguing that the aged were becoming second class citizens. The Council wholeheartedly endorsed Kennedy's proposal for hospital insurance, claiming that it was not even a major reform. The Federal Government was already spending 17 billion dollars for 18 million seniors, but that amount was not enough. (Of that amount, 13 billion was going for Social Security and Civil Service retirement payments.) The report added that, contrary to current publicity, most of the nation's elderly did *not* have adequate resources for medical care or even food and housing. Exactly one-half of the couples over 65 lived on incomes less than $2,530 per year. Single older people lived on less than $1,255. Both figures were below the nation's minimum income. Furthermore, the report stated, the AMA's claim that 53 percent of the elderly had medical insurance protection was about 100 percent inflated![29]

While Mills and Smathers planned to expand the role of the states by strengthening Kerr-Mills, at least one state, New York, did not respond favorably to its growing responsibility. On May 3 Governor Rockefeller presided over a Governors' Conference on Aging held at New York's Waldorf-Astoria. The conference was sponsored by New York State's Office for the Aging. Over 1,000 people attended. Rockefeller told the audience that the need for Federal health insurance "grows more urgent daily." In New York, the state medical aid program (MAA) would be paying benefits for up to ten percent of its population next year. This aid, the Governor insisted, would be more efficiently delivered by Social Security financing. Rockefeller added that he was generally in favor of the Kennedy Administration's hospital insurance bill, but preferred to keep Senator Javits's 1962 provision for the beneficiaries to "opt out" of the system. Those chosing to stay out of the system would receive a Social Security cash credit to purchase private health insurance.[30]

New York City was host to another pro-Medicare political gathering to celebrate Senior Citizen's Month. On May 17, 1963, approximately 2,640 seniors gathered at an Assembly sponsored by the Golden Ring Council of New York (an affiliate of the National Council for Senior Citizens). Under Secretary of HEW Ivan Nestingen was the guest speaker. He received loud applause every time he mentioned the word "Medicare."[31]

By June the Ways and Means Committee had completed its work on Kennedy's tax bill. Mills, instead of suggesting that the Committee take up hospital insurance, sponsored his own bill to increase Social Security benefits and correspondingly raise Social Security taxes. In a very rare news conference (Mills seldom spoke to reporters) the Chairman of the Ways and Means Committee stated the obvious: that he did not intend his new Social Security bill to be used as a vehicle for any version of the President's medical care program. Instead, Mills said, his bill was designed to increase the monetary reserve of the trust fund. He stated, "My only intention in introducing the bill is to get the fund on an actuarial sound basis and to call attention to the fact that it is not actuarially sound now.''[32] Mills's explanation was interpreted as a warning to pro-Medicare people who wanted to expand the Social Security system in order to pay hospital benefits. Mills's proposed increase in Social Security taxes created some difficulty for Medicare supporters. There was little perceived room left to raise taxes even *more* for Medicare.[33]

The Kennedy team had barely responded to Smather's anti-Medicare statement and Mills's new legislative threat when the pro-Medicare group itself broke rank. Up to 1963, the trouble within HEW between Cohen and Nestingen and the competition in the Senate between McNamara and Anderson were kept reasonably quiet. In the spring of 1963, the quiet ended.

Senator Wayne Morse introduced a resolution to establish a permanent health subcommittee on aging under the auspices of the Special Committee on Aging which was itself within the Senate Committee on Labor and Public Welfare. Senator Pat McNamara announced his intention to be the head of the proposed subcommittee. Senator Smathers, who was a member of both the Labor Committee and the Finance Committee, announced his support of Morse's resolution.

The resolution was interpreted by Clinton Anderson as a direct challenge to his leadership and response to his inability to get any action out of the Finance Committee. The Morse resolution was also a challenge to Wilbur Cohen who supported the strategy of concentrating on the Finance Committee as a vehicle for passing Medicare.[34] Cohen went directly to Anderson's office and explained that even though he was opposed to the new subcommittee, he did not want to involve the Administration in a fight with its own supporters.

Cohen indicated that there were other long-range considerations. When Medicare did pass Congress, Smathers and Long would almost definitely be on the conference committee that would resolve the differences between the House passed bill (i.e., a Mills version), and the Senate bill (the Administration version). The Administration would surely need their cooperation. Cohen suggested that Anderson try to change precedent and get five Democrats from the Senate side on future conference committees.

Cohen thought it best to let the Morse resolution ride—particularly so as not to antagonize either Smathers or Long. While Smathers was publicly critical of King-Anderson, he had privately given President

Kennedy his word that he would work something out when the bill came to the floor in the Senate. Long was currently favoring a more radical bill than the President's, but the positions of both Senators were quixotic. Only the year before, Long had favored a more conservative program.

Cohen's logic did not alter the bitter feelings that surfaced among Medicare supporters. Cruikshank reported to Cohen that the AFL-CIO wanted to stay out of the argument over the Morse resolution. Cohen assured Anderson that he would be in on any major strategy session regardless of which Committee was involved and that the President was still committed to routing Medicare through the Finance Committee. Cohen added that Anderson and King were still the Administration's spokesmen in Congress for hospital insurance. The advocacy of other related bills that might come out of the new subcommittee did not affect either King's or Anderson's role.[35]

Two days after Cohen had talked with Anderson, the Health Subcommittee on the Elderly was established. The new Subcommittee chose the Kerr-Mills program as its first subject of inquiry. After holding hearings, the Subcommittee issued a report on four parts: a majority report, signed by Chairman Pat McNamara and members Edmund Muskie, Edward Long, Frank Moss, Maurine Neuberger, Wayne Morse, and Joseph Clark; a minority report signed by Everett Dirksen, Barry Goldwater, and Frank Carlson; and separate reports by George Smathers and by Hiram Fong.

In its introduction the majority report stated, "After three years of operation, the Kerr-Mills Medical Assistance for the Aged (MAA) program has proved to be at best an ineffective and piecemeal approach to the health problems of the nation's 18 million older citizens."[36]

The report listed the basic problems of the Kerr-Mills:

1. It was not a national program and the Majority report predicted that it never would be, only 28 states thus far had programs.

2. In the most recent month included in the study, July 1963, only 148,000 people received assistance. That represented less than one percent of all elderly. The Majority committee blamed the limited participation on "eligibility tests," lien type recovery provisions, and "responsible relative provisions."

3. The benefits varied so widely, only four states had comprehensive programs: Hawaii, Massachusetts, New York, and North Dakota.

4. The program generated unusually high administrative costs.

5. The distribution of Federal matching funds went disproportionately to the wealthier states; 88 percent of all funds were going to five states: New York alone received 42 percent of all Federal funds. The other four were California, Massachusetts, Michigan, and Pennsylvania. That left only 12 percent for the rest of the 20 states.

6. The intention of the law was to create a new category of medically indigent people eligible for assistance. That intention was frustrated by states' policy of transferring elderly persons from their welfare programs to MAA. The states could save money, but few *new* people were getting aid. The medically indigent category was originally intended to mean those not on OAA roles but who were unable to cope with the costs of health services. MAA was not reaching that type of person.

7. Because of the eligibility tests that required an individual to be near dependency to receive help, the law implied that it was for the same type of person already on OAA roles.[37]

In addition, the majority committee found that twelve states had "responsible family" provisions in which the state was allowed to investigate the assets of sons and daughters of the applicant. When proud older people found that their children had to be informed of their situation, they sometimes withdrew their applications. Nine states had lien laws that extended to the homes of the applicant. That meant that the home of the applicant was subject to state ownership after their death. The problem was that older people tend to equate ownership of a home with self-respect and the idea of the government taking a lien on their property was inconceivable. "In means test medicine, far too much emphasis is placed upon the means test and not enough upon the medicine."[38]

In a few states, such as Louisiana, applicants to MAA had to pay an "enrollment fee" to the fund before qualifying for reimbursement. Such fees were illegal. Too, there was no freedom of choice within the program. Many doctors and many hospitals would not participate because fees at which they were reimbursed were below the going charges. At least three states, New Mexico, Georgia, and Nevada, had passed legislation to establish a Kerr-Mills program but had no funds available to participate. Three more states, Indiana, Missouri, and Montana had passed legislation only to have their Governor veto it. Nine states, Alaska, Arizona, Colorado, Delaware, Mississippi, Ohio, Rhode Island,

and Texas had not even bothered to discuss Kerr-Mills in their state assemblies.[39]

In the minority report, the Senators claimed that the majority had come to unwarranted and premature conclusions. Not all potentially eligible seniors needed MAA services. At least 55 percent of all the elderly had private health insurance policies. (That figure, the same one that the AMA used, came from the Health Insurance of America). The Senators took issue with criticism of the family responsibility and property lien clauses. Families who are technically able to take care of their own members should do so, the minority said, before the state programs were invoked.[40]

Senator Smather's own opinion was more a caveat than anything else. While the majority report contained valuable information, he said, the MAA program still seemed to him the most practical means of assisting the needy elderly with their medical bills. Congress therefore should work on correcting the weaknesses in the law.[41] In the fourth separate statement, Hiram Fong ignored the majority and minority reports and endorsed his own bill calling for Federal-state sharing funds and offering three choices of insurance plans. (Fong's bill was co-sponsored in the Senate by Leverett Saltonstall, Aiken, Scott, Hale Boggs, Prouty, and Cotton).[42]

In the Fall of 1963, with the legislative session almost over, newspapers and periodicals around the country began calling hospital insurance the forgotten issue of that year. *Business Week* remarked:

Until the Kennedy Administration makes a real fight for its program of hospital care for the aged under the Social Security system—tens of thousands of the elderly will lack the safeguards they need and should have. This has become one of the great forgotten issues in 1963. It cannot stay forgotten in 1964.[43]

The *New York Times* referred to Medicare as "the most forgotten of all forgotten issues of 1963." Kennedy said almost the same thing at a news conference on foreign and domestic policy. The President told the press that he regretted not getting a bill out this year, and promised to do so next year. He added that he had discussed a bipartisan bill for 1964 with Senator Javits and Senator Anderson.[44] On November 15, 1963, President Kennedy told the AFL-CIO Convention in New York that the main legislative issue on his 1964 agenda was jobs. Right behind were Civil Rights, education, and Medicare. As for the latter, the President said:

I cannot tell whether we're going to get this legislation before Christmas, but I can say that I believe that this Congress will not go home next summer to the people of the United States without passing this bill. I think we should stay there till we do.[45]

What provided new confidence for 1964 was not so much the newly scheduled Ways and Means hearings for November, but the published results of a 12–member committee known as the National Committee of Health Care for the Aged. This was the original task force established by Javits a year before.

The Committee proposed a three-part concept of health care financing. Neither the government nor the private sector and surely not the elderly, it asserted, could do the job alone. All three groups had to work together toward a single program. While the Committee suggested a specific role for each part, it did not mention details in terms of amount of taxes or numbers of days. It only suggested that any plan cover about 70 hospital days.[46]

Senator Javits called for immediate legislation along the lines of the Committee report. Senator Anderson said that the report was quite significant, especially since it was released only five days before the Ways and Means Committee hearings. Not everyone was as enthusiastic. Senator Ribicoff called the report most encouraging, but said that he was working on a plan of his own and hoped it would be ready by next year. As expected, the AMA voiced immediate opposition to the Committee report.[47]

House hearings on Representative Cecil King's HR3920, authorizing the government to provide under the Social Security Program for the payment of hospital and related services to aged beneficiaries, were scheduled to begin on November 18. The Ways and Means Committee planned eight days of hearings and no vote at the conclusion. Hearings were expected to resume on the same subject on January 3, 1964. Testimony was supposed to cover the following topics: adequacy of medical programs under existing laws (Kerr-Mills); the extent and adequacy of coverage under private or no-profit health insurance programs; the President's proposal which was contained in HR3920; and 49 identical bills; and alternate legislative proposals.[48]

Secretary of HEW Anthony J. Celebrezze was the first witness. He was accompanied by Wilbur Cohen, Robert Ball, and Robert Myers. The Secretary remained on the stand from 9:30 a.m. to 8:00 p.m. Representative Howard Baker asked if the President and HEW could make the whole Medicare system voluntary to get away from the repugnant compulsory aspects. Celebrezze answered that if the people chose not to be included, they may be unprotected at age 65 and wish that they had coverage, and could end up as welfare cases.[49]

Celebrezze then engaged in a heated debate with Thomas Curtis (R-Missouri) over the HEW distribution of 100,000 copies of a report explaining the King-Anderson Bill of 1963. Curtis objected to using the taxpayers' money to promote a point of view. Curtis also was angry about an alleged connection between HEW and the Physician's Committee on Health. Twenty-seven doctors on that committee, Curtis charged, were the recipients of large Federal research grants.

Celebrezze answered calmly and methodically. Finally Curtis aroused the Secretary's wrath by saying that the committee studying the Social Security structure was loaded with advocates of Medicare, and therefore not an objective committee. Celebrezze responded angrily, "I pride myself on my integrity. I don't load Committees."[50]

Curtis proceeded to harass Robert Ball and Wilbur Cohen about their future plans to expand Medicare to cover orphans and such as soon as the bill passed for the elderly. The conservative Republican from Missouri concluded by defining fundamental differences in philosophy between the Administration and himself. He believed that the private sector should supply the insurance base, and that the government offer the supplement for those who could not afford private coverage. The Administration, on the other hand, wanted the government to provide the base and the privates to be supplemental.[51]

After Curtis, Chairman Mills expressed his own concern about the financing of Medicare. If the Forand Bill had passed in 1958, Mills said, it would have been 100 percent under-financed today. If the Kennedy-Anderson Bill had passed in 1960, limited only to those over 68, it would be 33 percent under-financed. Mills thought that there was something very wrong with HEW's cost estimates.[52]

Robert Myers explained that the cost assumptions in the earlier bills were that hospital costs would rise and eventually wages would catch up. Mills replied that this had not proven to be the case and, if hospital costs continued their dramatic rise, the program would be in trouble.

Myers responded by saying that in the future, the earnings base will be adjusted and the dollar deductible can also be adjusted. Mills then asked, "Why not simply start out with a one percent tax increase so that the American people will know what they are getting into?"[53]

At approximately 7:30 p.m., when Celebrezze, Cohen, Myers, and Ball had been answering questions for nine hours, Mills yielded to Bruce Alger, a right-wing Republican from Texas. The first thing Alger said was that "the hearings were going to get tougher." He was glad, Alger said, to see Dr. Cohen there, since "I don't know of anybody I enjoy differing with more. . . . My objections to what you have said today are so intense that it is difficult for me to be objective."

Mills interrupted Alger, saying, "Let the record show that the Committee kept the Secretary there until around 7:50 p.m. . . . and that some of us have stayed here with you." That concluded the first day.[54]

Over the next four days Alger and Curtis kept up a continual barrage about the immorality of people getting "something for nothing," and the danger of passing a bill that will let a "foot in the door." (The "foot" was socialism.) Eighty percent of the elderly, Curtis continued, did not need assistance with their medical bills. Representative Al Ullman (D-Oregon) observed that he was tired of Curtis's 80 percent, and tired of hearing him call for meaningless statistics that cluttered up the records. At that point Representative Perkins Bass of New Hampshire claimed that he used to live in Curtis's Missouri district and found it to be the wealthiest in the state. Bass added that Clayton, Missouri, was certainly not a good place in which to judge the economic situation of the elderly.[55]

The Republicans meanwhile initiated a campaign to convince the public that the Kennedy Administration had sabotaged Kerr-Mills in order to create a demand for King-Anderson. Republican spokesmen reported to the press that the three-year-old Kerr-Mills program was not given a fair chance. If the Administration would try to make it work, Medicare would not be necessary.[56]

The culmination of this campaign was Senator Karl E. Mundt's (R-South Dakota) testimony before the Ways and Means hearings. Mundt accused HEW of "deliberate sabotage." HEW, Mundt claimed, gave no help to the public to explain how to use the program. Worse, HEW staff members "maligned, ridiculed and described in half-truths and false generalities the law." Mundt cited particular speeches made by HEW staff: Mr. Cohen had called Kerr-Mills "socialized medicine with a vengeance"; Mr. Nestingen had called the law an "administrative monstrosity." In Mundt's own state of South Dakota, Kerr-Mills was in trouble because, he claimed, of administrative difficulties set up by HEW. In conclusion, Mundt said that HEW, and Congressional members who supported Medicare, and state and local welfare workers, had engaged in "a planned program of interference" with regard to Kerr-Mills.[57]

Toward the end of the hearings, Senator Frank T. Bow presented his alternative bill, HR21, to the Committee. This bill provided for the medical and hospital care of the aged through a system of voluntary health insurance programs. Bow agreed that the elderly had inadequate resources for illness. While only about half the elderly population in this country had insured themselves, coverage of all the senior citizens was a desirable national objective. Bow claimed that private insurance could be made available to all, regardless of medical history—without government interference and without compulsion. Bow specifically proposed government subsidies to the insurance companies.

Representative James A. Burke (D-Mississippi) asked Bow if any insurance policy today offered the provisions that Bow recommended. Since none did, Burke asked if Bow could provide a statement that the insurance companies could guarantee that all of the people that Bow claimed would be covered; and that there would be no questions asked. Bow responded by saying that he could provide evidence that the insurance companies would be willing to work something out.[58]

Dr. Edward Annis, representing the AMA, took about 40 minutes to summarize the AMA's 12–page statement against Medicare:

1. The basis for high quality health care is the voluntary relationship between patient and doctor. That would disappear if the government became the purchasor of health services.

2. The government would proceed to fix prices for services to protect the public purse. The financial incentives of medicine as a career would disappear.

3. Incentives or competition would also disappear.

4. This would result in a decline of professionalism—doctors would be like government employees.

5. This would lead to assembly-line medicine.

6. Young people would no longer enter into the medical field.[59]

Dr. Annis was queried about the role of AMPAC, AMA's political arm. AMPAC had recently distributed to medical and community organizations a phonograph record, allegedly of a speech given by Paul Normile, an AFL-CIO official, at a meeting of steel workers in western Pennsylvania. The cover of the record said that the speech was handed to AMPAC by a labor union member who objected to the high pressure technique of COPE (Committee of Political Action, affiliated with the AFL-CIO), and "its attempt to dominate government at every level in the United States."[60]

Normile, district director of United Steel Workers from Coraopolis, Pennsylvania, had never made such a speech and filed a $400,000 damage suit for fraud and libel. The papers were served on Dr. Donald E. Wood, Chairman of the Board of AMPAC, while the Ways and Means Committee were holding hearings. Representative Eugene Keogh wondered how much Dr. Annis knew about the scandal. Annis responded that the lawsuit was ridiculous and a publicity stunt particularly in as much as Dr. Wood was also supposed to testify at the hearings.[61] In general, the temper of the hearings were even more heated than previous hearings on the same subject, prompting Representative Martha Griffiths to announce, "I would like to say that I am one of the few people in this place who thinks that the proponents have overstated their case but I also think that the opponents have overstated their case."[62]

The most significant change during the 1963 hearings was in the attitude of Wilbur Mills. Mills now said that he was not quarreling at this point with the basic philosophy behind Medicare. His concern was that, if the program were enacted, it should be at a tax rate that would make it sound for the future and not dependent upon future Congresses. His reservations, Mills said, concerned the financing of the bill, "and of course it is no fault of Mr. King's at all." Mills insisted that the bill presumed a static economy, and did not allow enough flexibility for increase of costs in the future.[63]

What Mills did not tell the Committee that day was that in the morning before the hearings, Mills and Henry Hall Wilson had finally reached a tentative agreement on a formula to finance Medicare. Wilson had left Mills's office to find Larry O'Brien. A while later, while Mills had the floor, he was informed of President Kennedy's assassination. The Chairman abruptly cancelled the hearings.[64]

7

Politics First

Lyndon Johnson adopted most of John F. Kennedy's unfinished legislation and incorporated it into the Great Society. After civil rights, Medicare was second in priority along with fair housing and full employment on Johnson's list of legislative "musts." Medicare appealed to Johnson in a special way. Health insurance for the elderly was not only an essential part of a war on poverty: it was also a project first taken up by Johnson's hero, Franklin Roosevelt. Johnson, who had received his political education during Roosevelt's Administration, still took the goals of the New Deal very much to heart.

There was more: "Johnson," wrote Doris Kearns, "seemed to regard the program of the Great Society in the way overly fond parents look at their children."[1] As a son Johnson was very serious about his filial obligations to his parents and to everyone else's parents. Health insurance for the elderly was one concrete means to demonstrate that obligation. At a news conference Johnson told reporters, "I can think of no single piece of legislation that I would be happier to approve."[2] On another occasion he said, "It does not seem fair to ask older people to stoop and bend and plead for funds to be shoveled out of the state and Federal treasuries by means of a mean's test."[3] In his 1964 State of the Union message, Johnson said, "Let this session of Congress be known as the session which finally recognized the health needs of our older citizens."[4]

After hearing the President's speech, AMA spokesman Dr. Edward Annis was outraged. President Johnson, Annis said, "apparently has been grossly misinformed by his advisors on medical legislation."[5] But the AMA was no longer the main obstacle to getting Medicare passed. The Chairman of the Ways and Means Committee, Wilbur Mills, now held the most power with regard to Medicare. To get his legislative program passed, Johnson spent hours on the telephone, "talking, cajoling, persuading members of Congress," but he could not push the Chairman of the Ways and Means Committee.[6] Mills had his own ways of operating and his own reasons for not rushing into a national Medicare program.

Even Mills was actually no longer the obstacle that he appeared. A timely article in *America* said that old people could not afford medical care. They felt a loss of dignity in asking for charity. They waited for an emergency to force them into hospitals instead of seeking financial assistance to pay to prevent such an emergency.[7] Mills was almost ready to publicly agree. In a January 1964 memo to the President, White House Special Assistant Lawrence O'Brien described Mills as "on the brink" of accepting Medicare.[8] Mills was as much an expert on Social Security as the Secretary of HEW. He understood the inevitability of Medicare, but he was interested in a workable, financially sound bill that would pass his Committee and the House with a decent majority.

Many details needed working out. HEW staff members had been rewriting a bill to present to Mills at the time of Kennedy's death. HEW and the White House staff wanted to offer solutions to the problems that troubled Mills.

Unlike Kennedy, Johnson did not get involved with the details of individual bills such as Medicare. He was only interested in the final results.[9] In the meantime, there were a few changes within the White House staff. Ted Sorensen resigned as Special Assistant, as did Myer Feldman, who had been Kennedy's link to HEW and Congress on Medicare. The key figure now was Larry O'Brien, along with his Senate liaison, Mike Manatos, and House liaison, Henry Hall Wilson.[10]

O'Brien was more than equal to the task. He was raised in a political environment. His father made the O'Brien home Democratic Party headquarters for Boston leader James M. Curley. O'Brien had worked for the Democrats from the age of 15. When John Kennedy challenged Senator Henry Cabot Lodge for the Massachusetts senatorial seat in 1952, O'Brien was in charge of the campaign, creating a state-wide organization that helped Kennedy win by 70,000 votes. O'Brien again ran Kennedy's campaign for Senator in 1958, directed his presidential campaign in 1960, and served as Special Assistant to the President for Congressional Liaison for Kennedy and then Johnson.[11]

Within HEW, Wilbur Cohen continued to take charge of the Medicare effort, especially since Ivan Nestingen was not popular with the new President. Cohen, on the other hand, had a long relationship with Johnson. In Johnson's mind, Cohen *was* Social Security. The association had grown through the years with the help of Elizabeth Wickenden, a close friend of Johnson's. Through the 1940s and 1950s Wickenden constantly urged Johnson to go to Cohen for information on Social Security and later Medicare. Johnson came to trust Cohen. In 1964, memos and instructions flowed from Cohen in HEW to O'Brien in the White House, or from Congress to Manatos and Wilson, then to O'Brien and ultimately to the President.[12]

While the Medicare advocates were making changes on the King-Anderson Bill, Senator Jacob Javits, along with his liberal Republican colleagues Clifford Case, Kenneth Keating, Thomas Kuchel, John Sherman Cooper, and Margaret Chase Smith, introduced their own version of health insurance for the elderly. This bill, S2431, was based on the National Health Committee report of November 1963. Stressing simplicity, it proposed 45 days of hospital insurance, 180 days of skilled nursing coverage, or 240 days of home care visits. There were no deductible or options. Everyone over 65 was eligible to participate in the benefits. Javits said that his bill would serve as a minimum base of health protection and permit private insurance companies to offer further protection and additional coverage for such services as doctors' fees, dental fees, and drugs.[13] The bill was introduced in the House by New York Congressman Seymour Halpern. The *New York Daily News* applauded the Javits-Halpern Bill, claiming, "If private enterprise can be induced to enter the field let's bring it in!"[14]

The Ways and Means Committee hearings, begun in November 1963, were scheduled to resume in January. The hearings covered the increases and changes in the Social Security system proposed earlier by Mills, as well as various Congressional proposals for health insurance for the elderly. The January hearings were accompanied by great publicity and rallies for many of the witnesses. Before Mayor Wagner left New York City to testify on behalf of King-Anderson, 1,000 older persons demonstrated in front of City Hall. The rally, organized by local chapters of the National Council for Senior Citizens at the request of the Mayor, served as a public statement of the city's support for the King-Anderson Bill. Mayor Wagner considered the demonstration a mandate. He told the crowd: "I am for it, period."[15]

Dr. Benjamin Spock attracted the most attention when he arrived in Washington to testify on behalf of the King-Anderson Bill. Dr. Spock was met by large crowds of well-wishers. He told the committee, "Babies and children are deprived of things when parents' savings are wiped out by paying for illnesses for grandparents."[16]

AFL-CIO President George Meany also received wide press attention when he testified. Answering rumors that working men were not going to like the increase in their taxes that would accompany Medicare, Meany said, "Labor has revised the slogan of the airline industry. They want to pay now and fly later."[17] The *New York Times* reported, "With the possible exception of Civil Rights, no domestic issue in recent years has produced a response from a greater cross-section of American opinion than Medicare."[18]

The fanfare clouded the reality. The public hearings changed no votes on the Ways and Means Committee. The count was still 11–14 against a Social Security-financed health insurance program for the elderly. Frustrated by lack of progress Representative Eugene Keogh (D-New York) reminded his colleagues, "Patients have been known to die while the specialists are conferring."[19] Mills postponed the executive session on Social Security amendments until April. February and March were taken up by the foreign security tax bill.

Throughout the hearings Mills had listened attentively to witnesses. In private, he detailed his major reservations about King-Anderson to Wilbur Cohen and Larry O'Brien. Mills did not like the idea of including commercial insurance and even Blue Cross as fiscal intermediaries. He did not like the inequities that resulted when everyone over 65 received Medicare benefits, while many could not qualify for Social Security checks because they were still working. To make it equal to Social Security requirements, Mills thought that some kind of retirement test should apply to Medicare also.[20] Most important, Mills worried that hospital costs were rising faster than wages. He was particularly concerned about the large discrepancy between the HEW estimate that Medicare would cost $1.6 billion and the $2.7 billion predicted by private insurance companies. Mills was not willing to jeopardize the entire Social Security fund by guessing which figures were more accurate.[21]

After only five days of hearings, the Committee adjourned. No bill was reported out of the Ways and Means Committee. Johnson assured the nation, "We have just begun to fight."[22] Yet the editorial board of the *New York Times* wondered if Medicare was becoming nothing but a "hardy perennial." The *Times* admonished the President that a "working plan" such as the one the Administration submitted to Mills, cannot be implemented "without effective leadership." Johnson's statement, "We have just begun to fight" reveals "that the Administration has not yet made the necessary effort to assure a victory. If the bill is to pass this year Mr. Johnson will have to be prepared for a fight to the finish."[23]

By February, Johnson was ready to follow the Kennedy tradition and deliver a major speech to Congress on the "Health Needs of Our Nation." The President had budgeted into his Great Society at least 19 bills for health benefits and services related to the elderly. Regarding Medicare Johnson said, "Government should provide a base that related private programs can supplement.... The cost to the average worker would only be one dollar a month during his working years."[24] Johnson stressed the need for cooperation by private insurance companies. He also called for an expansion of the Kerr-Mills program.

For most of February and March, the Administration's attention was on Civil Rights legislation in the House and on a major tax bill in the Senate. Ironically, a reminder of the need to pay attention to Medicare came from the Republicans. Six Republicans, led by Massachusetts Senator Leverett Saltonstall, introduced a voluntary medical program for the elderly. Saltonstall intended his bill as a substitute for both King-Anderson *and* Kerr-Mills. Kerr-Mills, Saltonstall explained, imposed a burdensome means test requirement and does not reach all aged people who need assistance with their medical bills. The Republicans wanted to replace the means test by an income formula. Medical assistance would be available to anyone over 65 whose income is under $3,000 per year. The program would be voluntary. About 15.7 percent of the older population would be eligible. In addition, there would be a fee ranging from $10 to $120 per year charged to beneficiaries.[25]

The *New York Times* called the Republican bill "costly, and unrealistic." Its only value the *Times* reported was "as a confession that Kerr-Mills was not working. In a year when the nation is addressing itself to a frontal attack on poverty, it is unthinkable that Congress should adjourn without having had an opportunity to vote on a Medicare program so basic to the alleviation of human suffering.''[26] Congress adjourned anyway for Easter recess. When the legislators returned, Mills called an executive session in the Ways and Means Committee to determine what to do about Medicare and the Social Security Amendments for 1964.

Cohen, Robert Ball, Robert Myers, and the rest of the HEW staff prepared a new and complete package for the executive session. The revisions included the following: a five percent increase in Social Security benefits, financed by raising the taxable earnings base to $6,000. Also, the language of Kerr-Mills was rearranged to emphasize the *most needy* category first, followed by the other categories, such as the disabled. This served to identify Kerr-Mills as primarily a welfare program—and not an alternative to Medicare.

The changes were clearly made for the benefit of Mills. The tax increases admitted at the outset that the costs of a health insurance program were going to put Social Security taxes at the 10 percent limit. (No law kept the payroll tax limit at 10 percent. Rather, it was Abraham Ribicoff's suggestion in 1960 that 10 percent was a psychological limit. Thereafter it became a "Rubicon" beyond which Medicare advocates dared not cross.) By raising the wage base from $4,800 to $6,000, HEW hoped it was creating a package of fiscal solvency. HEW also included part of Mills's desired cash increase of Social Security benefits.[27]

In a private memo to the President, Larry O'Brien noted that, from the requests for technical information that Mills was making to HEW, it was beginning to appear that Mills was getting ready to justify an endorsement of Medicare. Mills was requesting information about altering Kerr-Mills to assure broader and more uniform use by the states. Mills also indicated to HEW that he had abandoned the idea of including an option for cash benefits instead of health insurance.[28]

Others on the Ways and Means Committee were also requesting information from HEW. The senior Republican member, John W. Byrnes of Wisconsin, asked the estimated cost of increasing Social Security benefits to $10 per applicant. Since it was the first time that a Republican ever requested information about such a large benefit increase, HEW staff became suspicious. They interpreted Byrnes' request as a last ditch effort to price Social Security benefits so high as to forever eliminate the possibility of affording Medicare.[29]

Representative Joel Broyhill (R-Virginia) even suggested to Mills that they "sweeten up" Kerr-Mills so that nobody would want Medicare. Significantly, Mills defended the Medicare advocates. He told Broyhill that the people who advocate health insurance want to *prevent* people from going on relief, not to expand the relief system.

The executive session of the Ways and Means Committee remained in session until mid-June. During that time, Senator Smathers decided to go ahead with the Senate Special Committee on Aging's hearings on the ability of private insurance to meet the needs of older people. Smathers's Committee requested that Robert Ball testify. Ball, who was concentrating his energies on Mills and the Ways and Means Committee, declined to appear, ruffling feathers and further driving a wedge between the two factions in the Senate: Senator Clinton Anderson on the Finance Committee who understood Ball's strategy and Senator Pat McNamara on the Labor and Public Welfare Committee of which the Aging Committee was part. McNamara resented the attention given to Mills. Yet Ball had sound reasons for not wanting to testify in the Senate. He did not want to find himself in the position of making harsh statements to the Aging Committee about the private insurance companies and then having to compromise during the executive session of the Ways and Means Committee by creating a role for the private insurance industry.[30]

The efforts of HEW, O'Brien, Henry Hall Wilson, and AFL-CIO leaders Nelson Cruikshank and Andrew Biemiller to propose a compromise package for Mills were in vain. The Ways and Means Committee made no progress. Wilbur Mills was not going to vote yes until he had a clear majority on his committee. Of the four Democrats on the Committee who still refused to support Medicare, A. Sidney Herlong (Florida), Mills, Clark W. Thompson (Texas), and John C. Watts (Kentucky), the President was able to persuade only Thompson.

Thompson was from Johnson's home state, and Johnson reminded him of the personal appearances and letters that he had made on Thompson's behalf in the 1962 election.[31] John Watts was unable to change his mind, at least not until after the 1964 election. Watts was from tobacco country in Kentucky, and the AMA was using all of its resources to make sure the tobacco industry opposed Medicare. Dr. Annis even went on a personal speaking tour throughout Watt's district.[32] A. Sidney Herlong was stubbornly and philosophically opposed to Medicare. Wilbur Cohen even tried to convince Smathers "to push" Herlong into line. Herlong would not go along. He owed his allegiance to the AMA.[33]

With only 11 votes, King-Anderson was short of a majority. Mills, as always, refused to be a swing vote. Henry Hall Wilson asked the

Chairman what he could do. Mills said that he might be able to convince Watts, but he needed more assurances about Herlong. Wilson agreed to continue talking to Watts, Thompson, and Herlong. In case the bill came up on the House floor, Wilbur Cohen lobbied other Democrats, such as Martha Griffiths (D-Michigan), who might oppose the bill.

Mills told O'Brien, Cohen, and Cecil King that he had on paper the names of 220 House votes against Medicare. The Johnson Administration was not about to argue with Mills over tallies, even though *The New Republic* believed that Medicare would pass the House by as much as 20 votes. If Medicare had enough votes, the plan was for King to make a motion to report out the Social Security Amendments with Medicare, and Al Ullman would back him up. Since King was unwilling to risk defeat, there was no vote. The executive session reported out several Social Security amendments, including an across-the-board five percent increase of benefits which would affect 19.5 million people in Title II of the Social Security program. The Ways and Means Committee ended its executive session on June 23, 1964.[34]

The next opportunity for Medicare was in the Senate. The Senate Democrats needed organization and strategy to attach a King-Anderson Amendment to the Social Security Bill sent over by the House. On June 12, House Majority Whip Hale Boggs asked White House Assistants Bill Moyers and Douglass Cater at a British Embassy dinner to tell the President to move ahead with Medicare in the Senate as soon as possible.[35]

Senator Abraham Ribicoff took the initiative. On July 20, Ribicoff described to Johnson Medicare's situation in the Senate. The five percent increase in benefits in the final House version, he said, was going to cause a serious tactical problem. Senators would be understandably reluctant to vote against Social Security increases. On the other hand, if passed, the five percent increase would foreclose any chance for Medicare in 1964.

Ribicoff proposed a compromise. Why not, he asked, give Social Security beneficiaries a choice: either a cash increase or hospital insurance. That choice would leave financing at the 10 percent limit and the wage base stable at $5,400. Benefits would be available to everyone over 65. Nobody would be "forced" to accept health insurance. They could choose cash instead. If the President was interested, Ribicoff concluded, he would take the necessary action in the Finance Committee—recognizing that Clinton Anderson had leadership responsibilities for that legislation. Also, Ribicoff warned, without strategy Medicare was not going to make it this time around. If the President wanted something to pass, Ribicoff's version had a better chance of succeeding than the King-Anderson Bill. Ribicoff added that someone had to make a tactical decision either to go with King-Anderson, go with a compromise plan like Ribicoff's, or give up for 1964. The only person to make that decision was the President.[36]

Ribicoff's plan was not what Johnson, Anderson, and the HEW people or Nelson Cruikshank and AFL-CIO wanted at the start. In actuality, HEW had drawn up an almost identical compromise but was holding it as a last resort. Ribicoff, however, did not wait for a response from the President. During a Democratic Freshman Senator lunch, Ribicoff showed his plan to Senate Majority Leader Mike Mansfield, arguing that, if the Senate could pass a compromise, then the burden to act would again be on Mills.[37]

In the meanwhile, the Medicare forces argued about strategy: whether to present King-Anderson only in Finance Committee during its hearings, or to attach it as an amendment directly on the Senate floor. Nelson Cruikshank and Andrew Biemiller believed that George Smathers and Russell Long would support Medicare in the Finance Committee this time. Wilbur Cohen was skeptical. He felt that they were better off trying Medicare as an amendment on the floor.[38]

Once again, Wilbur Cohen's strategy proved the most effective. On August 6, 1964, the House sent HR11865 (Social Security Amendments) to the Senate. Clinton Anderson was not present that day. Senator Albert Gore, who happened to have the floor, quickly added King-Anderson as a floor amendment to the House bill. Because it was added on to the House increases, Gore's amendment put the cost of the bill over the ten percent payroll tax limit. Senator Pat McNamara joined Gore in introducing King-Anderson as an amendment to HR11865, as did Hubert Humphrey, Joseph Clark, and eventually Clinton Anderson.

Ribicoff, who had never received a response to his memo from the President, also introduced his proposal as a floor amendment to HR11865. To confuse matters, both Clinton Anderson and Hubert Humphrey co-sponsored Ribicoff's amendment. Pat McNamara did not like Ribicoff's plan at all. McNamara did not even like some features in the Gore Amendment, such as using Blue Cross as an administrative agency, although he went along with it. Another feature in the Gore Amendment that did not appeal to McNamara was the inclusion of an "automatically adjusted cost sharing principle" which was Robert Myer's idea to keep the system financially sound.[39] If hospital costs rose too fast, then a higher deductible would automatically be imposed.

Vance Hartke (D-Indiana) was even less satisfied than McNamara with Ribicoff's Bill. In a letter to Johnson, Hartke said that the House bill pending before the Senate (HR11865) whose purpose it was to liberalize Social Security benefits, was *not* the proper vehicle on which "to ride a watered down version of Medicare." First of all, any Medicare amendment would slow down the passage of the Social Security increases. More important, the voluntary aspect of Ribicoff's "watered-down" version would endanger the principle of the Social Security program.[40]

The Republicans added two amendments of their own to HR11865. Senator Javits wrote his bill (S2431) in amendment form. Javits's Bill gave elderly beneficiaries a choice between increased cash benefits or health insurance of the type described in his bill. With Javits's Bill, the cost of financing was over the ten percent limit on payroll taxes. Ribicoff noted that, in order to stay within the ten percent limit for both King-Anderson and Javits's amendments, the coverage of dependent children in college could be changed to coverage of children up to age 21 but only if they were enrolled in high school. Senator Hugh Scott (R-Pennsylvania) then offered voluntary health insurance as an amendment.[41]

On August 6, 1964, the Senate Finance Committee opened hearings. Votes on the Committee had not changed since 1960. Chairman Harry F. Byrd was still totally committed to blocking Medicare. Secretary Celebrezze testified that

HR11865 is seriously lacking in the area of the highest priority need. It fails completely to offer those past 65 an avenue through which they can afford and obtain adequate basic health insurance protection. It thus fails to come to grips with the gravest threat to financial security and peace of mind in old age. What is needed to provide security in old-age in sickness as well as in health is . . . First and most urgent, hospital insurance for the aged provided under the social security program so that older people would be assured of being able to meet this major item of expensive health care in a way consistent with dignity and self-respect.[42]

Byrd asked Celebrezze which of the bills pending before the Finance Committee the Administration preferred. Celebrezze answered that the Administration preferred King-Anderson on top of the House bill. If they had to choose one, then King-Anderson would take priority. Byrd then asked if the Secretary was concerned that the total tax rate for both measures would reach 10.4 by 1971. Robert Ball answered that there was nothing magical in the figure of ten percent.[43]

The tone of the Finance Committee hearings revealed more of an interest in the mechanics of Medicare than in the customary debate on morality. Vance Hartke asked AFL-CIO representatives Nelson Cruikshank and Andrew Biemiller if the labor unions were willing to accept Ribicoff's option plan. Biemiller answered that they were flexible if that was the only way they could meet the need of the elderly for health insurance.

An argument ensued between Hartke, who did not want to jeopardize the Social Security increases in the remaining two weeks (August 22) of the session, and Ribicoff, who insisted that they could get a compromise plan accepted.[44] It was an argument that the AFL-CIO and HEW were also drawn into. The AFL-CIO and Cohen (speaking for HEW) wanted to try for a King-Anderson version of Medicare and the Social Security cash increases. They did not want the latter alone for fear that it would preclude the former. Anderson, who agreed with the AFL-CIO and Cohen, was not present to support his side. In Anderson's place, Albert Gore performed well. Finally Republican Wallace Bennett said, "We Republicans have been interested sitting here today silent while our Democratic colleagues are fighting over the dilemma in which their party finds itself."[45]

As the hearings went into a second week, White House representatives held a strategy session. O'Brien and Manatos were present, along with Senators Mansfield, Humphrey, Anderson, and Ribicoff. O'Brien assured the Senators that the President was "four-square" behind King-Anderson. However, no one realistically believed that King-Anderson would survive a conference committee. The consensus was that Ribicoff's plan had a better chance. The Senators thought that Presidential pressure was needed to get an immediate meeting with Senate Democratic leaders Russell Long, Herman Talmadge, William Fulbright, and George Smathers to determine what their position was going to be in case of a floor vote. The Senators also agreed that, if Mills was not in full support of the Administration's position, then the Administration should allow the Social Security amendments to die! Otherwise, Medicare might be permanently lost.[46]

Another argument between diverging Democratic positions before the

Finance Committee was over the role of Blue Cross. Walter J. Mc-
Nerney, President of Blue Cross, equivocated on King-Anderson.
McNerney seemed to be against Medicare. Ribicoff favored the use of
Blue Cross as the administrative intermediary between the Federal Government and hospitals. Ribicoff had gone so far as to tell representatives
of the Kaiser plan and other Group plans not to upset the situation and
fight for inclusion. Cohen, Ball, and Myers expressed anxiety about
giving Blue Cross the key role.[47] The AFL-CIO on the other hand was
definitely in favor of using Blue Cross, if only for George Meany's
oblique reason of allowing the public to "get a hold on" Blue Cross.
Anderson favored using a number of the major insurance groups as
intermediaries, each having responsibility for a different region. Hartke,
speaking for himself and McNamara, definitely opposed giving any
private group a role. Complicating the whole business was the unclear
position of Blue Cross itself. Senator Douglas, in his usual caustic
fashion, told McNerney, "Your comments remind me of a novelist who
said he led the public up to the bedroom door and slammed it in their
faces."[48]

The Finance Committee rejected all four amendments. The Gore
Amendment was defeated 6–11. Ribicoff's Amendment was defeated
5–12. (Hartke was the one Democrat who voted for Gore's proposal
and against Ribicoff's.) Both Javits's and Scott's Amendments were
defeated by a voice vote. The Committee reported out HR11865 in
almost the form in which it had received it from the House. The minority
said that the majority report failed to meet "the most desperate and
urgent need of our older people." Congress recessed for ten days while
the Democrats held their presidential nominating Convention.[49]

On August 30, 1964, when HR11865 came up before the Senate, the
Democrats still did not unify their efforts. Senator Long, along with
Senators Smathers and Hartke, immediately added an amendment to
liberalize cash benefits beyond what was in HR11865. Their intention
(except for Hartke) was to reach a payroll tax limit of 10 percent so
that there was no room left for a King-Anderson Amendment. Hartke
wanted more of a cash increase for the elderly. Long's move was not
expected, either by the White House or by other Democrats advocating
Medicare.

Fortunately, Senator Douglas was a fast thinker. No sooner had Long
finished introducing his amendment than Douglas jumped to his feet

and accused Long of sabotage. Douglas, followed by Gore, continued to talk and hold the floor while Anderson, Humphrey, and Mansfield, rushed to Mansfield's office to rewrite an amendment for Medicare to make it "germane as a substitute to Long's amendment."[50]

Douglas, with characteristic eloquence, told his Senate colleagues that he was "struck with admiration and sorrow that the Senator from Louisiana would produce such an adroit parliamentary maneuver."[51] After Douglas, Gore continued to filibuster until Anderson, Humphrey, and Mansfield were ready with their amendment. They almost didn't make it because the Senate was about ready to adjourn. Since Gore was still holding the floor, he went ahead and introduced the substitute that called for 90 days of hospitalization with a deductible range from $20 to $90; or, 45 days with no deductible; or, 180 days with a flat deductible of $92.50; 60 days of nursing home care; 240 home health visits; outpatient services with $20 deductible; plus, $7 cash increase to Social Security beneficiaries only. The new amendment carried with it taxes that went up to 10.4 percent on a salary base of $5,600. Long denounced the plan as a "Federal giveaway." The advocates of Medicare hoped that, if the Senate would start with the above plan, they would force a compromise in conference and end up with Ribicoff's less expensive plan.[52]

The debate and political maneuvers that followed Gore's introduction of a new version of Medicare were complicated by factors unrelated to Medicare. As soon as a vote for HR11865 was taken, the Senators returned to a troublesome debate over a rider that Everett Dirksen had attached to a foreign aid bill. Dirksen's rider was designed to delay Congressional reapportionment—a delay that the Democratic liberals very much did not want to happen. Some therefore thought it better to put off Medicare in order to postpone the Dirksen issue. As the *New York Times* complained, the four issues (Social Security increases, Medicare, the Dirksen rider, and the foreign aid bill) were "tied up like a pretzel."[53]

On September 2, the debate ended. Many Senators, particularly the Democrats, were absent during the first roll call. The Gore Amendment stood at 42–42. Barry Goldwater, now the Republican presidential candidate, dramatically flew from Arizona to Washington, D.C., to cast his negative vote. Goldwater believed that the Gore Amendment was an "insult to the intelligence of the American people." It presumed that American workers were incapable of knowing how to spend their money. The Arizona Senator told his colleagues, "I face with deep foreboding the consequences of our embarking on this course. . . ."[54]

After two more roll calls, the Gore Amendment was approved 49–46. The margin would have been larger had all Democrats been present. All the Republicans, except for Javits's group of four, voted against the Gore Amendment. On the Democratic side, most of the South, including Senators Long, Smathers, Byrd, and Fulbright, voted against the Gore Amendment. Surprisingly, especially since the medical profession rebuffed his 1962 election, Lister Hill refused to say which way he was voting. When the roll calls were taken, Hill was not present.

The whole bill, HR11865, including the Gore Amendment, was accepted 60–28. In a statement to the press Anderson said, "I suspect that the bill will go to conference and a man named Wilbur Mills will sit down with the conferees from the Senate and agree something will have to go and then agree on a modified version that won't cost too much."[55]

The next step was for a Senate-House Conference Committee to work out the differences between the Senate and House versions of HR11865. The Senate conferees were Democrats Harry F. Byrd, Russell Long, George Smathers, Clinton Anderson, and Albert Gore, and Republicans John J. Williams (Delaware) and Frank Carlson (Kansas). Although Senate conferees were expected to vote as a bloc and uphold the position of the Senate, this tradition was not mandatory. Only two of the seven Senate conferees—Anderson and Gore—had actually supported Medicare. The House sent five conferees: Democrats Wilbur Mills, Hale Boggs, Cecil King, and Republicans John F. Byrnes and Thomas Curtis. Only two of the five from the House had voted for Medicare. If ever there was a time for President Johnson to intervene, this was it. Bill Moyers called Ken O'Donnell and asked him to "pull out all of the stops" on White House lobbying.[56]

The principal differences between the two versions were as follows: The Senate *deleted* from HR11865:

1. the five percent across the board increase in benefits based on a taxable wage base of $5,400 and changed it to a seven percent limited increase on a taxable base of $5,600.

The Senate *added*:

2. Social Security coverage for doctors.

3. Social Security coverage for tip income.

4. elimination of the prohibition against covering policemen and firemen. (The House had made the prohibition on grounds that policemen and firemen have their own retirement fund.)

5. a health insurance program for Social Security recipients—and a cost saving device if costs got too high.

6. the imposition of a deductible in 1969 or after hospital costs rose without a commensurate increase in wage base.[57]

Mike Manatos met with House Speaker Carl Albert and Majority Whip Hale Boggs to see what the House conferees were planning to do. Boggs said that he and Cecil King would not sign a conference report that did not make a provision for Medicare. Carl Albert agreed with that stand. Boggs pointed out to Manatos that their position left Mills in the predicament of having to side with the Republicans. Manatos then discussed the situation by phone with Gore and Anderson and they too said that they would not sign a report that left out Medicare. Gore advised that, even though it was a tough decision, the Senate should act to kill the whole bill as a last resort rather than accept a bill without Medicare. In Gore's view, it was better to fight it out this year rather than to request another increase in Social Security taxes next year to finance Medicare. Mike Manatos reported the conversations to Larry O'Brien.[58]

The conferees made no progress. Smathers told the press, "We're at complete loggerheads."[59] Compromises were offered to Mills, discussed, and finally rejected. HEW staff was busy making proposals and counter-proposals—none of which were acceptable to Mills. The House was 3–2 against any of the compromises and the Senate was 4–2 against a retreat from its position. Harry F. Byrd was caught in the middle. He could not ignore the mandate of the Senate. At the same time his conscience prevented him from supporting the Senate's position. On the final vote, he abstained.[60]

Smathers and Long, on the other hand, surprised everyone by voting to uphold the Senate's bill. Smathers was personally pressured by the President. Long had other reasons.[61] He was interested in becoming the next Senate Majority Whip, if Hubert Humphrey vacated that post for the Vice Presidency. He not only needed to prove that he could be a loyal party man, but he also needed the votes of Anderson, Gore, and other liberal Democrats. Anderson exchanged his support for Long as Majority Whip for Long's support in the conference.[62]

The same morning that Anderson reported that the conferees were about to end their deliberations and simply quit, Mike Mansfield held a private meeting with Mike Manatos and Senators Smathers, Long, Mike Monroney, John Pastore (D-Rhode Island), Alan Bible (D-Nevada), and legislative assistant Frank Valeo. Manatos suggested a recess for the Conference Committee until after the November election. The purpose was to preserve an untarnished record for Medicare and the pending Aid to Appalachia for the Democratic campaign. Also, by forcing a recess at that point, the Democrats would postpone the current Bobby Baker hearings.[63]

Mills had other plans. He wanted finished business and a completed record. On the final day of meeting, he told the conferees to return for one more morning. No one knew why. The next morning he asked for a final vote on the record. The Senate conferees were 4–2 in favor of their version. Byrd abstained. The House conferees were 3–2 against the Senate version. The conference could not report out a bill.[64]

The President and the press blamed Mills for refusing to pass Medicare. The *New York Times* wrote, "The chief reason the country does not now have a Medicare program is the one man blockade exercised for four years by Chairman Wilbur Mills."[65] The *Times* was also angry that the Democrats had decided to risk losing the rest of the Social Security Amendments. No legislative tactics, the newpaper proclaimed, were morally justified that forced old people to live "through another winter on the edge of penury."[66]

In a speech in Arkansas, Mills justified his position by saying that he was primarily concerned about the financial soundness of the system. Under the current Medicare proposals, he said, the taxable wage base would have to be increased annually just to keep up to costs—up to $7,200 by 1976! Mills had another reason for not letting HR11865 with the Gore Amendment get to the House floor for a vote. Many House members had privately beseeched him not to force a public vote before the election. They did not want to get caught between the wrath of the medical profession and the business community on one side and of the old folks and labor on the other. Mills saved his friends from embarrassment and took the blame himself. Ultimately, each colleague so spared owed a debt to Mills.[67]

Clinton Anderson was heartbroken. It was the second time that he had witnessed a version of his original King-Anderson almost pass, and then lose. He had gone into the conference with several compromises, including one that put a ceiling on benefits and one that did not allow for the usual "blanketing in" of eligible persons who did not contribute. Mills considered each compromise, and then rejected them one by one.

President Johnson was personally not so willing to compromise. On more than one occasion his direction to the Democrats was to stand pat. Johnson was expecting a landslide in the November election and did not want to give away more than necessary.[68]

The American Medical Association congratulated itself on another successful lobbying effort (or so its leaders believed) even though Smathers and Long had betrayed their wishes. The doctors had hired a new public relations firm, Fuller, Smith and Rem, Inc., with a 1 million dollar budget while the conferees were in Committee. The AMA wanted one-minute commercials on ABC, CBS, and NBC but the major networks would not sell one-minute time for controversial issues. The money went instead for local networks and radio.[69]

Although the joint conference could not report out a bill, Medicare was still a good campaign issue. On a paid TV political advertisement, Johnson was asked by a reporter, "Mr. President, is Medicare going to be on the list of your "must" legislation next year?" The President replied, "Just top of the list!"[70] During the first week of November, the White House published a nine-page summary of Johnson's goals for the Great Society. His legislation for education was on the top of the list, followed by programs for conservation. The health goals, one of which was Medicare, came third.[71] Both Johnson and Vice Presidential candidate Hubert Humphrey mentioned Medicare frequently. Humphrey said in a campaign speech in southern California that he personally had a number of improvements for the Social Security system. Humphrey wanted to see the Social Security system modified so that it would be linked to the cost of living index. Humphrey naturally endorsed Medicare, and suggested a new program, the creation of a National Senior Citizens' Corps. "Retired persons constitute a huge reservoir of skill, talent, experience and energy seeking useful and constructive outlets."[72]

As expected, the Democrats received an overwhelming victory on November 2, 1964. The 89th Congress was composed of 295 Democrats in the House (67 of them new) and 140 Republicans (19 of them new). Three Republican members of the Ways and Means Committee were replaced by Democrats. Even if Chairman Mills was inclined to bottle up Medicare again, the Administration supporters had enough votes in the House to force the bill out of Committee. The election had given Medicare at least 54 votes in the Senate. Mike Monroney, who had voted against Medicare in the Finance Committee, told Anderson that Medicare was the most popular issue in Oklahoma and Monroney now would support Anderson.[73]

On November 11, the headline in the *New York Times* read "Mills Gives Way in Aged Care Bill." In a telephone statement to the press from his home in Arkansas, Mills said that he was ready to bring up the long stalled measure immediately after Congress convened in January if President Johnson wanted him to.[74]

Newspapers around the country predicted that Medicare would clear Congress by Easter. The AMA meanwhile was silently awaiting the Administration bill. However, they reduced their Washington lobby staff, intending to shift their emphasis away from the Capitol and directly to the people. The new head of the AMA, Dr. Donovan T. Ward, told the House of Delegates during their annual December meeting that "the battle must go on." Delegates from Michigan and D.C. offered compromises for the AMA but Dr. Ward wouldn't listen: "We do not, by profession, compromise in matters of life and death. Nor can we compromise with honor and duty."[75]

By law, uncompleted legislation cannot be carried over from one Congress to another. An entirely new bill had to be introduced. In light of the Administration's strong position, a less compromising version could now be written.[76] Secretary Celebrezze told the President that during the December recess Wilbur Cohen was keeping in close touch with Anderson, King, Speaker McCormack, and Majority Leader Carl Albert. Cohen was also in touch with AFL-CIO leaders Cruikshank and Biemiller. Celebrezze sent along a summary of the last version of King-Anderson to the President.[77] Meanwhile, Cohen, Robert Ball, Robert Myers, Cruikshank, Biemiller, and their staffs sat down to rewrite the bill. Senator Anderson put in an early request with Mansfield that the "S1" designation be reserved for Medicare, implying Medicare as the first order of business. Cecil King did the same, requesting the designation of "HR1" for the House version.[78]

8

The Three-Layer Cake

I feel certain that historians will mark this year as the turning point in our long struggle to solve the major part of what has become one of the most urgent issues of public policy—the problem of financing the costs of hospital care for the aged—costs which now remain the major cause of personal financial disaster faced by our aged citizens.[1]

With the above pronouncement, Senator Clinton Anderson introduced S1 in the Senate. Anderson had 41 co-sponsors for his bill, including three Republicans, Jacob Javits, Thomas Kuchel, and Clifford Case. Javits had suggested a joint bill with himself, Anderson, and Albert Gore, but neither the President nor Anderson was interested.[2] The same day, January 6, 1965, Representative Cecil King introduced HR1 in the House of Representatives. The new Medicare bill had been recommended by President Johnson in his State of the Union Message the day before. Johnson received loud applause from his Congressional audience every time he mentioned the word Medicare. On January 7, the President received the same enthusiastic reaction to Medicare during his Special Health Message to Congress.[3]

The revised King-Anderson Bill, S1, had become a 6 billion dollar package. It was drafted partly along guidelines suggested by an Advisory Council on Social Security, a 13–member panel of non-government experts called together by HEW Secretary Anthony Celebrezze. The rest of S1 was written by a team from HEW, headed by Wilbur Cohen, and a team from AFL-CIO, headed by Nelson Cruikshank. The new bill proposed 60 days hospital benefits, 60 days of nursing home benefits, and 240 home health visits. Also, a certain number of diagnostic out-patient services were covered with a $20 deductible. The package included the seven percent increase in Social Security benefits that had passed the Senate in 1964. For the hospital benefits, a flat $40 deductible was imposed.

The $40 deductible was arrived at after considerable discussion and disagreement. Budget Director Kermit Gordon recommended a $60 deductible, reasoning that with a higher deductible the system was better assured of economic solvency. Senator Anderson and Nelson Cruikshank wanted a $20 deductible so that access to hospital care was more available. During the 1964 House-Senate conference on Medicare Senator Russell Long had insisted that the deductible be at least $40. Cruikshank on behalf of the AFL-CIO finally agreed to $40 as a reluctant compromise.[4]

In accordance with the wishes of Wilbur Mills and the recommendation of the Advisory Council, the new Medicare program was to be financed by a separate payroll tax (separate from Social Security deductions) and kept in a separate trust fund (separate from the Social Security Trust Fund). "This way," said Mills, "the tax payer can see where his money is going."[5] The tax payer would be able to clearly identify on the W2 form the amount of money going to Social Security and the amount going to Medicare. Since the money for Medicare was kept in a separate trust fund, the public did not have to worry about the rumors that hospital insurance jeopardized the Social Security system.[6]

S1 and HR1 were the Medicare advocates' opening proposal. The White House saw Medicare as a legislative certainty for 1965. The President was well aware of the momentum produced by the November election. He was also aware how short lived that mandate might be. Johnson wanted to rush through as much legislation as he could during his "honeymoon" session in order to "exploit the historical moment."[7] The only question remaining for Medicare was in what shape the final bill was to emerge as law; or how much of the 6 billion dollar package would pass.

Ironically, it was the Republicans and anti-Medicare groups like the American Medical Association that defined the shape of the final bill. The opponents of Medicare made a momentous decision in 1965. They chose, as their course of action, not to trim the new package down, but instead to criticize the Administration's bill for *not doing enough*!

The opponents believed that their only hope was to scare the public into thinking that the Administration's Medicare plan would confer no real benefits. Their message via television, radio, journals, newspapers, and speeches, was that the public was being hoodwinked by the Johnson Administration. If this campaign succeeded, it would leave the door open to alternative bills that offered wider benefits but were based on alternative methods of financing.

The leading advertiser of this message, the American Medical Association, was the first to recommend another bill, known as "Eldercare." The AMA's bill was sponsored in the House by A. Sydney Herlong, Jr. (D-Florida) and Thomas Curtis (R-Missouri) and in the Senate by Leverett Saltonstall (R-Massachusetts). Dr. Donovan F. Ward, President of the AMA in 1965, claimed that "Eldercare would provide far more to our elderly citizens than is proposed in the Administration's Medicare tax program."[8] In January the AMA proceeded to launch a 1 million dollar national education campaign to kill Medicare by insisting how limited it was. Instead, Eldercare was praised as covering 100 percent of all health expenses including surgery and drugs.[9]

To anyone who read the actual bill, Eldercare was a myth. Even its sponsor, Herlong, politely commented to his Congressional colleagues that the AMA was probably trying to oversell its bill to the public and Congress and in doing so was giving misleading information. Eldercare, said Herlong, didn't offer quite so much as 100 percent.[10] The executive council of the AFL-CIO was not as reticent. They called Eldercare unworkable and said that the AMA's bill consisted of empty promises.[11]

Eldercare was simply an enlargement of the Kerr-Mills program. The program would offer only those services authorized by the individual states. Furthermore, Eldercare would offer nothing to the elderly living in the twenty states that had no provisions for Kerr-Mills. In the states that had passed legislation Eldercare would apply only to those elderly who were willing and able to pass a means test sponsored by state welfare departments. The Kerr-Mills law did in fact legislate the opportunity for states to cover *all* health services, but only three or four states came even close to doing so. Nevertheless, the AMA was using the literal language of the 1960 Kerr-Mills to advertise the potential benefits for Eldercare.[12]

The AMA was not alone in sponsoring legislation that claimed to offer *more* benefits than Medicare. The Republicans in the House, led by the new Minority Leader Gerald Ford, wanted to be on record as creating positive alternatives. If Medicare passed and the public was disappointed, then the Republicans could point to the record and say that their bill was better and more liberal. Senior Republican on the Ways and Means Committee, John F. Byrnes (R-Wisconsin) sponsored a bill, dubbed "Bettercare" that went beyond Medicare and Eldercare in advertised services. Byrnes's Bill included such items as drugs and doctor's fees that the Medicare bill left out. Senior citizens who wanted comprehensive coverage could purchase a special plan put out by private insurance companies. The elderly would be reimbursed for the cost of their premiums, depending on their income, out of general revenues of the U.S. Treasury, While Byrnes's Bill was administrated on a national level (as opposed to Eldercare which was administrated on a state level), it was a voluntary program. Byrnes's Bill was co-sponsored in the Senate by Hugh Scott (R-Pennsylvania), Thruston Morton (R-Kentucky), Norris Cotton (R-New Hampshire), George Aiken (R-Vermont), and Winston Prouty (R-New Hampshire).[13]

The Byrnes Bill and Eldercare were only the major representatives of many others. Many members of Congress were jumping on the bandwagon with bills that offered more services than Medicare. Vice President Hubert Humphrey jubilantly acclaimed the rush of his Congressional colleagues to sponsor bills. On January 11 he told a crowd of 800 council members of the AFL-CIO "Don't tell me it doesn't pay to win elections!"[14]

The psychological climate of Congress was shifting from "why so much?" to "why so little?" when the Ways and Means Committee opened public hearings on HR1. The new mood was not lost on Chairman Wilbur Mills. With Mills clearly committed and in charge, the Committee went to work on the details of creating a new law. Except for brief digressions from Representative Thomas Curtis on the unfairness of including everyone in on the benefits, the Committee lost no time arguing morality or ethics. They went directly to specific issues.

The first of several problems that the hearings addressed was that the Administration's package had gone beyond the 10 percent withholding tax "Rubicon." The new tax, pegged at 10.4 percent, worried many Congressmen. Representative Eugene Keogh (D-New York) said that he would like to see a definite ten percent limit placed on Social Security taxes. As an alternative, Keogh said that he would prefer instead to see the wage base raised—even to $7,500.[15] Mills's response to Keogh and others was that he never thought there was any determinable dollar limit to a tax rate. Mills defined the situation by saying that a tax rate is based on the willingness of the tax payer to pay.[16]

Robert Ball, part of the HEW team testifying earlier at the hearings, reiterated his position that there was nothing magical in the ten percent limit. Curtis wanted to know why the Administration could not figure out a way to stay within ten percent. Keogh suggested pushing the Social Security cash increases down to five percent in order to save money.[17] Wilbur Cohen tried to assure the Ways and Means Committee that HEW had consulted the Council for Economic Advisors as well as Budget Director Kermit Gordon to see if the higher tax might be excessive to employers and put them at a disadvantage in the world market. Cohen was told that the one-quarter of a percentage point wouldn't make a difference.[18]

The Ways and Means Committee left the issue of the tax rate and went to the next major hurdle put forth by Curtis: the degree of government control in the new bill. Referring to phrases such as "adequate nursing care and physical supervision" and "approval for accreditation," Curtis wanted to know *who* was going to determine what was adequate, *who* would do the approving and exactly *how* much power would the Federal Government have? Curtis found out that the final authority for "approving" hospitals and nursing homes would rest with the Secretary of HEW, but that the Secretary was authorized to delegate that authority to proper state agencies.[19]

The new Medicare bill established one criteria for hospitals as a condition for accreditation: each hospital had to set up a utilization review committee—that is, a group of staff doctors who met regularly to review the length of time each patient was required to stay in a hospital. The committee would also review admissions and prescribed treatment. It was *not* an outside overseer. It was a function of the hospital staff. The Federal Government, Wilbur Cohen assured Curtis, would not get involved in the process at all. "If a review board makes a mistake, there is nothing we can do about it, because that is the professional decision of the doctors."[20]

The Medicare bill also required minimum conditions for nursing home accreditation: 24–hour nursing service, maintaining health and safety standards, and adequate recordkeeping. The writers of the Medicare law were concerned that Federal money would be collected by nursing homes who did not observe nominal fire and health precautions. Curtis wanted to leave the responsibility of oversight in the hands of the state licensing bodies. There was, however, mounting evidence in 1965 that the states were not doing their jobs. The conditions in many nursing homes were deplorable even before the 1965 Medicare/Medicaid Act became law.[21]

Chairman Mills clarified the bill's intent for his Committee. He said that "we are setting up certain conditions" that have to be met. State agencies could review observance, but monitoring and enforcement would be in the hands of HEW.[22]

Walter J. McNerney, president of Blue Cross, raised another problem. The nursing home field, he testified, was currently in the rudimentary state of development. A lot of the care was pegged to Social Security income. If 60 days of Medicare coverage was suddenly pumped into the system, nursing home developers would proliferate to take advantage of the new law. Nursing homes already in existence were going to expand, maybe too rapidly to maintain quality. McNerney stressed the need for very *high* Federal standards.

Blue Cross's most recent experience with nursing homes was in connection with the auto industry. Blue Cross, the American Hospital Association, and the American Medical Association were trying to decide whose business it was to oversee standards. Neither the state, nor the hospitals nor the doctors were ready to assume supervisory responsibilities. There was a current void of control in the nursing home field that McNerney feared was only going to get worse.[23]

In his testimony, McNerney proceeded to the next detail of concern. The new Medicare bill proposed 240 home health visits. However, a home health visit was not defined. Did it mean one-half of a visit by a doctor, a two-hour visit by a nurse, a visit from a physical therapist or what? If the home health visit was defined as professional care, then that care *could not* be produced. There were not enough professionals around the country available for such services.[24] Mills asked if the 240 visits should be too much, were 120 visits more realistic? The Committee postponed the subject for a later time.[25]

McNerney's presence led to a discussion about the role of Blue Cross in the Medicare law. The bill proposed choice in administrative agencies appointed by HEW. Blue Cross might be one choice. The members of the American Hospital Association, represented by Associate Director Kenneth Williams and legislative assistant Lacey Sharpe preferred a single national agency, such as Blue Cross, to handle administration. The AHA wanted no choice in regional carriers.[26]

Representatives of the AFL-CIO, on the other hand, opposed Blue Cross as an administrative agency, contending that Blue Cross had not been successful in keeping up quality of care or in its utilization work. The experience of many of the unions, particularly the steelworkers, in working with Blue Cross was poor. Blue Cross never had consumer representatives on their boards; Blue Cross maintained a strong anti-union attitude toward their own employees.[27] The AFL-CIO suggested instead state health departments be given the responsibility. As with the other problems, no final decision was made during the executive hearings of the Ways and Means.[28]

As the bill was nearing completion in the House, Senator Abraham Ribicoff (D-Connecticut) wrote a worried letter to the President. Medicare, Ribicoff feared, was going to disillusion millions of the elderly. This disillusionment would be felt before the 1968 election. Too many senior citizens believe that all of their medical bills will be paid. He added, "What is more, Republicans are presenting many more comprehensive variations, so that they will be able to say 'I told you so.' "[29]

Ribicoff need not have worried. Wilbur Mills was fully aware of what the Republicans were doing. As the Ways and Means hearings came to an end on March 3, Mills surprised everyone with an astonishing "legislative coup." He suggested putting together all three of the major bills: King-Anderson, the AMA's Eldercare, and the Byrnes Bill. The result would be a three-layer program, or, as it was fondly called by HEW, a "three layer cake." Mills requested that Cohen create a package that would include all three bills. With that new development, the hearings ended, and the Ways and Means Committee went into closed session.[30]

Cohen left the hearings and dashed off a memo to the President advising him of Mills's latest suggestions. Cohen added in the memo, "At least nobody will vote against it." The next day, Bill Moyers of the White House staff informed Cohen that the President had read the memo.[31]

It did not take Cohen and his staff long to put together a new three-part package. Getting it through the Committee was another matter. Mostly because of Curtis's continual introduction of amendments, the closed session of the Ways and Means Committee did not end as soon as was expected. The problem, Larry O'Brien told the President, on March 23, was that, with the exception of Al Ullman, none of the Democratic committee members "are totally familiar with the bill, thus the tendency is to yield to Mills."[32] Cohen, who sat with Mills during the sessions, made daily reports on the Committee's progress to O'Brien, Celebrezze, Kermit Gordon, and White House assistant Douglass Cater.

Only one significant area of disagreement arose between Cohen and Mills.[33] On March 17, Cohen met privately with Carl Albert, Hale Boggs, and Wilbur Mills to discuss that problem: the inclusion of hospital-specialists, pathologists, radiologists, anesthesiologists, and psychiatrists under Medicare reimbursements. Mills was adamantly opposed to their inclusion. HEW and the AFL-CIO wanted their inclusion. Since the situation was at an impasse, everyone yielded to Mills's wishes. Mills's purpose was to keep all doctors out of the Medicare part of the bill, including hospital specialists.[34]

Finally, the bill was ready. The Ways and Means Committee approved it 17–8 in a straight party vote. Mills's Bill was referred to, for lack of a better name, by the acronym Elder-Medi-Better-Care. Mills called it "Social Security Amendments of 1965." In its first section, the bill included a basic plan of hospital coverage, nursing home and home-health coverage, under the Social Security program but with a separate payroll tax financing and a separate trust fund to hold the money. The second part (adapted from Byrnes's Bettercare) was a voluntary plan covering doctor's fees (including the four specialists in question) financed by a $3 a month premium deducted from Social Security benefits and matched by money from general revenue. The third part (from AMA's Eldercare) was an expanded Kerr-Mills program that paid for medical care for the recipients of welfare outside of the Social Security system, as well as the medically needy defined by the MAA part of Kerr-Mills. This third part was eventually called Medicaid. In addition, the bill provided for a seven percent increase in Social Security payments.

Mills spent 39 minutes, mostly without notes, explaining the provisions of the new bill to his House colleagues. "Let us be sure that the design of benefits is not defined by whatever it takes to get a bill passed with the feeling that details can be solved later."[35] Medicare passed the House on April 8, 1965, 263–153.

President Lyndon Johnson was pleased with the Medicare bill. That and other parts of his Great Society were progressing well. The bill on education had also passed the House. Voting Rights was doing well in hearings. He enthusiastically endorsed the three-level approach, calling it "a tremendous step forward for all of our senior citizens."[36]

Mills was acclaimed a hero. *Newsweek* described the bill as one which "aimed to please all of the people some of the time."[37] *Fortune* praised the new package, especially the financing that specified separate payroll tax, a separate fund, and the tax raises in graduated steps. *Fortune* thought that this might wisely prevent a build-up of cash which might motivate Congressional raids on the funds. Dr. Harold Meyers, who wrote the article in *Fortune*, thought that the private insurance companies should be pleased. They not only received an administrative role but got rid of their high risk beneficiaries. *Fortune* also praised a little discussed feature of the new bill, that individual persons could deduct one-half the cost of purchasing health insurance from their income tax up to $250.[38]

Mills gave a luncheon in the Ways and Means Committee room for a 70–member delegation of the New York Golden Ring Council of Senior Citizens. The elderly guests gave Mills a standing ovation for his role in Medicare, and called him the chief architect in a plan that was "more workable, more effective, than anything foreseen."[39] Mills's Republican colleague on the Ways and Means Committee, John Byrnes, said about Mills's new popularity, "I assume Wilbur saw the election returns and he could see he was being left behind. The troops were rushing right past him. He figured he'd better give his horse some oats and get up there in front where a leader belonged."[40]

Despite the fact that Eldercare was part of the new bill, the AMA was horrified. Dr. Donovan Ward exclaimed that the bill would take this country "not one, but two steps down the path to socialized medicine." Dr. Ward added, "It is the most revolutionary social welfare package to come out of Washington since the New Deal."[41] *Business Week* said that the AMA shouldn't be so upset. The AMA spent $900,000 to say that Medicare was not enough and that Eldercare was better. Mills took them at their word.[42]

The new three-part Medicare package, having passed the House, went next to the Finance Committee in the Senate. The Senate Finance Committee did not receive the new package with open arms. Medicare advocates sensed that there would be trouble. Even before the new bill was sent to the Senate, Wilbur Cohen tried his best to dissuade Russell Long from amending the basic hospitalization part of the bill. It did not look good, Cohen insisted, for the Majority Whip to make fundamental changes in the Administration's legislation. After much begging and arguing, the most Cohen could get from Long was a promise to think about it. Cohen requested that if Long wanted to make amendments, he make them on the supplemental part of the bill relating to physicians' services and not on the basic King-Anderson hospitalization. Since Cohen was not reassured, he asked Nelson Cruikshank and Andrew Biemiller to urge Long not to tamper with the bill. This they did, with as little success as Cohen had had.[43]

Obstruction was not only going to come from Long but also from Chairman of the Finance Committee Harry F. Byrd. In a bold political maneuver, however, President Johnson neutralized Byrd. Johnson invited Harry Byrd to a meeting at the White House without telling him why. Byrd thought the discussion would have to do with Vietnam. At first Byrd declined, saying that he would be on his Virginia farm, but then agreed to attend when the President promised private transportation to and from Virginia. The meeting began in the President's office and then moved to the Cabinet room. Johnson had invited nine other Democrats, including Mills, King, Speaker McCormack, Hale Boggs, Majority Leader Carl Albert from the House, and Anderson, Smathers, Majority Leader Mike Mansfield, and Byrd from the Senate.

In the Cabinet room, Byrd discovered that the meeting was going to be in front of television cameras. The President made a public statement about Medicare, and asked each person to comment on the new bill. When it was Byrd's turn, the President said, "I know that you will take an interest in the orderly scheduling of this matter and give it a thorough hearing." The President asked Byrd if there was any reason he knew of to delay the hearings and if he could schedule them promptly. A red-faced and "barely audible" Byrd said yes. Johnson banged his fist on the table in front of the Congressmen and said "Good." After that meeting Byrd said to O'Brien, "if I had known what you had in mind I would have dressed more formally."[44]

In order to speed the hearings, Anderson sent a written request to Byrd to require witnesses to submit testimony 48 hours in advance. Anderson also asked that only national organizations be allowed to testify.[45] Byrd replied that he would ask testimony to be submitted 24 hours in advance, but would not deny anyone if they could not comply. Also, he would not restrict testimony to national organizations. In particular, he would not rule out the patriotic representation of the "little man." Anderson knew that the "little man" meant individual doctors from various state medical associations. Byrd scheduled hearings for April 29–May 7.[46]

Once again, and for the last time, HEW Secretary Celebrezze, and HEW staff Wilbur Cohen, Robert Ball, Commissioner of Social Security, Robert Myers, Chief Actuary of Social Security Administration, Charles Hawkins, legislative reference officer of the Welfare Administration, Irwin Wolkstein, Chief of Disability Benefits, and Lisbeth Bamberger, special assistant to Cohen, came before the Finance Committee to discuss Medicare: "Public assistance cannot prevent dependency. It can only provide for relief after the dependency has occurred. A key to the solution of the Problem is the approach taken by our well established contributory social security program."[47] Celebrezze summarized the latest bill as including: 60 days of hospital care for a $40 deductible; 100 days of skilled nursing home payments after release from a hospital; 100 home-care visits following discharge from either of the above. Also, out-patient diagnostic services were included with a deductible of $20. A second part of the bill, a voluntary one, covered doctors' fees up to 80 percent of all costs after a $50 deductible, and $3 monthly premium. Celebrezze pointed out to the Finance Committee that the controversial stipulation that nursing homes had to be affiliated with hospitals had been dropped and replaced by "arrangement" with a hospital. Celebrezze said that another issue, the reimbursement to the hospital by a third party, was the "subject of extensive and painstaking consideration." Such a reimbursement principle was widely accepted by hospitals. Also after a great discussion, it was decided that the Secretary of HEW was responsible for administrating the whole program with two advisory groups: one, a group of experts outside of the government called in for general policy matters much like the Social Security Advisory Council; two, another group of experts to study and report on utilization of hospitals and other services.[48]

Unlike the Ways and Means Committee, the Senate Finance Committee did not get right down to details. The members of the Committee seemed unable to leave the issue of Medicare philosophy and basic morality. Senator Hartke said that the principle on which Medicare was based discriminated against people who worked for a living. Benefits went also to those who lived on their investments, interest, dividends, and rent. Celebrezze agreed that the philosophy of social insurance was to insure against loss of wages, but it extended to other methods of earning a living. Hartke responded that the basic philosophy was perhaps wrong. Albert Gore pointed out that Social Security was also supposed to induce early retirement from the work force.[49]

This discussion gave Carl Curtis an opportunity to interject his opinions. Curtis said that his own unofficial polls showed that people in the 20–40 year age bracket were busy paying off their homes and educating their children and could not possibly pay bills for elderly making in excess of $10,000 a year. Celebrezze answered that in his own travels he never met anyone in that age category who objected. Curtis said, ''We have been meeting different people.''[50]

Later in the hearings, the Senators resumed talk on average incomes of the elderly and need for Medicare. Anderson asked Douglas if he remembered the famous example of a study of five families living in a certain area. Four of the five had incomes of less than $1,000. One man retired with an income of over a million. The study showed that the average income for the area was $200,000.[51]

The Finance Committee hearings were attended daily by those on the committee who were interested in the bill: Byrd, Long, Smathers, Anderson, Douglas, Gore, Talmadge, McCarthy, Hartke, Ribicoff, and three Republicans, Curtis, Williams, and Carlson. Douglas prepared an amendment, endorsed by HEW and co-sponsored by Moss, Neuberger, Hartke, and Javits, that included the four hospital specialists as part of the basic Medicare plan. The Douglas Amendment was endorsed by American Hospital Association, although it was not favored by the professional organizations of the four groups. The radiologists, for example, said that their payment arrangement would lead to loss of professional dignity. The anesthesiologists said that they typically had their own billing arrangement, separate from the hospitals, in 85 percent of the cases.[52]

After Douglas's amendment, it was Long's turn to bring up his objections. Long's concern was about persons over 65 who had to stay in the hospital more than 60 days. Celebrezze said that in such cases, Kerr-Mills funds would enter in. Long then protested that many states had no Kerr-Mills provisions. Celebrezze stated emphatically that Medicare was not a program for chronic illness or custodial protection. The average hospital stay for persons over 65 was 14 days. Therefore, 60 days was more than ample. Long disagreed. Long thought that the people who stayed over 60 days in the hospital should have the primary protection. It was *their* bills that could not be paid. Surprisingly, Douglas agreed with Long. He told the Finance Committee that he had supported catastrophic coverage as far back as 1950, as a substitute for the Wagner-Murray-Dingell Bill.[53]

The professional reaction to both the Long Amendment and the Douglas Amendment was mixed. The American Nursing Home Association endorsed the House bill and the Douglas Amendment. Both the Physicians Forum and the National Medical Association (an organization of black physicians) supported Medicare and the Douglas Amendment. Dr. Edward Young, director of Physicians Forum and head of Massachusetts General Hospital, testified strongly against the *lack* of adequate standards that went with the nursing home provisions. Young said that the nursing home situation in this country was a "national disgrace." The majority might as well say "abandon hope, all of you who enter here." Dr. Young was also in favor of stricter standards for surgeons' reimbursements. "There are many poor surgeons out there," he told the Finance Committee.[54]

Dr. Donovan Ward, President of the AMA, said that, according to the Opinion Research Corporation of Princeton, New Jersey, in a poll taken in March, 1965, 74 percent of the population favored the AMA's Eldercare, 14 percent favored Medicare, and 12 percent had no opinion. Anderson could not resist asking Dr. Ward, "Do you suppose that is why Congress is supporting it?" Dr. Ward categorically opposed Medicare and the Douglas Amendment.[55]

The President of Health Insurance of America said that the new bill went far beyond what was needed to protect the elderly. The bill was so inclusive now that he said he even appreciated the old King-Anderson Bill more.[56] Charles Schottland, representing the American Public Welfare Association, and Commissioner of Social Security between 1954 and 1958, testified on behalf of the new bill and the Douglas Amendment. Schottland said that he had been testifying before the Committee for the last 30 years. Long asked if he had anything new to add, "to what you told us in the last 30 years." Responding to Long, Douglas said, "Samuel Johnson said once: 'men need not so much to be informed as to be reminded.' "[57]

By the time that the Finance Committee concluded its public hearings, it was apparent that the biggest threat to Medicare was Russell Long. Long was determined to mold the bill into his own version much as Mills had done in the House. Unlike Mills, whose major concern was fiscal solvency, Long's interests were in changing the bill to create a catastrophic or long-term illness insurance system. Long criticized Mills's version as inadequate because it failed to deal with long-term illness. Long proposed to get rid of specific time limits, such as 60 days hospitalization, and substitute unlimited coverage.

As a second issue, Long did not believe in the equitability of the social insurance principle: equal benefits for all who paid into the system. Long wanted deductibles pegged to income as well as a new feature called "coinsurance" where those able to pay would pay ten percent of all costs up to 50 percent of their income. This was in addition to the deductible.[58]

Long's version appealed to some liberals such as Vance Hartke and Abe Ribicoff. It was totally unacceptable to the President, HEW, the AFL-CIO, Anderson, and, most important, Wilbur Mills. The *New York Times* speculated that Long was either making a graceful retreat from his previous opposition to Medicare, or attempting to sabotage the whole program.[59] *The New Republic* commented that Long couldn't expect to win his amendments, "but it does his Louisiana heart good to see his friends squirm." *The New Republic* added that Long "continues to confound the Congressional world by his ability to court both the liberal and conservative poles at the same time."[60]

Wilbur Cohen explained the implications of Long's amendment to Larry O'Brien. The variations on deductibles would look something like: ten percent deductible on $1,000 gross income; 15 percent on $4,000 gross income; 20 percent on $5,000 gross income; and 30 percent on $10,000 gross income. Basically, middle and upper income senior citizens would pay a proportionately higher percentage of their hospital bills. Cohen explained further to O'Brien that the basic principle of Social Security—the principle that Medicare advocates had been fighting for, that there be no means test—would be violated by Long's amendments. Furthermore, the cost of Long's program, which he estimated at 560 million dollars, would be much more than the Medicare package that passed the House. Long's stipulation that income tests be based on previous year's income and not the current income would cause problems for many who are newly retired. Long also changed the language to read non-contributors. The result was that there would be no incentive to contribute into the Social Security system.[61]

HEW believed that Long's plan was impossible to administer. It would require a new Federal income reporting system for 20 million aged, dual to the one administered by the U.S. Treasury Department. The deductible range was going to be difficult to determine since most of the income of the elderly was in the form of savings. Long's bill would penalize savings. His co-insurance feature was also very complicated. It has the government subsidizing up to 40 percent of costs. In short, Long's amendments, according to HEW, were unworkable and unfair.[62]

Clinton Anderson told his colleagues on the Finance Committee, Douglas, Smathers, Talmadge, Fulbright, McCarthy, Hartke, and Gore, that Long's amendments would end up imposing two times the deductible of King-Anderson, cost much more, and only help a fraction of one percent of the elderly. Only a very small number of senior citizens used hospitals more than 60 days. Anderson pleaded with the other Democrats on the Committee not to support Long.[63]

As a last resort, Wilbur Cohen went directly to Byrd. Byrd would never support Medicare, but Cohen hoped to persuade the Chairman to at least vote against Long. After listening to Cohen during the course of three visits, Byrd said, "It's a bad amendment to a bad bill." Cohen laughed and said, "I didn't mean for you to go that far, but I'm grateful for your voting against Long's amendment."[64]

During the course of the Finance Committee's closed session in June, Long wandered in and out several times daily to check the line-up of votes. On June 17, Long walked into the Committee room, quickly explained his amendments, saying that he had no copies to hand out. Long told the Committee that the Administration was not opposed to his changes, and then called for a vote before anyone could check on Long's word. The vote came out 7–6 in *favor* of Long's two amendments. At this point Anderson held up a proxy of Fulbright's and used it to vote against Long. Long responded that Fulbright had given him a more recent proxy. Both Senators handed their proxies to the clerk for a check on dates. Long's was more recent. The vote was 8–6 in favor of Long's two amendments.[65]

After the Finance Committee adjourned, Anderson asked the clerk to see the proxies. The one Long had submitted was more recent but pertained to an entirely different matter! When Fulbright returned from Arkansas, he and Anderson went directly to Long. Mike Mansfield also went to Long in anger. Long, however, merely said that there must have been some misunderstanding and agreed to another vote.

Due to the speed with which Long explained his amendments and then called for a vote, Fulbright's proxy was not the only mix-up. Douglas had voted for the amendment, and then went back to his office to figure out the implications of his vote. He quickly realized that he had made a mistake in supporting Long. Douglas said, "Long's proposal would turn the nation's hospitals into warehouses for the senile."[66] Albert Gore was not present for the vote that day but had given his proxy to Ribicoff. Gore had intended Ribicoff to use it against Long. Ribicoff thought that he was free to use it according to his best judgment. Ribicoff's best judgment was to support Long. Gore returned from Tennessee extremely upset over the misuse of his proxy.[67]

President Johnson was even more perturbed. He expressed his anger by telephone, personally calling Democrats on the Finance Committee to reprimand them for supporting Long. Johnson regarded Long's action as an affront. Long was challenging Johnson for personal reasons. It seemed that Long, who as Majority Whip had supported Johnson on the Civil Rights Voting Act, felt he needed to regain credibility in Louisiana. Long used Medicare to express his independence of the President's Great Society.[68] The *New York Times* criticized Long's amendments as "so disastrous that it is hard to believe it was put forward with any aim except to kill any prospect of Medicare in this session of Congress."[69]

A team consisting of Cohen, Cruikshank, Biemiller, and Elizabeth Wickenden, backed up by lobbyists of the A.H.A., set out to change votes on the Finance Committee. Cohen held an emergency strategy session, with Douglas, Cruikshank, Ball, Leonard Lesser (Walter Reuther's assistant), Mike Manatos, and Anderson's assistant Howard Bray. The group agreed as a last resort to increase the hospital coverage by another 60 days.[70] Anderson, however, refused to compromise. Although Hartke warned Anderson that he would not be able to defeat Long without that extra 60 days compromise, Anderson refused the change. The team of advocates was effective.[71] On June 23 Anderson won. On a second vote Long's amendment was defeated 10–7. The President was elated. George Meany sent Anderson a congratulatory note stating, "we considered these the most serious threats that have arisen this year to an equitable and workable program of Health Insurance for the elderly."[72] On June 24, 1965, The Senate Finance Committee reported out the Medicare package by a vote of 12–5. The Committee added 75 amendments to the House bill.

Clinton Anderson was worried about the excessive number of amendments. He also worried that Long was going to be floor manager for the bill. Anderson did not protest, however, reasoning that Long would probably speed the bill through more quickly than anyone else. On the other hand, if Long should allow more amendments from the floor, then the bill would again be deadlocked in conference.[73] Anderson wrote directly to the President, complaining that not the Republicans but the Democrats were going to wreck the bill. Anderson told the President that Long would probably do nothing on the Senate floor, but that Long had gotten Ribicoff and Hartke to again offer the "crippling" amendments of unlimited benefits. Anderson said that he would hate to see Hartke and Ribicoff offer the amendments, and then Long as floor manager raise no objection to them. Anderson asked that the White House put whatever pressure they could on Long, Ribicoff, and Hartke to see that they didn't seriously amend the bill and jeopardize its final passage, the "passage that we've all been working on."[74]

Anderson then requested that Long allow Robert Ball, the Commissioner of Social Security, and one of his assistants to be on the Senate floor to assist on technical information during the floor debate. Ball and Irwin Wolkstein were present. The debate lasted three days. On July 9, at 8:00 p.m., the Senate passed the bill, 68–21, with no less than 513 amendments![75]

After the Senate victory, Marion Folsom, member of the Social Security Advisory Council, wrote Clinton Anderson expressing delight that Long's amendments were thrown out. Folsom said

I would have favored the original Administration Bill without the voluntary program for financing medical fees as I (and others on the Council) felt that this field should be left to voluntary agencies. Also I feel that your Committee went *too far* in liberalizing the work test provisions. Otherwise it is a good bill and I hope it will be passed.[76]

As a gesture of good will, Anderson's office sent out a copy of the Senate version to every doctor, dentist, nursing home organization, hospital, osteopathic hospital, and county welfare director in the country.[77]

The Medicare package went into final conference on July 19, 1965. The members of the conference, particularly Mills, Boggs, Long, and Smathers, wanted so many amendments that the White House thought they were trying to obstruct the conference. Only the Bill's original sponsors, King and Anderson, maintained loyalty to the Johnson Administration. At the end of the second day of deliberations, Cohen reported optimistically to O'Brien that "on most of the important matters we were able to work out reasonably accepted compromises.'' Cohen detailed for O'Brien the basic areas of contention that remained:

1. Reduction of the retirement age to 60 at actuarially reduced rates. This was Harry Byrd's (D-Virginia) amendment. If a worker retired at age 60 he would get $60 per month. When he reached 65 he would *not* get his normal $89 but continue to receive $60.

2. Eugene Keogh (D-New York) amendment to the Bill on tip income. Long opposed.

3. Vance Hartke wanted his amendment liberalizing Social Security payments to the blind.

4. Long liberalized public assistance provisions. Mills was opposed.

5. Problem of the four medical specialists not resolved.

6. There was disagreement on increase of wage base to $6,600.

7. There were also about 10–15 small technical problems.[78]

One small technical problem related to the administration of the enlarged MAA program (Title XIX). The American Public Health Association was lobbying to move the program from the jurisdiction of state welfare departments to the jurisdiction of state health departments, regarding the state health departments as in most cases captives of the state medical societies.[79] Clinton Anderson suggested as a compromise that perhaps it could be up to the State Governors to decide. The outcome was to leave the MAA program where it was.[80]

The Conference Committee was essentially stuck on cutting out 1.2 billion dollars of costs of the 1.5 billion dollars that was added on by Senate amendments. Anderson and the Senate side lost the battle on the issue of the four hospital specialists. Mills, Boggs, Long, and Smathers voted against Anderson and King on that issue. Mills, Boggs, and Long, tried to assure Cohen that the defeat was not so monumental because if leaving out the specialists didn't work, it could always be amended in at a later date. The Conference Committee ended in compromising Hartke's amendments to the blind by passing some liberalization of benefits but not as much as Hartke wanted. The Conference Committee reported out Medicare on July 21, 1965.

Anderson told the President that the bill came out in generally "good shape," Anderson was still upset about the non-inclusion of the specialists but thought that perhaps he and Douglas would offer a separate bill after Medicare became law. The House passed the new bill July 27 by a vote of 307–116. The Senate passed the bill July 28, 70–24.[81]

All that remained was for the President to sign the bill into law. Johnson's staff offered three suggestions for the location of the ceremony: the Truman Library in Missouri, the FDR house in Hyde Park, New York, and the White House. President Johnson preferred the Truman Library. Johnson envisioned the signing in Missouri as a dramatic and generous gesture toward the 82–year-old former President.

Not everyone in the White House was as enthusiastic as the President over flying half of the Cabinet and half of the Congress out to Missouri. White House assistant Horace Busby complained that it was not such a good idea to associate Medicare with Truman's 1945 bill. Such an association would imply a "grotesque distortion, with very impolitic overtones." The conclusion might be drawn that the next step would be to enlarge the Medicare program to cover the whole population. Furthermore, the AMA would boycott the ceremony, and Truman might make a few "distasteful" remarks about doctors. As an alternative, Busby wanted a newsworthy event in Washington. He suggested that the President invite about 700 people to the White House as a possible counteraction to bad news from Vietnam.[82]

Wilbur Cohen was also against the idea of going out to Missouri. There would not be enough room in the Truman Library for all of the people whom Cohen thought should be invited to the signing ceremony. Cohen suggested waiting until August 15 and then quietly signing the bill at Hyde Park on the anniversary of the original Social Security Act.[83]

President Johnson had his mind made up. He was going to sign the Voting Rights Bill in the Capitol and Medicare in Missouri. Bill Moyers, Horace Busby, Doug Cater, Harry McPherson, Marvin Watson, and Jack Valenti of the White House staff wired him that the idea to sign in Missouri was a marvelous one. "It brings out the relationship between the first bill for Medicare and the final passage."[84]

On the morning of July 30, the President flew to Missouri with 47 guests from the Capitol. Altogether there were 200 witnesses in the Harry S. Truman Library Auditorium. The guests included: Vice President Hubert Humphrey, Congressional members Carl Albert, John McCormack, Mike Mansfield, Russell Long, Abraham Ribicoff, Wilbur Mills, Clinton Anderson, Cecil King, Hale Boggs, James Roosevelt,

George Smathers, Emmanuel Celler, and John Dingel, Jr., as well as Governor of Missouri Thomas Hearns, former Secretary of HEW Anthony Celebrezze, Wilbur Cohen, Aime Forand, and Larry O'Brien. In addition to those present, the President listed the names of those who played a major role in the passage of Medicare: John F. Kennedy, John Dingell, Sr., Robert Wagner, and James Murray.

Truman was the first to speak. "I am glad to have lived this long and to witness today the signing of the Medicare bill."[85] The President said:

I'm so proud that this has come to pass in the Johnson Administration.... And through this new law ... every citizen will be able in his productive years, when he's earning, to insure himself against the ravages of illness in his old age.... No longer will old Americans be denied the healing miracle of modern medicine. No longer will illness crush and destroy the savings that they have so carefully put away over a lifetime so that they might enjoy dignity in their later years.[86]

President Johnson later recalled that President Truman said that no single honor ever paid to him had touched him more deeply.[87]

9

Medicare Becomes a Reality

The bill that President Lyndon Johnson signed into law on July 31, 1965, was an ambitious combination of three very different programs: Medicare—a hospital, nursing home, and home health insurance plan; Part B—a voluntary major medical plan; and Medicaid—a total health package for the poor. In addition to the "three-layered cake" the new law provided a seven percent increase in Social Security benefits. Application of Medicare to 20 million persons, Wilbur Cohen once said, was probably the largest single government operation since D-Day in Europe during the Second World War.[1] Senator Clinton Anderson told White House Assistant Larry O'Brien that anyone who had presented a bill of the 1965 nature in 1960 would have been committed to St. Elizabeth's.[2] HEW now had the tremendous task of putting all parts of the new law into operation.

Robert M. Ball, Commissioner of Social Security, was placed in charge of Medicare. Ball was well trained for his new responsibilities. He began his government career in 1939 in the Bureau of Old Age and Survivors in the Social Security Administration, meeting other Social Security professionals, Wilbur Cohen, I. S. Falk, and Robert Myers. Ball became Assistant Director of the Bureau, 1949–1952, and then Deputy Director, 1953–1962. He was appointed Commissioner of Social Security in 1962, and served until 1973.[3] Ball was the recipient of numerous public service awards and honorariums. His recent book, *Social Security: Today and Tomorrow*, is a major contribution to the understanding of the problems of Social Security.[4]

In addition to Ball, HEW appointed a 16-member Advisory Council on Health Benefits, headed by former Budget Director Kermit Gordon. Nelson Cruikshank was appointed to the Council to represent the interests of organized labor. The other 14 members were from the medical and hospital community. This Advisory Council reported to the Secretary of HEW. HEW also hired 1,800 new employees and established 21 branch offices and 71 temporary service centers during 1965–1966.[5]

To cope with the enormity of the program, HEW staggered the starting dates for the new services. After the increase in Social Security benefits were sent out, Medicaid was scheduled to begin January 1966. HEW gave itself 11 months to set up the administration for the hospital insurance part of Medicare. July 1, 1966, was the target date. The nursing home benefits and Part B (doctor's fees) were delayed until January 1, 1967—a full one and one-half years after the signing of the law.[6]

The first part of the law that went into effect, the seven percent cash increase, was a bellwether for the degree of cooperation that HEW was going to get from the states. The cash increase was made retroactive to January 1965 and paid out in one lump cash bonus so that the elderly would have immediate benefits. That was one of President Johnson's main concerns. To insure that the cash bonus would really be a bonus, HEW advised the states' welfare agencies to ignore at least $5 of the bonus in computing public assistance payments. (Public assistance supplements took care of many of the elderly for whom Social Security payments did not cover basic needs.) However, only nine states agreed to cooperate with the government. The others saw Federal cash bonuses as a means of reducing state expenditures. Several state welfare agencies immediately cut their relief budgets by the exact amount of the Social Security increases. This action nullified any effect of the new increases for those elderly dependent on public assistance as additional means of support.[7]

But this action also awakened senior citizens organizations to serve as watch dogs for the elderly. The National Council for Senior Citizens recognized this responsibility immediately. Local affiliates spent the Autumn of 1965 using the passage of Medicare to enlarge their organization. Membership jumped to 2 million in 1965 and four million in 1984. The affiliates hoped to provide a vigilant power base from which to rectify state transgressions.[8] Other senior citizen groups have successfully increased their memberships. AARP has 14 million members; a newer organization, the Gray Panthers, has 110 chapters.

Of all the parts of the 1965 law, hospital insurance ran the smoothest.

Hospitals had only to be licensed by their state and set up "utilization committees" in order to be approved for Medicare reimbursement. Beginning hospital insurance benefits on July 1, 1966, was one of the most important administrative decisions made by Wilbur Cohen. I. S. Falk, Cohen's former associate in the Social Security Administration, pointed out that hospital usage was 10–20 percent lower in July than during the height of the flu season in January and lowest of all during the July Fourth weekend. The slow season enabled the 10,000 hospitals around the country to eaae into the new program.[9] The feared result that hospitals would be flooded with patients never materialized.

Elderly patients checked into the hospitals at the usual rate. Their bills were submitted to one of the HEW-selected area fiscal intermediaries. These agencies, usually Blue Cross, processed, reviewed, and paid the claims directly to the hospitals.

According to the new law, an elderly patient who had been admitted to the hospital for at least three days was entitled to 100 days of nursing home benefits. Establishing the administration for that nursing home coverage was the most complicated and difficult part of the Medicare program. In 1965, there were 16,000 nursing homes and health care agencies in the United States. A private organization, known as the Joint Committee on Accreditation of Hospitals' was given the task of clearing nursing homes for participation in the Medicare program. By the time that the administrative apparatus was working, only 740 nursing homes met Medicare qualifications. The Social Security Administration allowed about 3,200 more facilities to qualify under a newly created category, "substantial compliance."

Substantial compliance was a controversial term. It had originated from HEW's insisting on civil rights desegregation codes. Many rural southern hospitals refused to desegregate even after being threatened with withdrawal of Medicare reimbursement. HEW was faced with two bad choices—allow Medicare to handle segregated hospitals which frequently were the only hospitals in rural areas, or refuse money and risk leaving thousands of elderly people without a hospital to enter. HEW chose the former course, creating a new category of compliance, "substantial compliance." HEW was forced to use that category in the nursing home industry.[10]

According to nursing home expert Bruce Vladeck, "once the door was open to 'substantial compliance' Medicare became liable for payment for facilities that its framers never intended to support."[11] Allowing for less than total compliance to minimum standards led to a lowering of quality of care. Although Congress criticized HEW in various special investigations, Vladeck writes that the blame belongs with Congress. "Congress had attempted to legislate an impossibility." In 1965 most nursing homes in the country could not meet, even to a partial extent, Medicare's requirements. If the standards were kept, then millions of elderly would be denied benefits to which they thought they were entitled. Vladeck concluded that "the administrative actions that resulted, however unwise, represented a reasoned effort to cope with that impossible contradiction."[12]

The second "layer" of the 1965 Medicare law, known as Part B, required a major advertising campaign. Part B was voluntary, and in order to participate the elderly had to sign up. The drive to describe Part B medical benefits began in September 1965. HEW sent out about 20 million kits containing leaflets explaining that Part B was a major medical insurance program, covering 80 percent of all surgical and other physician fees. Included in the kit was a simple application form for those eligible to check off and sign if they did or did not want to participate. In addition to the kit, which were published in 22 languages and delivered to some locations by horses and dog sleds, HEW also engaged a public relations firm to advertise the services of Part B in newspapers and television commercials.[13]

President Johnson was looking for a 100 percent response. He was pleased with HEW's entire advertising effort. He especially liked the simple application form that the elderly had to return to Washington.[14] Vice President Hubert Humphrey, however, complained to Jack Valenti at the White House that the campaign showed a "total lack of imagination." He was amazed, Humphrey said, to find not a single picture of the President in the leaflets and applications. To Humphrey, even the television advertisements were poorly done. Who was the spokesman for the government, he asked—not the President or even John Gardner, Secretary of HEW, but "a Mr. Ball."[15]

By December 1965, only 8 million people had returned yes applications and HEW redoubled its efforts. By the end of March, 90 percent of the 17 million eligible had returned an application with yes checked off. The deadline for signing up for Part B was initially set for March 31, 1966. Johnson asked Congress to extend the deadline for two more months. By then, the HEW drive was a success. After May 31, only

1 million persons (about five percent of the elderly) declined to participate.[16]

Not only could the elderly choose to participate in the major medical programs, but doctors whose fees were being covered also had a choice between two modes of reimbursement for their services. They could bill the patient directly in the usual fee-for-service manner, and leave it to the patient to submit the doctor's bill to the fiscal intermediary. Or they could fill out the forms and submit the bills directly to the intermediary, usually Blue Shield. Medicare promised to reimburse 80 percent of all reasonable charges. At the 1965 AMA convention the doctors voted for the former method of reimbursement, preserving their usual doctor-patient relationship.[17]

Setting Medicaid (also known as Title XIX) in motion was a major undertaking. Medicaid, the third "layer" of the 1965 law, was a program for medically needy persons of all age groups. "Medical indigence in the murky language of welfare administrators, means that one has enough money barely to live from day to day but not enough to pay the doctors when sickness hits."[18] The intent was to offer uniform health services to all persons in federally funded public assistance programs. Medicaid did not cover all persons on all welfare rolls. Only the following three categories were eligible:

- All persons in public assistance programs funded partially by Federal money. These included persons in Old Age Assistance (OAA) programs, in the blind programs, the disabled, and families with children where one parent was absent or incapacitated.

- People in the above category who needed only medical aid and who were able to handle other basic necessities.

- All medically needy children under 21 in all public assistance roles. (This category owed its existence to Senator Abraham Ribicoff.)

Medicaid replaced the 1960 Kerr-Mills law. In so doing it attempted to correct the former law's problems. Kerr-Mills was a state program that had allowed many variations even from one part of a state to another. Medicaid was intended to be more uniform. The old Kerr-Mills program was funded by complicated Federal-state matching formulas. The new Medicaid was financed by a simpler method. The Federal Government paid between 50 percent and 80 percent of expenses based on a per capita income calculation.[19]

Title XIX removed certain restrictions that had hampered the effectiveness of Kerr-Mills. First, states could no longer hold adult children responsible for medical expenses of parents. This was important. Many old people had testified in the Kerr-Mills hearings that they were afraid to apply for badly needed medical aid because they did not want their children to know or be held responsible. Second, states had to remove all residence requirements for applicants. This was an advantage for those elderly who moved from one state to another for retirement. Third, states had to provide reimbursement for comprehensive services: hospital care, nursing home care, home health visits, doctor's fees, drugs, and diagnostic work. In 1965 only five states offered those services under Kerr-Mills.[20]

State governments retained significant responsibilities. State participation in Medicaid was not mandatory. States could choose to participate. States, moreover, had the task of defining their own medical indigent levels. California thus set its income level at $3,804. Other states stayed in a similar range: Illinois at $3,600, Michigan, Minnesota, and Hawaii between $3,000 and $4,000. New York, at the behest of Governor Rockefeller, wanted minimum income for Medicaid eligibility to be $6,600. That meant a serious drain on Federal funds before the program was in operation a full year. Rockefeller defended his level, but HEW began a special investigation to see if such high income levels were warranted.[21]

While Medicaid's roots were in America's welfare tradition, the law itself was poorly conceived. Hospital Insurance, or Medicare Part A, had been discussed over a seven-year period, debated in thousands of pages of hearings, and written about in numerous special reports and investigations. But Mills and other Democrats were worried about the AMA's claims that Medicare was insufficient to handle the health needs of the elderly. According to a survey taken in January 1965, and circulated in Congress, most Americans believed that Medicare would offer more services than it actually did.

Medicaid, Title XIX was casually added as an after thought in March 1965. It was Mills's attempt to include the opposition. Medicaid was an application of the AMA's own Eldercare Bill, which was in turn an elaboration of the 1960 Kerr-Mills program. The Kerr-Mills program, itself a hastily passed law without benefit of much congressional discussion, was not working well, and Mills was happy to find a way to dispose of it. Also, according to an HEW staff member, Theodore Marmor, Medicaid was "another means of 'building a fence' around Medicare by undercutting future demands to expand medical and hospital insurance to cover all income groups."[22]

Medicaid included payment for poor elderly (those not entitled to Social Security benefits) in nursing homes. The predicament for Medicaid patients in these homes was even worse than the nursing home situation under Medicare. Licensing of Medicaid-reimbursed nursing homes was supposed to be done by state agencies. However, thousands of potential Medicaid beneficiaries were already in custodial facilities paid for by Kerr-Mills or other public assistance programs. These custodial homes, frequently referred to as "extended care" facilities, could not come close to meeting even "substantial compliance" standards. HEW was forced to choose between refusing to qualify these institutions, with the inhuman consequences of seeing thousands of elderly poor without a place to live, or shutting its eyes and allowing the significantly lower state standards to supersede.

Wilbur Cohen once commented that the American people will accept an ideological revolution *if* the ideological revolution works.[23] The implication of all the parts of the new Medicare and Medicaid law was enormous. Having lost the battle to stop Medicare, many of the bill's critics were at least willing to try to make it work. In a conciliatory spirit, Congressman John Byrnes addressed his colleagues:

Mr. Speaker. The job now before us is to try to make the system that is established under this bill work as best it can. There will be no advantage to anyone in trying to sabotage the program. The program contains enough dangers to the basic social security system and to the quality of health in this country without adding additional problems and dangers. I would therefore at this point urge all who have anything to do with the administration of this program or the health needs of our people, if they have any hatchets to bury them, and if they have any disagreements or animosities from the past that they bury them and that all do their utmost to make the program work as well as possible.[24]

As Robert Ball explained, everyone in government felt that high quality health care was impossible without the cooperation of doctors.

The Johnson Administration tried as hard as possible to enlist the aid of the medical profession in structuring the new Medicare program.

HEW named 45 doctors to serve on administrative committees and appointed two full-time physicians as consultants to the Social Security Administration. On July 30, 1965, the day before the President flew to Missouri to sign Medicare into law, he met with 11 AMA leaders, headed by Dr. Francis Blassingame, Executive Vice President. Johnson gave the doctors a half hour pep talk and excused himself, turning the meeting over to Wilbur Cohen. After explaining the administrative aspects of Medicare, Cohen asked the doctors to think about the program and come back in two months for an exchange of ideas.

The response of the medical profession was mixed. At the AMA's 115th annual convention, held in Chicago on July 4, 1965, shortly before Medicare passed the Senate, Dr. Charles Hudson, the new President, called for cooperation with the government. Hudson "urged doctors to make the most of the new program." For the most part, the keynote mood was moderation.

However, many state delegates, especially from states like Texas and Oklahoma with powerful medical societies, thought doctors should continue to fight Medicare even after it became law. The American Association of Physicians and Surgeons, AAPS, a right-wing elite group of about 50,000 surgeons, spearheaded the opposition. The AAPS urged members not to cooperate in any way with the new program: not to serve on committees, not to fill out required forms, even to refuse Medicare patients.[25] This last suggestion so appalled even the most conservative AMA leaders that Dr. James A. Appel, the AMA's outgoing President, warned that reaction to Medicare *could not* include unethical tactics such as boycotts, strikes, or sabotage.[26]

Criticism of the final bill was not limited to conservatives. Liberal critics like Senator Pat McNamara criticized the numerous compromises in the Medicare program. McNamara accused Wilbur Cohen of giving away 65 percent of the original bill.[27] Considering the power that the conservative Senate Finance Committee and House Ways and Means Committee had and the major role that Russell Long and Wilbur Mills played in their respective Committees, a pure McNamara-type bill was unlikely. Since Mills and Long were intent upon keeping the "shackles" off the medical profession, many compromises were thought necessary. At least some of those compromises have created difficulties for Medicare and Medicaid since 1965.

HEW had so feared a reaction of the sort proposed by the AAPS that the medical community was given enormous latitude in every aspect of administration that concerned doctors.[28] *The Nation* observed that "the eagerness of those who framed the Medicare Act to avoid a confrontation with the medical profession has created many openings for domination by physicians." In the more than fifteen years that Medicare and Medicaid have been in operation, the two most serious problems that have appeared are high costs and fraud. The "customary and reasonable" fee reimbursement policy has contributed to those problems. In 1965 Congress wanted to stay clear of any suspicion of controlling fees. As a concession to the medical profession, Congressional leaders worded the reimbursement procedure so that doctors could claim their "customary and usual rates."[29]

However, the "customary and usual" principle backfired. Washington had no idea of what was customary for a doctor to charge. The doctors were worried that their profits would freeze at current levels. Between the day of the signing of Medicare and the day that Part B began operation, the usual rates rose 300 percent beyond the normal rate increase. As a result Medicare bills came in *much* higher than anticipated.[30]

The responsibility for determining what was reasonable was left to the fiscal intermediary—in most cases, Blue Shield. Since Blue Shield was a doctor-controlled organization, giving it final say on charges was further appeasement of the medical profession. When the final bill was being discussed in conference, Medicare advocates Clinton Anderson, Robert Ball, and Robert Myers, as they wrote the provisions for private insurance carriers into the 1965 bill, worried that they were making a mistake. They believed that the government could not expect private insurance carriers to be very vigorous in protecting government interests such as saving money. However, they did not think that Medicare would pass Congress *without* giving insurance companies a role as fiscal intermediary.[31]

While high costs of health care are probably the main concern of the nation, a secondary problem concerns abuse and fraud in the Medicare program, and even more so in Medicaid. Since Medicare is more of a middle class operation, the proportions of abuse have not been as great as they are in health care services dealing with poor people or those on welfare. However, the Medicare law allows considerable opportunity for exploiting the system. Doctors, for example, are reimbursed on a per capita basis. Many have exclusive arrangements with a nursing home and may make one "sweep" and submit bills for all the patients in rooms on the corridors.[32]

Ironically, it is *not* the recipients of Medicaid who are misusing funds, but the purveyors of services. Instead of evidence that the poor are receiving quality care, headlines after Congressional investigation describe Medicaid services in derogatory terms such as "medicaid mills." Health care facilities that have grown to deal with the demand for Medicaid services are frequently crooked in operation. HEW is reimbursing bills for services never performed, not needed, and, more frightening, not wanted. One doctor collected 2 million dollars from Medicaid for performing abortions on women who were not even pregnant. The women were routinely misled on pregnancy tests.[33] In 1968 alone, 4,300 individual doctors and 900 health groups collected illegal fortunes from Medicaid.

Congressman Claude Pepper's House Select Committee has frequently investigated Medicaid fraud. Pepper's Committee listed the following common methods of abuse: 1. Cash kickbacks to doctors and nursing home operators made by other health services; 2. Doctors ordering many unnecessary blood tests and other lab work for Medicaid patients; 3. The kickbacks involved doctors, clinical labs, nursing homes, and pharmacies; and 4. An inordinately high number of injections given to Medicaid patients. Pepper's Committee charged that the Medicaid program is losing at least 2 billion dollars a year to outright fraud.[34] Recently even the FBI stepped in to investigate organized crime's penetration of the Medicaid health care industry.[35]

Since 1965 Congress has made some progress in resolving the major problems of Medicare and Medicaid. Congress has directed its efforts toward placing controls and limits on the system. In 1971, the Senate Finance Committee mandated the establishment of Professional Standards Review Organizations (PSRO's). The country was divided into 203 areas, each with its own PSRO that would supersede all state and fiscal intermediary review policies. The goal was for the medical profession (since PSRO's are composed of local doctors) to review its own service to Medicare and Medicaid patients. In most parts of the country, the doctors were glad to comply. Senator Wallace Bennett (R-Utah), one of the sponsors of PSRO's, felt he was doing doctors a favor in pushing the legislation that set up the PSRO program, since it placed review of care in physicians' hands. Not all the doctors were appreciative. State medical societies in Florida, Georgia, Illinois, Louisiana, and Texas wanted nothing to do with the Congressional program.[36]

In 1974, the National Health Planning and Resources Development Act again divided the country into 200 areas. The intent of this act was to control construction of facilities in order to avoid duplication and waste that tend to drive up costs. The National Health Planning Board was also charged with the responsibility of coordinating health services. It is hoped by many members of Congress that the Health Planning Board will eventually be the foundation for a Health Security Board. Such a Board would take on functions similar to those of the Federal Reserve Board in coordinating health care in the United States.

Despite these efforts, the basic problem with Medicare is that medical costs are rising faster than payroll tax revenue. Tremendous inflation has affected money allocated to Medicaid, too. Between 1972 and 1982, costs of medical services rose 18 percent per year. In 1983 Congress passed a number of measures that eased the financial strain on the Medicare Trust Fund. For example, medical withholdings for those self-employed doubled. The first day deductible for hospital services increased. Monthly premiums for Part B increased.

Even more important was a provision passed in 1983 that created a new method for hospital reimbursement. Illnesses were broken down to 467 diagnostically related groups. Illnesses within the same group are reimbursed at the same fixed amount of money, no matter how long a patient remains in a hospital. Secretary of Health and Human Resources, Margaret Heckler, expects this approach to save the government at least 2.8 billion dollars annually.[37]

Critics of this approach have two complaints. A study published in the *New England Journal of Medicine* warned that this plan may backfire. While it is intended to give hospitals an incentive to send patients home sooner, the study threatens that doctors could easily "admit more patients if they thought their hospitals needed the business."[38]

Another point, even more serious, is that hospitals will and have already shifted the financial burden to non-Medicare patients. Non-Medicare hospital rates have gone up, followed by hospital insurance premiums. Not wanting to foot the increases, many corporations have passed the higher premiums on to their employees. When pressed with this problem, President Ronald Reagan hoped "private insurance will negotiate similar fixed payments."[39]

While insurance companies do not stand on a strong historical record for initiating cost saving methods, another solution is slowly surfacing from the private sector. This is the Health Maintenance Organizations, or HMOs. Corporations can choose to drop insurance premiums altogether and join an HMO for a flat annual fee. In 1984 there were 280 HMOs servicing 12.5 million people. By 1990, membership is expected to increase to 50 million.[40]

One problematic area that needs reform is the nursing home industry covered by both Medicare and Medicaid programs. As of 1982, the Medicare program spent 36 billion dollars for health care covering 26 million Americans; of that, 7.3 billion went for nursing home services.' As early as 1966, and again in 1967, 1968, and 1969, Senator Frank Moss (D-Utah) and Senator Edward Kennedy (D-Massachusetts) sponsored a series of amendments to create enforceable standards for Medicare and Medicaid reimbursed homes. The standards required full record keeping systems, the observation of fire, safety, and environmental codes, transfer agreements with hospitals, and the employment of at least one full-time registered nurse. In 1965 many states did *not* have those minimum requirements. Those that did found them difficult to enforce.

Enforcing standards remains an elusive problem. HEW was given authority to withhold Federal funds for institutions not meeting those requirements. With Federal investigators, and the threat of withholding funds, nursing homes have improved. Greater public awareness as well as press attention has accomplished a lot. However, nursing homes and extended care facilities have a long way to go in meeting uniform quality standards. Unfortunately, in the 1980s, deaths of elderly people in fires in these homes, as well as inhumane treatment and lack of sanitation, are still front page news.[41]

Since 1965, Congress has sponsored various types of legislation to either expand the medicare system or to significantly change its focus. These legislative proposals generally fall into three categories: A Comprehensive National Health Insurance program all at once (Kennedy-Corman) or in steps beginning with mothers and children (Javits); Federal subsidies for the purchase of private health insurance (Nixon, Ford, Packwood, Fulton-Carter-Duncan-Murphy-McIntire-Burleson); and a catastrophic insurance program for the entire population (Long-Ribicoff and, most recently, Reagan).

Expanding Medicare to provide a comprehensive national health insurance system had been the goal of the AFL-CIO, Walter Reuther's National Committee for Health Insurance, and the National Committee for Senior Citizens since the late 1960s. Walter Reuther, the late President of the United Auto Workers, "was among the first to see that financing programs like Medicare and Medicaid..." was not enough to resolve the "spiraling cost of health care" for the rest of the population. In 1968, Reuther formed the Committee of One Hundred for National Health Insurance. Several health care leaders joined the committee including I. S. Falk, Charles Schottland, Dr. Michael E. deBakey, Mrs. Mary Lasker, Nelson Cruikshank, and Senators Edward Kennedy, John Sherman Cooper, William Saxbe, and Ralph Yarborough, and Representative James Corman.

Based upon the Committee's recommendations, Kennedy and Corman introduced a national health insurance bill in August 1970. The two have introduced similar legislation every year since. The Kennedy-Corman Bill, usually referred to as the Health Security Act, was written into the Democratic National Platform in 1976 and 1980.

The Kennedy-Corman bills are financed by payroll contributions and will cover about 95 percent of the population. There is no deductible. One of the major features of the bill is that it covers "first dollar expense" making it equally available to all income groups. The more recent Kennedy-Corman bills have emphasized cost standards and controls as well as reforms for the delivery of health care.[42]

Numerous bills reflect the popularity of the mostly Republican second alternative to health care. The most prominent is known as the Packwood Bill after its sponsor, Robert Packwood (R-Oregon). The bills call for a variety of government subsidies either directly or indirectly to the private health insurance industry. For example, the Federal Government would mandate employers to purchase comprehensive health insurance for their employees. Or the government would give tax credits for the purchase of private policies. Other methods include Federal-state cost sharing of the purchase of individual policies. All of the measures stress voluntary participation. The above bills are usually supported by the AMA, the Health Insurance Industry, and the American Hospital Association.[43]

The third alternative in legislative options is catastrophic coverage for the entire population. Russell Long favored such legislation as far back as 1964 when he tried to seriously amend Medicare to extend its benefits for unlimited duration. Since Harry F. Byrd's retirement in

1967, Long has been Chairman of the powerful Senate Finance Committee, and introduced his Long-Ribicoff Bill with great frequency. The bill would be financed out of general revenues, but applicable only to the small percentage of the population who required much longer than average hospital stays. The bill has been popular in conservative Democratic circles as a way of adding some benefits without changing anything but the cost. In 1974 President Ford's administration backed an effort to add catastrophic coverage to the Medicare law.

A catastrophic program has won the support of the Reagan Administration, possibly more for its ideological appeal than fiscal responsibility. In March, 1984, a Federal Advisory Council headed by Republican Governor of Illinois Otis Bowen, studied ways to change the Medicare program. Their goal was to avert future insolvency. The Council recommended moving up the age for receiving benefits to 67 years old, raising the deductibles, taxing employer paid health benefits, and shifting the emphasis of the Medicare program to catastrophic coverage.

The Reagan Administration has also discussed plans to drastically alter the social insurance principles inherent in the Medicare program. Reagan prefers going back to a pre–1965 means test approach, or "layering benefits according to income." However, the amount of money saved by this approach is questionable. According to Assistant Secretary of Human Services Robert T. Rubin, the average income of Medicare beneficiaries is $15,000.[44]

The programs suggested above have one thing in common: they acknowledge the necessity for a change in the American health system. *Business Week* observed a "public perception that the costs are out of hand and the quality and quantity of supply are wanting."[45] In 1980 Americans spent 200 billion dollars on health care. That represents 8.2 percent of the Gross National Product. Americans spend more of their per capita income on health care than any other industrial nation. As the cost of health care rises, so do premiums for private policies. Senator Edward Kennedy once commented that General Motors pays more to Blue Cross/Blue Shield than it does to U.S. Steel.[46] Yet insurance protection is unevenly distributed throughout the United States. Many people have no health insurance protection at all. Thousands of others have only minimal protection. Senator Kennedy warned, "There are no simple solutions to the problem of rising health costs."[47] But clearly, "a new approach to national health care is urgently needed."[48]

Before we can sensibly proceed to solve present and future health care problems, we must take a good hard look at the current three layers of services that compose the Medicare and Medicaid programs. We must examine the choices, options, *and* compromises made during the entire Medicare debate. The enactment of the 1965 Medicare and Medicaid law showed that the American democracy had some capacity for innovation in meeting the health needs of the people. Many of the health problems predicted by the opponents have not come to pass: hospitals are not overflowing with elderly patients; hospitals have not become vacation spots for those looking for a free ride; the number of students seeking a medical career has not diminished; American doctors have not fled the country; America has not become socialized.

Other difficulties, in part the consequence of concessions to the medical profession and the insurance industry, have arisen: high costs; quality standards in nursing homes; overutilization; fraud; and lack of planning for facilities. In addition, there is a recent problem that is growing unchecked and making control of health costs vexing. This is the growth of malpractice lawsuits and insurance policies. Very recently, as part of a 1984 Deficit Reduction Act, the Reagan Administration has initiated a policy of fixed reimbursements to doctors for Medicare patients. This pertains only to those doctors who agree to participate in the new Medicare plan. Many of the doctors, however, are forced to pay as much as a 100 percent increase in malpractice insurance premiums. The future experience in dealing with these problems should ease the way for a more equitable and affordable health care system in the United States.

Notes

INTRODUCTION

1. Oslo Peterson, "Financing a Medical Care Program Through Social Security," *New England Journal of Medicine* 265 (September 14, 1961): 526–528.

2. Richard Harris, *A Sacred Trust* (New York: 1966), 55.

CHAPTER 1

1. Richard Harris, *A Sacred Trust* (New York: 1966), 73.

2. Wilbur Cohen in a personal interview with the author, March 8, 1977.

3. "Paying Health Costs of the Aged," *Business Week* (January 31, 1959): 33.

4. Nelson Cruikshank in a personal interview with the author, May 24, 1976.

5. Raymond Munts, *Bargaining for Health Care: Labor Unions, Health Insurance and Medical Care* (Madison: 1967), 90–91.

6. Jerome Pollack, "A Labor View of Health Insurance," *Monthly Labor Review* 81 (February 1958): 145.

7. "Medical Care for Retired Workers?" *Fortune* 62 (July 1960): 211.

8. "Resources and Health Status of OASI Beneficiaries," *Monthly Labor Review* 82 (August 1959): 882.

9. Aime Forand in a recorded interview with Peter Corning, 1966, Princeton, New Jersey in the Columbia University Oral History Program, 11. Hereafter identified as COH.

10. Eugene Feingold, *The Politics of Medicare* (San Francisco: 1966), 24.

11. William Reidy in a recorded interview with Peter Corning, 1966, COH.

12. Forand, Corning interview, 1965, COH.

13. *New York Times*, March 21, 1960, 15.

14. Forand, Corning interview, COH, 25.

15. Harris, *A Sacred Trust*, 73.

16. *New York Times*, March 21, 1959, 15.

17. Forand, Corning interview, COH, 8.

18. Ibid., 25.

19. Harris, *A Sacred Trust*, 83.

20. Forand, Corning interview, COH, 8.

21. Ibid., 31.

22. Ibid., 32.

23. U.S. Congress, House, Ways and Means Committee, *Hearings on HR4700*, 86th Cong., 1st Sess., 1959, 310.

24. I. M. Rubinow, "Standard of Sickness Insurance," *Journal of Political Economy* 23 (March 1915): 226.

25. Cohen's testimony before House, Ways and Means Committee, *Hearings*, 86th Cong., 1st Sess., 345.

26. Standard definition used by social insurance experts, such as I. S. Falk, Edwin Witte, Oscar Ewing, I. M. Rubinow.

27. House, Ways and Means Committee, *Hearings*, 305.

28. Ibid., 306.

29. Ibid., 155.

30. Ibid., 156.

31. Ibid., 374.

32. Ibid., 374.

33. Ibid., 375.

34. Ibid., 377.

35. Ibid., 405.

36. Cruikshank interview with author.

37. House, Ways and Means Committee, *Hearings*, 91.

38. Ibid.

39. Ibid., 111.

40. Harris, *A Sacred Trust*, 65.

41. House, Ways and Means Committee, *Hearings*, 270.

42. Ibid., 278.

43. Ibid., 281.

44. Ibid., 284.

45. Harris, *A Sacred Trust*, 65.

46. U.S. Congress, House, Ways and Means Committee, *Hearings on Unemployment Insurance Amendments*, 85th Cong., 2d sess., 1958, 8.

47. House, Ways and Means Committee, *Hearings on HR4700*, 86th Cong., 1st Sess., 1959, 11.

48. "Paying Health Costs," *Business Week*, 33.
49. President Eisenhower message to Congress, *Congressional Quarterly Almanac* 16 (January 1959): 618.
50. "Paying Health Costs," *Business Week*, 33.
51. *Political Profiles* 3, 6.
52. As an example of Mason's remarks, see House Ways and Means Committee, *Hearings on HR4700*, 377.
53. Wilbur Cohen in a recorded interview with David McComb, December 8, 1968, Lyndon B. Johnson Oral History Program, Austin, Texas, 5.
54. Wilbur Mills in a personal interview with the author, June 24, 1981.
55. Forand, Corning interview, COH, 25.
56. Cohen, interview with author.

CHAPTER 2

1. Nelson Cruikshank in a recorded interview with Peter Corning, 1966, Columbia University Oral History Program.
2. Paul Douglas, *In the Fullness of Time* (New York: 1972), 392.
3. U.S. Congress, *Congressional Record* 105 (February 2, 1959): 1495.
4. Aime Forand in a recorded interview with Peter Corning, Princeton, NJ, 1966, COH.
5. U.S. Congress, House, Ways and Means Committee, *Hearings on HR4700*, 86th Cong., 1st sess., 1959, 244.
6. Douglas, *Fullness of Time*, 230–232.
7. Arthur M. Schlesinger, Jr., *A Thousand Days* (Boston: 1965), 650.
8. Doris Kearns, *Lyndon Johnson and the American Dream* (New York: 1976), 155.
9. *Who's Who in America* 34th ed., 964; *Political Profiles* 3, 224.
10. Lister Hill in a recorded interview with T. H. Baker, February 1, 1971, Lyndon Baines Johnson Oral History Program, Austin, Texas, 6.
11. William Reidy in a recorded interview with Peter Corning, 1966, COH, 59.
12. Ibid., 64.
13. Ibid., 71.
14. Ibid., 77.
15. Ibid., 69.
16. Forand, Corning interview, COH.
17. Reidy, Corning interview, COH, 78.
18. Wilbur Cohen in a recorded interview with Charles T. Morrissey, November 11, 1964, John F. Kennedy Library Oral History Program, Boston, 46.
19. Reidy, Corning interview, COH, 77.
20. *Who's Who in America*, 4th ed., 645; *Political Profiles* 3, 333.

21. Lister Hill in a recorded interview with T. H. Baker, 1971, LBJ-OH, 5.

22. Reidy, Corning interview, COH, 77.

23. Henry Hazlitt, "Age, Needs and Votes," *Newsweek* 55 (April 25, 1960): 95.

24. "Wave of the Future," *Nation* 190 (April 9, 1960): 306.

25. U.S. Congress, Senate, Subcommittee on Aged and Aging, *Report*, 86th Cong., 1st sess., 1960, Intro.

26. Richard Harris, *A Sacred Trust* (New York: 1966), 100.

27. *New York Times*, March 24, 1960, 25.

28. *New York Times*, April 12, 1960, 16.

29. Charles Odell in a recorded interview with Peter Corning, 1966, COH, 9.

30. Reidy, Corning interview, COH, 90–92.

31. U.S. Congress, Senate, Subcommittee on Aged and Aging, *Hearings*, 86th Cong., 2d sess., 1960, 4.

32. *New York Times*, March 24, 1960, 32.

33. Senate, Subcommittee on Aged and Aging, *Hearings*, 86 Cong., 15.

34. Ibid., 16.

35. Ibid., 22.

36. Ibid., 24.

37. Ibid.

38. Ibid.

39. Ibid., 269.

40. Gilbert Harrison, "Those Old Folks Back Home," *New Republic* 142 (April 18, 1960): 9.

41. U.S. Congress, *Congressional Record* 106, 86th Cong., 2d sess. (April 1960): 16914, 16915.

42. Wilbur Cohen in a personal interview with the author, March 8, 1977.

43. Ibid.

44. Ibid.

45. This opinion was voiced by several sources: Jay Constantine, who was on the Labor staff, in a personal interview with the author, April 1976; Wilbur Cohen, in a personal interview with the author, March 8, 1977; Fred Arner, in a telephone interview with the author, April 1976; and William Reidy, in his recorded interview with Peter Corning, 1966, COH.

46. A good discussion of the background material for the Ten Point Program is in Wilbur Cohen's Oral History recorded by David McComb, 1968, in LBJ-OH.

47. U.S. Congress, *Congressional Record* 104, (August 19, 1958): 18422.

48. Cohen, Morrissey interview, JFK-OH, 43.

49. Cruikshank, Corning interview, COH, 7.

50. Harris, *A Sacred Trust*, 102.

51. Russell Long's comments on the subject are peppered throughout the Senate Finance Committee Hearings, 1960–1965; also discussed with Nelson Cruikshank in a personal interview, May 1976.

52. Claude Pepper in a recorded interview with Peter Corning, 1966, COH, 41.

53. Robert Myers in a recorded interview with Peter Corning, 1966, COH, 59.

54. Cohen, interview with author.

55. *New York Times*, November 12, 1975, 46: also, Clinton Anderson, *Outsider in the Senate* (New York: 1970).

56. *Current Biography*, 1945, 6–7.

57. Memo, Howard Bray to Clinton Anderson, July 15, 1960, Clinton P. Anderson Papers, Box 236, Library of Congress.

58. "Health Insurance—No Action," *New Republic* 142 (May 2, 1960): 5–6.

59. Harrison, "Folks Back Home," 9–10.

60. J. J. Linder, "Which Bill is Best?" *Nation* 190 (May 28, 1960): 356.

61. *New York Times*, April 11, 1960, 1.

62. "Old Age and Health Care," *America* 103 (June 25, 1960): 387.

63. Edward T. Chase, "Medical Aid for the Aged," *Commonweal* 72 (May 20, 1960): 199.

64. "Showdown in the Medical Care Issue," *Business Week* (August 20, 1960): 25.

65. Harrison, "Folks Back Home," 9.

66. *New York Times*, February 21, 1960, 48.

67. Chase, "Aid for Aged," 199.

68. Harrison, "Folks Back Home."

69. *New York Times*, April 13, 1960, 27.

70. U.S. Congress, Senate, Finance Committee, *Hearings*, 86th Cong., 2d sess, 1960.

71. J. J. Linder, "Which Bill is Best?," *Nation*, 356.

72. The telegram was read aloud to the Finance Committee during its *Hearings*, 86th Cong., 2d sess., June 30, 1960, 161.

73. Ibid., 80.

74. *Congress and the Nation* 1: 1253, 1254.

CHAPTER 3

1. *New York Times*, August 21, 1960, 4–6.

2. Robert and Rosement Stevens, *Welfare Medicine in America: A Case Study of Medicaid* (New York: 1974), Prologue.

3. "Health Insurance—No Action," *New Republic* 142 (May 3, 1960): 5–6.

4. Eugene Feingold, *Medicare: Policy and Politics* (San Fransisco: 1966), 108–109.

5. *New York Times*, April 17, 1960, 1.

6. Richard Harris, *A Sacred Trust* (New York: 1966), 108–109.

7. *New York Times*, April 20, 1960, 27.

8. "Chairman Mills," *Time* 74 (September 7, 1959): 11.

9. Wilbur Cohen in an interview with the author, March 8, 1977.

10. Cohen, in a recorded interview with David McComb, May 10, 1969, Lyndon Baines Johnson Oral History Program, 7.

11. Monte Poen, *Harry S. Truman Versus the Medical Lobby* (Columbia: 1979), 96.

12. Stevens, *Welfare Medicine in America*, 21.

13. U.S. Congress, Senate, Committee on Labor and Public Welfare, *Hearings*, 81st Cong., 1st sess., 949, 1950, 12.

14. Poen, *Truman Versus Lobby*, 185.

15. Stevens, *Welfare Medicine in America*, 23.

16. Ibid., 24.

17. "Should Medical Aid be Added to OASDI?" *Congressional Digest* 39 (March 1960): 67.

18. "Which Bill is Best?" *Nation* 190 (May 28, 1960): 465–68.

19. *New York Times*, June 6, 1960, 31.

20. Aime Forand in a recorded interview with Peter Corning, Columbia University Oral History Project, 1965.

21. Robert Myers in a recorded interview with Peter Corning, COH, 1967.

22. Robert Kerr Papers, University of Oklahoma, copy of speech prepared for Kerr, Box 226.

23. "The Salami Slicer," *Time* 91 (April 5, 1968):24, 25

24. Cohen to author, March 8, 1977.

25. U.S. Congress, *Congressional Record* 109 (January 2, 1963):39.

26. Cohen to author, March 8, 1977.

27. Kerr Papers, memo of speech delivered on Senate floor on August 15, 1960, Box 226.

28. Daniel Seligman, "Senator Bob Kerr—The Oklahoma Gusher," *Fortune* 59 (March 1959):136.

29. Cohen in a recorded interview with Peter Corning, COH, 1966, 16.

30. U.S. Congress, Senate, Finance Committee, *Hearings on HR12580*, 86th Cong., 2d sess. 1960, 200.

31. U.S. Congress, *Congressional Record* 106 (August 16, 1960):16542.

32. Myers, Corning interview, COH, 51–52.

33. John Samuel Ezell, *Innovations in Energy: The Story of Kerr-McGee* (Norman: 1979), 36.

34. Ibid., 39.

35. "Senator Bob Kerr," 135.

36. "The Salami Slicer," 24.

37. Cohen, Corning interview, COH, 62.

38. *New York Times*, August 14, 1960, 42; also, Cohen to author, March 8, 1977.

39. "Showdown on Medical Care Issue," *Business Week* (August 20, 1960):25.

40. Harris, *A Sacred Trust*, 112.

41. *New York Times*, August 15, 1960, 11.

42. *New York Times*, August 16, 1960, 16.

43. *New York Times*, October 15, 1960, 1.

44. *New York Times*, August 23, 1960, 28.

45. Forand, Corning interview, COH; also, U.S. Congress, *Congressional Record* 106 (1960): 16425.

46. Murphy, T.E. *Saturday Evening Post* 232 (March 19, 1960):12.

47. *New York Times*, August 21, 1960, Sec. 4, 4.

48. *New York Times*, August 14, 1960, 42.

49. *New York Times*, September 8, 1960, 17.

50. *New York Times*, June 6, 1960, 31.

51. *New York Times*, September 8, 1960, 17.

52. Robert J. Myers, *Medicare* (Bryn Mawr: 1970), 34.

53. Ibid.

54. Stevens, *Welfare Medicine in America*, 34.

55. "Politics of Medicine," *Harper's* 221 (October 1960): 124.

56. U.S. Congress, House of Representatives, *Congressional Record* 106 (1960):16425. Speech made by Aime Forand.

57. Subcommittee on Problems of Aged and Aging, *Hearings*, "Special Report on Kerr-Mills Medical Assistance for the Aged" (June 1964):1.

58. Ibid., 2.

59. *Wall Street Journal*, December 28, 1960, 1.

60. *Wall Street Journal*, December 28, 1960, 4.

61. "Health Care for the Aged," *Reporter* 24 (February 2, 1961):25.

62. "Medicare for the Aged," *Newsweek* 57 (January 23, 1961):51.

63. "Aging with a Future," *America* 104 (January 28, 1961):559.

64. Harris, *A Sacred Trust*, 121; also, Nelson Cruikshank in interview with author, June 13, 1976.

65. "Aging with a Future," 559.

66. It was Representative John Fogarty's idea to set up the White House Conference. Bill Reidy (Reidy, Corning interview, COH, 1966) who was handling most of the health legislation as staff assistant for the Labor Committee tried to "sit on" Fogarty's bill. Fogarty wanted to schedule the conference for October 15, 1960, which would mean Vice President Nixon would chair it. "It'll win the god-damned election for him." Reidy had the date changed to January.

67. "Medicare for the Aged," 51.
68. "Health Care for the Aged," 24.
69. "Aging with a Future," 558.
70. Ibid., 559.
71. "Medicare for the Aged," 52.
72. "Health Care for the Aged," 24.
73. Elizabeth Wickenden in interview with author, January 13, 1982.
74. "Hope for the Aged," *New Republic* 143 (September 12, 1960):5.

CHAPTER 4

1. Wilbur Cohen in recorded interview with David McComb, May 10, 1969, Lyndon Baines Johnson Oral History Program, 36.
2. Cohen in recorded interview with Charles Morrissey, November 11, 1964, John F. Kennedy Oral History Program.
3. *New York Times*, January 11, 1961, 4.
4. Cohen, Morrissey interview, JFK-OH.
5. Cohen, McComb interview, LBJ-OH, 45.
6. Ibid., 40.
7. *New York Times*, January 11, 1961, 4.
8. T.E. Murphy, "Ribicoff," *Saturday Evening Post* 224 (June 21, 1952):30.
9. Arthur M. Schlesinger, Jr., *A Thousand Days: John F. Kennedy in the White House* (Boston, 1965), 126.
10. *New York Times*, January 14, 1961, 1.
11. Cohen, McComb interview, LBJ-OH, 38.
12. Ibid., 36.
13. Ibid., 42.
14. Cohen, Morrissey interview, JFK-OH, 56.
15. Cohen in interview with author, March 8, 1977.
16. Cohen in recorded interview with William Moss, May 24, 1971, Part II, JFK-OH, 4.
17. Ibid., 74.
18. *New York Times*, January 31, 1961, 3; also *Vital Speeches*, Vol. 28, 1961.
19. *Congressional Quarterly* (1961):263.
20. Ibid., 263.
21. *New York Times*, February 10, 1961, 6.
22. Richard Harris, *A Sacred Trust* (New York, 1966), 123.
23. "King, Cecil," *Current Biography* (1952), 309–310.
24. *New York Times*, February 14, 1961, 1.
25. Cohen, interview with author, March 8, 1977.
26. *New York Times*, February 11, 1961, 1.

27. Cohen in recorded interview with Peter Corning, 1966, Columbia University Oral History Project, New York.

28. Wilbur Mills in interview with author, June 24, 1981.

29. "Adam Smith, M.D.," *Commonweal* (March 24, 1961): 654.

30. Ibid., 655.

31. "Health Plan Battle: The AMA or JFK?" *Newsweek* 57 (May 8, 1961):101.

32. *A.M.A. News* (February 15, 1961).

33. "Health Plan Battle," 101.

34. *New York Times*, April 25, 1961, 3.

35. *New York Times*, April 30, 1961, 1.

36. "Health Plan Battle," 101.

37. Harris, *A Sacred Trust*, 134–135.

38. "Family Doctor's Fight Against Socialized Medicine," *Look* 25 (May 23, 1961):75.

39. Ibid., 81.

40. "Health Plan Battle," 100.

41. Cohen, interview with author.

42. Harris, *A Sacred Trust*, 136.

43. J. David Greenstone, *Labor in American Politics* (New York: 1969), 336–338.

44. William Reidy in recorded interview with Peter Corning, 1966, COH, 90–92.

45. Charles Odell in recorded interview with Peter Corning, 1966, COH, 11–12.

46. Reidy, Corning interview, COH, 93.

47. Cohen, interview with author.

48. Nelson Cruikshank in interview with author, May 24, 1976.

49. *New York Times*, April 22, 1961, 8.

50. *New York Times*, April 2, 1961, 41.

51. *New York Times*, April 29, 1961, 1; also, Odell, Corning interview, COH, 71.

52. U.S. Congress, House, Ways and Means Committee, *Hearings on HR4222*, 97th Cong., 1st Sess., 1961, 32–33.

53. Ibid., 36.

54. Ibid., 40.

55. Ibid., 40–45.

56. Ibid., 493.

57. Ibid., 1647.

58. Ibid., 1656.

59. Ibid., 1648.

60. Ibid., 1853.

61. Ibid., 328.

62. Ibid., 609.

63. Ibid., 379–380.
64. Ibid., 1138.
65. Ibid., 1140.
66. Ibid., 1313–1404.
67. Ibid., 1409.
68. Ibid., 1583.
69. Ibid., 1787.
70. Cohen, Corning interview, COH, 31.
71. Claude Wood to CPA, memo, Clinton P. Anderson Papers, Box 224–230, July 1966.
72. House, Ways and Means Committee, *Hearings*, 327.
73. Robert Myers in recorded interview with Peter Corning, 1967, COH.
74. House, Ways and Means Committee, *Hearings*, 934.
75. John F. Kennedy to Pat McNamara, letter, Clinton P. Anderson Papers, Box 220, August 5, 1961.

CHAPTER 5

1. Clinton P. Anderson to Harry F. Byrd, January 17, 1962, in Clinton P. Anderson Papers, Library of Congress, Box 233.
2. Howard Bray to Clinton Anderson, January 20, 1962, CPA Papers.
3. Nelson Cruikshank in a recorded interview with Peter Corning, 1966, Columbia University Oral History Project, 82.
4. Cruikshank, Corning interview, COH, 87.
5. U.S. Congress, *Congressional Record* 108 (February 28, 1962):3061.
6. *Wall Street Journal*, March 1, 1962, 16.
7. *Congressional Quarterly* 18 (1962):194; also, *New York Times*, April 3, 1962, 26.
8. *Congressional Quarterly*, 195.
9. Ibid.
10. Allen Lesser in a recorded interview with Peter Corning, 1966, COH, 72.
11. *Congressional Record* 108 (April 12, 1962):6675.
12. Jacob Javits in a recorded interview with Peter Corning, COH, 1966, 6, 7.
13. Cruikshank, Corning interview, COH, 159.
14. *Wall Street Journal*, May 4, 1962, 9.
15. Clinton Anderson to Howard Bray, CPA Papers, May 4, 1962.
16. Lesser, Corning interview, COH, 69.
17. Robert Ball to Clinton Anderson, CPA Papers, May 10, 1962.
18. Lesser, Corning interview, COH, 71.
19. "The Great Medicare Debate," *Newsweek* 59 (June 4, 1962):33.
20. *Vital Speeches* 28 (June 15, 1962):516.

21. Cruikshank, Corning interview, COH, 162.

22. "Great Medicare Debate," 33.

23. Ibid., 34.

24. *Vital Speeches*, 517.

25. "Medicare: Second Round," *Nation* 194 (February 17, 1962):91.

26. "Rebel Without a Cause," *Nation* 194 (May 19, 1962):429.

27. "Ad Battle," *Newsweek* 59 (May 28, 1962):91.

28. *Vital Speeches* 28 (June 16, 1962):631.

29. *Nation's Business* 50 (July 1962):34.

30. *New York Times*, January 4, 1962, 20.

31. *New York Times*, January 7, 1962, 44.

32. Edward T. Chase, "What Care for the Aged," *Commonweal* 55 (March 2, 1962):591–593.

33. "First Aid to Medicine," *America* 107 (July 14, 1962):479.

34. "Great Medicare Debate," 34.

35. "Judgment on Medicine," *America* 107 (June 9, 1962): 372.

36. *Wall Street Journal*, March 1, 1962.

37. *New York Times*, June 12, 1962, 1; also, Cruikshank, Corning interview, COH, 90.

38. Richard Harris, *A Sacred Trust* (New York: 1966), 147.

39. Cohen to author, March 8, 1977.

40. U.S. Congress, *Congressional Record* 108 (June 9, 1962):11271.

41. Cruikshank, Corning interview, COH, 167.

42. *New York Times*, July 6, 1962, 52.

43. Ibid., July 7, 1962, 1; also, *Congressional Quarterly*, July 16, 1962.

44. Ibid., July 14, 1962, 7.

45. Howard Bray to Clinton Anderson, CPA Papers, July 12, 1962.

46. Lesser, Corning interview, COH, 43.

47. Wilbur Cohen in interview with author, March 8, 1977.

48. Clinton Anderson to John Kennedy, July 16, 1962, CPA Papers.

49. There are several facets to this account. References are found in Harris, *A Sacred Trust*, 170; Cruikshank, Corning interview, COH, 170; Bobby Baker's side of the story is in Bobby Baker, *Wheeling and Dealing* (New York: 1978), 140–141. All material related to the subject is missing from Robert Kerr's papers on deposit in Norman, Oklahoma.

50. Robert Kerr to Fred Arner, Kerr Papers on deposit at University of Oklahoma, Norman, July 14, 1962, Box 227.

51. Cruikshank, Corning interview, COH, 173.

52. Telegram on file in CPA Papers, July 14, 1962, Box 223, Library of Congress.

53. Anderson to John Kennedy, CPA Papers, July 17, 1962.

54. U.S. Congress, *Congressional Record* 108 (July 16, 1962):13603.

55. Ibid., 13630.

56. Ibid., 13666.
57. Ibid., 13667.
58. Ibid., July 17, 1962, 13785.
59. Ibid., 13787.
60. Ibid., 13791.
61. *New York Times*, July 18, 1962, 1.
62. Ibid., 14.
63. Ibid.
64. Nelson Cruikshank in a recorded interview with Peter Corning, Colombia University Oral History Project, 1966, 180; also, Cohen to author, March 8, 1977.
65. Anderson to John Kennedy, July 18, 1962, Box 233, CPA Papers.
66. Anderson to Pat McNamara, July 26, 1962, Box 233, CPA Papers.
67. Jay Constantine in interview with author, April 1976.
68. Howard Bray to Clinton Anderson, November 28, 1962, Box 233, CPA Papers.
69. Ibid.
70. *New York Times*, November 14, 1962, 18.
71. Anderson to Birch Bayh, November 17, 1962, Box 234, CPA Papers.
72. *New York Times*, August 23, 1962, 14.
73. Cohen to author, March 8, 1977.
74. Myers, "Medicare: The Cure," 131.

CHAPTER 6

1. Harold B. Myers, "Medicare: The Cure That Could Cause a Setback," *Fortune* 67 (May 1963):131.
2. *Gallup Polls* 2; polls taken: January 9, April 3, October 2, 1963, 3.
3. *Wall Street Journal*, February 27, 1963, 3.
4. Ibid.
5. Celebrezze's biography is found in the following sources: *Current Biography*, 1963, 62–64; *Newsweek* 60 (July 23, 1962): 15; *Washington Post*, July 15, 1962, 6.
6. Accounts about the hiring of the Secretary are in: Arthur M. Schlesinger, Jr., *A Thousand Days: John F. Kennedy in the White House* (Boston: 1965), 608; Theodore Sorensen, *Kennedy* (New York: 1965), 265. Wilbur Cohen's opinions about his superiors are in his recorded interview with Peter Corning at the Columbia University Oral History Program (COH) in 1966.
7. Memo in Clinton Anderson Papers, Library of Congress, Box 229–231, January 17, 1963.
8. Howard Bray's notes on the meeting, Anderson Papers.
9. Howard Bray to Clinton Anderson, January 30, 1963, Anderson Papers.

10. Nelson Cruikshank to Lawrence O'Brien, January 30, 1963, Anderson Papers.

11. *New York Times*, February 8, 1963, 11.

12. Ibid.

13. Ibid., February 22, 1963, 2.

14. U.S. Congress, *Congressional Quarterly* 19 (1963):232–234.

15. *Wall Street Journal*, February 27, 1963, 1.

16. *New York Times*, February 25, 1963, 13.

17. Notes in Anderson Papers, dated February 20–28, 1963, Box 234.

18. *New York Times*, February 20, 1963, 1.

19. Ibid., February 7, 1963, 6.

20. "Coverage for Aged," *America* 109 (August 10, 1963): 128.

21. *Wall Street Journal*, May 10, 1963, 19.

22. Myers, "Medicare: The Cure," 167.

23. *New York Times*, April 25, 1963, 12.

24. Anderson to Cohen, May 14, 1963, Anderson Papers.

25. Cohen to Anderson, May 24, 1963, Anderson Papers.

26. *New York Times*, May 18, 1963, 1.

27. "Focus on Aged," *America* 108 (May 11, 1963): 658.

28. *New York Times*, May 18, 1963, 1.

29. "Focus on Aged," 658.

30. *New York Times*, June 1, 1963, 50.

31. Wilbur Cohen in a recorded interview with Charles Morrissey, November 11, 1964, Lyndon Baines Johnson Oral History Library, Tape 4, 29.

32. *New York Times*, June 2, 1963, 1.

33. *Business Week* 36 (June 8, 1963):25.

34. Cohen, Morrissey interview, LBJ-OH, 30.

35. Memo about Cohen's thoughts to Anderson, Anderson Papers, May 9, 1963, Box 234.

36. U.S. Congress, Senate, Subcommittee on Health of the Aged, *Medical Assistance for the Aged*, 88th Cong., 1st sess., 1963.

37. Ibid., 1.

38. Ibid., 4.

39. Ibid., 5.

40. Ibid., 54.

41. Ibid., 53.

42. Ibid., 62–63.

43. "Who Pays for the Care of the Aged?" *Business Week* (November 5, 1963): 32.

44. *New York Times*, November 22, 1963, 30.

45. Ibid., November 15, 1963, 18–19.

46. Ibid., November 14, 1963, 15.

47. "Who Provides Welfare?" *Newsweek* 62 (November 25, 1963): 72.

48. U.S. Congress, House, Ways and Means Committee, *Hearings on HR3920*, 88th Cong., 1st sess., 1963.
49. Ibid., 26.
50. Ibid., 85.
51. Ibid., 114.
52. Ibid., 139.
53. Ibid., 145.
54. Ibid., 160.
55. Ibid., 445.
56. *New York Times*, November 20, 1963, 34.
57. *Hearings*, 270.
58. Ibid., 1106.
59. Ibid., 644–654.
60. *New York Times*, November 21, 1963, 33.
61. *Hearings*, 844.
62. Ibid., 918.
63. Ibid., 1148.
64. Lawrence O'Brien, *No Final Victories* (New York: 1974): 135.

CHAPTER 7

1. Doris Kearns, *Lyndon Johnson and the American Dream* (New York: 1976), 219.
2. *New York Times*, February 2, 1964, 1.
3. Ibid., January 16, 1964, 15.
4. *Vital Speeches* 30 (February 2, 1964):194.
5. *New York Times*, January 9, 1964, 16.
6. Wilbur Cohen in a recorded interview with Charles Morrissey, November 11, 1963, Tape 4, John F. Kennedy Oral History Program, 256.
7. Philip Portz, M.D., "The Elderly and Medical Care," *America* 110 (February 27, 1964): 276–278.
8. Lawrence O'Brien to Lyndon Johnson, January 27, 1964, Lyndon Johnson Papers, Legislative files Le: ISI.
9. Wilbur Cohen in interview with author, March 8, 1977.
10. Author's interpretation from notes and files at Lyndon Johnson Library.
11. *Current Biography Yearbook* (New York: 1961):346–348.
12. Wilbur Cohen Oral History in LBJ Library, Tape 1, 7–9.
13. Jacob Javits to the President, January 1964, in executive/legislative files, Le/ISI LBJ Library.
14. *New York Daily News*, January 20, 1964, 23.
15. *New York Times*, January 19, 1964, IV, 12.
16. U.S. Congress, House, Ways and Means Committee, *Hearings on*

HR11865, 88th Cong., 2d Sess., 1964. Dr. Spock's position on Medicare is further elaborated in an article in *Redbook* 23 (May 1964), Vol. 34.

17. *Hearings*, 1734

18. Ibid., 1954.

19. *New York Times*, February 16, 1964, section 4, 6.

20. O'Brien to Johnson, January 27, 1963, LBJ Library, Le/ISI, Legislative files.

21. "Health Care for the Aged: How the Democrat and Republican Plans Compare," *U.S. News and World Report* 58 (February 22, 1965): 46–48.

22. *New York Times*, January 26, 1964, 42.

23. Ibid., January 19, section 4, 2.

24. *Vital Speeches* 30 (February 2, 1964):194.

25. U.S. Congress, *Congressional Record* 110 (April 1, 1964):7716.

26. *New York Times*, April 3, 1964, 32.

27. "Age of Retirement," *New Republic* 155 (February 15, 1964):155.

28. O'Brien to President (private memo) executive files Le/ISI, February 1964.

29. Howard Bray to Clinton Anderson, April 15, 1964, memo in Clinton P. Anderson Papers, Library of Congress.

30. Ibid.

31. *New York Times*, April 23, 1964, 1.

32. "Age of Retirement," 155.

33. Henry Hall Wilson to Lawrence O'Brien, June 8, 1964, memo in LBJ Library, Le/ISI legislative files.

34. Cohen interview with author.

35. Douglass Cater to Lyndon Johnson, June 12, 1964, memo in Anderson Papers, Box 234; also in LBJ Library, Box 75 of legislative files.

37. Howard Bray to Clinton Anderson, July 27, 1964, Box 234, Anderson Papers.

38. Ibid.

39. Howard Bray to Clinton Anderson, August 7, 1964, Box 232, Anderson Papers.

40. Vance Hartke to Lyndon Johnson, August 10, 1964, memo in LBJ Papers, general legislative files, Box 77.

41. U.S. Congress, *Congressional Record* 110 (August 6, 1964):10482.

42. U.S. Congress, Senate Finance Committee, *Hearings on HR11865*, 88th Cong., 2d sess., 1964.

43. Ibid., 76.

44. Ibid., 200–203.

45. Ibid., 205.

46. Lawrence O'Brien to Lyndon Johnson, August 14, 1964, LBJ Papers, executive files Le/ISI, Box 75.

47. Senate, *Hearings*. McNerney's testimony begins on page 336. Also,

discussion about that testimony is found in a memo from Howard Bray to Clinton Anderson, August 22, 1964, in Box 234 of Anderson Papers.

48. Senate, *Hearings*, 344.

49. U.S. Congress, *Congressional Record* 110 (August 6, 1964):1173.

50. The most complete account of these events are found in Richard Harris, *A Sacred Trust* (New York: 1966), 166; also, Wilbur Cohen in a recorded interview with Peter Corning, Columbia University Oral History Program.

51. *New York Times*, September 2, 1964, 1.

52. Cohen, Corning interview, COH.

53. *New York Times*, September 2, 1964, 1.

54. Ibid., September 3, 1964, 1.

55. Ibid., 14.

56. Bill Moyers to Lyndon Johnson, September 8, 1964, in legislative files, Le/ISI, Box 75, LBJ Library.

57. Library of Congress Reference Service, copy in Box 232 of Anderson Papers, September 17, 1964.

58. Mike Manatos to Lawrence O'Brien, September 17, 1964, Manatos file, LBJ Library, legislative files.

59. *New York Times*, October 1, 1964, 1.

60. Clinton Anderson to Myer Feldman, October 1, 1964, Box 77, general legislative files, LBJ Library.

61. O'Brien to Johnson, September 18, 1964, legistlative files, LBJ Library.

62. Harris, *A Sacred Trust*, 171.

63. Mike Manatos to Jack Valenti, October 1, 1964, Manatos file, LBJ Papers, Box 4, general legislative files, LBJ Library.

64. Manatos to O'Brien, September 21, 1964, LBJ Papers.

65. *New York Times*, October 2, 1964, 16.

66. Ibid., October 3, 1964, 28.

67. "Medicare Set for the Next Round," *Business Week* October 31, 1964, 32.

68. Cohen in interview with author.

69. *New York Times*, October 3, 1964, 12.

70. "Medicare Set."

71. *New York Times*, November 1, 1964, 63.

72. Ibid., 55.

73. Mike Monroney to Clinton Anderson, November 10, 1964, Box 237, Anderson Papers.

74. *New York Times*, November 11, 1964, 24.

75. "Mills Terms for Medicare," *U.S. News and World Report* 57 (December 21, 1964):74.

76. *New York Times*, December 1, 1964, 28.

77. Anthony Celebrezze to Lyndon Johnson, November 25, 1964, legislative file Le/ISI, LBJ Papers.

78. Anderson to Mike Mansfield, December 1, 1964, Box 237, Anderson Papers.

CHAPTER 8

1. *Congressional Digest* 44 (January 15, 1965):71–72.
2. Jacob Javits to Clinton Anderson, December 30, 1964, Clinton Anderson Papers, Library of Congress, Box 237.
3. *New York Times*, January 8, 1965, 1.
4. Kermit Gordon to Lyndon Johnson, January 1, 1965, Le/ISI, Lyndon Johnson Papers, LBJ Library, Austin, Texas.
5. *New York Times*, January 3, 1965, 68.
6. Wilbur Cohen in a personal interview with author, March 8, 1977.
7. Cohen in a recorded interview with David McComb, May 10, 1969, Tape 3, LBJ Oral History Program, 7.
8. *New York Times*, January 10, 1965, 11.
9. "Eldercare vs. Medicare," *Time* 85 (February 19, 1965):22.
10. *New York Times*, February 24, 1965, 1.
11. Ibid., March 17, 1965, 39.
12. "Health Care for the Aged: How the Democrat and Republican Plans Compare," *U.S. News and World Report* 58 (February 22, 1965):46–48.
13. *Congressional Digest* 44 (March 15, 1965):65.
14. *New York Times*, January 12, 1965, 16.
15. U.S. Congress, House, Ways and Means Committee, *Hearings on HR1*, 89th Cong., 1st sess., 1965, 27.
16. Ibid., 29.
17. Ibid., 28.
18. Ibid., 30.
19. Ibid., 60–61.
20. Ibid., 62.
21. Ibid., 67.
22. Ibid., 68.
23. Ibid., 81.
24. Ibid., 183.
25. Ibid., 184.
26. Ibid., 223.
27. Ibid., 486.
28. Cohen, interview with author.
29. Abraham Ribicoff to Lyndon Johnson, March 3, 1965, Le/ISI, LBJ Papers.
30. Wilbur Mills's surprise approach recalled in several places: memos from Howard Bray to Clinton Anderson, March 2, 1965, in Anderson Papers, Box 237; Cohen to Lawrence O'Brien, March 25, LBJ Papers; also, Theodore

Marmor, *The Politics of Medicare* (London: 1970), 64; and Richard Harris, *A Sacred Trust* (New York: 1966), 186–187. Apparently, Mills spoke about his idea to no one except William Quay, John F. Byrnes's assistant.

31. Cohen to Lyndon Johnson, March 2, 1965, LBJ Papers.

32. O'Brien to Johnson, March 23, 1965, LBJ Papers.

33. Cohen to O'Brien, March 18, 1965, LBJ Papers.

34. O'Brien to Johnson, April 8, 1965, LBJ Papers.

35. *New York Times*, March 24, 1965, 1.

36. Ibid.

37. "Medicoup," *Newsweek* 65 (April 5, 1965):28.

38. Harold B. Meyers, "Mr. Mills' Elder-Medi-Bettercare," *Fortune* 71 (June 1965):166–168.

39. Ibid., 168.

40. Ibid.

41. "Biggest Change Since the New Deal," *Newsweek* 65 (April 12, 1965):88.

42. "Wrapping Up the Medicare Bill" *Business Week* (March 27, 1965):132.

43. Cohen to O'Brien, May 6, 1965, LBJ Papers.

44. O'Brien to Clinton Anderson, anecdote for his memoirs, one copy in executive files, Le/ISI in LBJ Papers; story also in Harris, *A Sacred Trust*, 190–191; also recalled in Lawrence O'Brien, *No Final Victories* (New York: 1974).

45. Anderson to Harry F. Byrd, April 13, 1965, Clinton P. Anderson Papers, Box 234, Library of Congress.

46. Byrd to Anderson, April 16, 1965, Anderson Papers.

47. U.S. Congress, Senate Finance Committee, *Hearings on S1 and Other Proposals*, 89th Cong., 1st sess. 1965, 93.

48. Ibid., 94–96.

49. Ibid., 114.

50. Ibid., 136.

51. Ibid., 137.

52. Ibid., 312.

53. Ibid., 182.

54. Ibid., 385.

55. Ibid., 625.

56. Ibid., 650.

57. Ibid., 836.

58. Cohen to Johnson, June 17, 1965, LBJ Papers.

59. *New York Times*, May 1, 1965, 11.

60. "Russell Long's Capers," *New Republic* 153 (July 3, 1965):6.

61. Cohen to O'Brien, June 16, 1965, Anderson Papers.

62. HEW staff memo to O'Brien, June 18, 1965, Anderson Papers.

63. Anderson to members of Finance Committee, June 18, 1965, Anderson Papers.

64. Cohen, recorded interview with Peter Corning, 1966, Columbia University Oral History Program.

65. Harris, *A Sacred Trust*, 198.
66. Paul Douglas to Anderson, June 23, 1965, Anderson Papers.
67. Anderson to Johnson, June 23, 1965, Anderson Papers.
68. Harris, *A Sacred Trust*, 199.
69. *New York Times*, June 25, 1965, 32.
70. Cohen, recorded interview with David McComb, Tape 4, May 10, 1969, LBJ Oral History Program.
71. Harris, *A Sacred Trust*, 202–203.
72. George Meany to Anderson, June 23, 1965, Anderson Papers.
73. Anderson to Abraham Ribicoff and Vance Hartke, July 1, 1965, executive files, Le/ISI, LBJ Library, Austin, Texas.
74. Anderson to Johnson, July 1, 1965, Anderson Papers.
75. Anderson to Russell Long, July 1, 1965, Anderson Papers.
76. Marion Folsom to Anderson, July 6, 1965, Anderson Papers.
77. Anderson to Anthony Celebrezze, July 12, 1965, Anderson Papers.
78. Cohen to O'Brien, July 19, 1965, LBJ Papers.
79. Howard Bray to Anderson, May 26, 1965, Anderson Papers.
80. Cohen to O'Brien, July 20, 1965, LBJ Papers.
81. Anderson to Johnson, July 21, 1965, Anderson Papers.
82. Horace Busby to Jack Valenti, Doug Cater, Bill Moyers, and Marvin Watson, July 23, 1965, LBJ Papers.
83. Cohen to Cater, July 21, 1965, LBJ Papers.
84. White House staff to President, July 16, 1965, LBJ Papers.
85. *New York Times*, July 31, 1965, 1.
86. Ibid., 9.
87. Lyndon Johnson, *The Vantage Point* (New York: 1971), 219.

CHAPTER 9

1. Wilbur Cohen in recorded interview with Charles Morrissey, November 11, 1963, Lyndon Baines Johnson Oral History Program, 11–12.
2. Lawrence O'Brien to Clinton Anderson, August 27, 1965, executive files Le/ISI, LBJ Library.
3. *Who's Who in America* 38th ed. (1974):144; *New York Times*, December 30, 1966, 26.
4. Robert M. Ball, *Social Security: Today and Tomorrow* (New York: 1978).
5. *New York Times*, November 12, 1965, 39.
6. Ibid., August 31, 1965, 12.
7. "Senior Citizens Organize," *America* 113 (November 6, 1965): 519.
8. Ibid.
9. Cohen, Morrissey interview, LBJ-OH.
10. Theodore R. Marmor, *The Politics of Medicare* (Chicago: 1974), 88.

11. Bruce Vladeck, *Unloving Care: The Nursing Home Tragedy* (New York: 1980), 54.

12. Ibid., 57.

13. "Great Salesmanship: Signing up for Medicare," *Time* 87 (April 8, 1966):27.

14. Jake Jacobsen (legal counsel to LBJ) to John Gardner, December 7, 1965, Le/exec. files in LBJ Library.

15. Hubert Humphrey to Jack Valenti, August 13, 1965, exec. files, LBJ Library.

16. "Great Salesmanship," 27.

17. Ibid.

18. D. Sanford, "Care for the Not So Poor," *New Republic* 154 (June 4, 1966):8.

19. "Medicare's Expensive Companion," *Business Week* (June 25, 1966):38–39.

20. "Not So Poor," 8.

21. "Medicare's Companion," 38–39.

22. John Gardner to Lyndon Johnson, December 13, 1965, executive files, LBJ Library.

23. "Great Salesmanship," 27.

24. U.S. Congress, *Congressional Record* 111 (July 28, 1965):17739.

25. *New York Times*, August 5, 1965, 1.

26. Ibid., August 7, 1965, 23.

27. Mike Manatos files, undated, Box 5, LBJ Library.

28. Howard Bray to Clinton Anderson, June 16, 1965, Box 235, Clinton Anderson Papers, Library of Congress.

29. Selig Greenberg, "The Medicare Bonanza," *Nation* 203 (November 14, 1966):513.

30. Memo, February 10, 1966, White House Central Files, Box 1, LBJ Library.

31. Bray to Anderson, June 18, 1965, Box 235, Anderson Papers.

32. Martin Feldstein, *Hospital Costs and Health Insurance* (Boston: 1981), 247–249.

33. *Washington Post*, July 23, 1980, C–3–1.

34. U.S. Congress, Senate, Special Committee on Aging, *Hearings*, 93d Cong., 1st sess., 1973.

35. *New York Times*, March 26, 1984, 3.

36. "Government Controls," *Medical Economics* (September 29, 1975):20.

37. *New York Times*, March 11, 1981, 1.

38. *New York Times*, August 3, 1984, 39.

39. *New York Times*, September 12, 1983, A22.

40. *New York Times*, August 26, 1984, 14.

41. Vladeck, *Unloving Care*, 59–62.

42. U.S. Congress, *Congressional Record* 121 (January 15, 1975):266.

43. Harry Paxton, "Four Prospects Under National Health Insurance," *Medical Economics* (September 29, 1975):129.

44. *New York Times,* March 11, 1984, 17.

45. "Curbing the Costs of Health Care," *Business Week* (April 4, 1977):82.

46. At Arthur D. Little Seminar, March 9, 1976, on Health Care Financing.

47. "Curbing the Costs."

48. Feldstein, *Hospital Costs,* 247.

Bibliography

BOOKS

Altmeyer, Arthur S. *The Formative Years of Social Security*. Madison: University of Wisconsin Press, 1966.

Anderson, Clinton P., and Viorst, Milton. *Outsider in the Senate*. New York: World Publishing Co., 1970.

Baker, Bobby. *Wheeling and Dealing*. New York: W. W. Norton Co., 1978.

Ball, Robert M. *Social Security, Today and Tomorrow*. New York: Columbia University Press, 1978.

Brown, J. Douglas. *An American Philosophy of Social Security*. Princeton: Princeton University Press, 1972.

Chambers, Clarke. *Seedtime for Reform*. Minneapolis: University of Minnesota Press, 1963.

Corning, Peter. *The Evolution of Medicare: From Idea to Law*. Washington: U.S. Government Printing Office, 1969.

Davis, Karen. *National Health Insurance: Benefits, Costs, and Consequences*. Washington, D.C.: Broakings Institute, 1975.

Davis, Michael M. *Medical Care for Tomorrow*. New York: Harper Brothers, 1955.

Donahue, Wallace, ed. *The Politics of Age*. Ann Arbor: University of Michigan Press, 1962.

Douglas, Paul H. *In the Fullness of Time*. New York: Harcourt Brace Jovanovich, Inc., 1972.

Duffy, John. *The Healers: A History of American Medicine*. Urbana: University of Illinois Press, 1970.

Epstein, Abraham. *Insecurity, A Challenge to America*. New York: Random House, 1937.

Evans, Rowland, and Novak, Robert. *Lyndon B. Johnson: The Exercise of Power*. New York: The New American Library, 1970.

Ezell, John Samuel. *Innovations in Energy: The Story of Kerr-McGee*. Norman: University of Oklahoma Press, 1979.

Falk, Isidore S. *Security Against Sickness*. New York: Doubleday, Doran and Co., 1936.

Feingold, Eugene. *Medicare: Policy and Politics*. San Francisco: Chandler Publishing Co., 1966.

Fischer, David H. *Growing Old in America*. New York: Oxford University Press, 1978.

Garceau, Oliver. *The Political Life of the AMA*. Boston: Harvard University Press, 1941.

Greenstone, J. David. *Labor in American Politics*. New York: Alfred A. Knopf, 1969.

Harris, Richard. *A Sacred Trust*. New York: New American Library, 1966.

Hirshfield, Daniel S. *The Lost Reform: The Campaign for National Health Insurance in the U.S. 1932–1943*. Boston: Harvard University Press, 1970.

Javits, Jacob, and Steinberg, Rafael. *An Autobiography of a Rich Man*. Boston: Houghton Mifflin Co., 1981.

Johnson, Lyndon Baines. *The Vantage Point*. New York: Holt, Rinehart and Winston, 1971.

Kearns, Doris. *Lyndon Johnson and the American Dream*. New York: Harper & Row, 1976.

Keller, Morton. *The Life Insurance Enterprise*. Boston: Harvard University Press, 1963.

Lubove, Roy. *The Struggle for Social Security*. Boston: Harvard University Press, 1968.

Marmor, Theodore R. *The Politics of Medicare*. Chicago: Aldine Publishing Co., 1970.

Morgan, Ann. *Robert S. Kerr: The Senate Years*. Norman: University of Oklahoma Press, 1977.

Munts, Raymond. *Bargaining for Health: Labor Unions, Health Insurance and Medical Care*. Madison: University of Wisconsin Press, 1967.

Myers, Robert J. *Medicare*. Bryn Mawr: McCahan Foundation, 1970.

O'Brien, Lawrence. *No Final Victories*. New York: Doubleday and Co., 1974.

Patterson, James T. *Mr. Republican: A Biography of Robert A. Taft*. Boston: Houghton Mifflin Co., 1972.

Poen, Monte M. *Harry S. Truman Versus the Medical Lobby*. Columbia: University of Missouri Press, 1979.

Pratt, Henry J. *The Gray Lobby*. Chicago: University of Chicago Press, 1976.

Rorty, James. *American Medicine Mobilizes*. New York: W. W. Norton Co., 1934.

Rubinow, Isaac M. *Social Insurance*. New York: Henry Holt Co., 1913.
———. *The Quest for Security*. New York: Henry Holt Co., 1934.
Schlesinger, Arthur M., Jr. *A Thousand Days: John F. Kennedy in the White House*. Boston: Houghton Mifflin Co., 1965.
Skidmore, Max. *Medicine: The American Rhetoric of Reconciliation*. Mobile: University of Alabama, 1970.
Somers, Herman, and Somers, Ann. *Medicare and the Hospitals: Issues and Perspectives*. Washington: The Brookings Institute, 1967.
Stevens, Robert, and Stevens, Rosemary. *Welfare Medicine in America: A Case Study of Medicaid*. New York: The Free Press, 1974.
Sorensen, Theodore. *Kennedy*. New York: Harper & Row, 1965.
Steiner, Gilbert. *The State of Welfare*. Washington: The Brookings Institute, 1971.
Vladeck, Bruce C. *Unloving Care: The Nursing Home Tragedy*. New York: Basic Books, 1980.
Witte, Edwin. *The Development of the Social Security Act*. Madison: University of Wisconson Press, 1962.
———. *Social Security Perspectives*. Madison: University of Wisconsin Press, 1962.

ARTICLES

"Ad Battle." *Newsweek* 59 (May 28, 1962):91.
"Anderson, Clinton." *Current Biography* (1945):67.
Anderson, Gilbert. "Those Old Folks Back Home." *New Republic* 142 (April 18, 1960):9–10.
Annis, Edward R. "Medical Care Through Social Security." *Vital Speeches* 28 (June 16, 1962):631.
"Biggest Change Since the New Deal." *Newsweek* 65 (April 12, 1965):88.
Campion, Donald R. "Aging with a Future." *America* 104 (January 28, 1961):558.
"Celebrezze, Anthony." *Current Biography* (1963):62–64.
"Celebreeze, Anthony." *Newsweek* 60 (July 23, 1962):15.
"Chairman Mills." *Time* 74 (September 7, 1959):11.
Chase, Edward T. "Adam Smith, M.D." *Commonweal*. 73 (March 24, 1961):654.
———. "What Care for the Aged." *Commonweal* 75 (March 2, 1962):591–593.
———. "Politics of Medicine." *Harper's* 221 (October 1960):124.
———. "What Care for the Aged." *Commonweal* 75 (March 2, 1962):591–593.
Coggeshall, Dr. Lowell T. "Commencement Address." *Vital Speeches* 28 (June 15, 1962):516.

"Coverage for the Aged." *America* 109 (August 10, 1963):128.

"Curbing the Costs of Health Care." *Business Week* (April 4, 1977):82.

"Eldercare Vs. Medicare." *Time* 85 (February 19, 1965):22.

"First Aid to Medicare." *America* 107 (July 14, 1962):479.

"Focus on the Aged." *America* 108 (May 11, 1963):658.

"Government Controls." *Medical Economics* (September 29, 1975):19–46.

Graham, J.J. "New Man at HEW." *Commonweal* 88 (May 3, 1968):608.

"The Great Medicare Debate." *Newsweek* 59 (June 4, 1962):33.

"Great Salesmanship: Signing Up for Medicare." *Time* 87 (April 8, 1966):27.

Greensberg, Selig. "The Medicare Bonanza." *Nation* 203 (November 14, 1966):513.

Harrison, Gilbert. "Those Old Folks Back Home." *New Republic* 142 (April 25, 1960):95.

Hazlitt, Henry. "Age, Needs and Votes." *Newsweek* 55 (April 25, 1960):95.

"Health Care for the Aged: An Unexpected Victory." *Reporter* 24 (February 2, 1961):24.

"Health Insurance—No Action." *New Republic* 142 (May 2, 1960):5–6.

"Health Plan Battle: the AMA or JFK?" *Newsweek* 57 (May 8, 1961):101.

"Hope for the Aged." *New Republic* 143 (September 13, 1960):5.

Johnson, Lyndon. "State of the Union." *Vital Speeches* 30 (February 1964):194.

"Judgment on Medicare." *America* 107 (June 9, 1962):372.

"King, Cecil." *Current Biography* (1952):309–310.

Lagomarcing, Paul. "Age of Termination." *New Republic* 155 (February 15, 1964):155.

Linder, J.J. "Which Bill is Best?" *Nation* 190 (May 28, 1960):356.

Mallory, Joseph R. "A Family Doctor's Fight Against Socialized Medicine." *Look* 25 (May 23, 1961):75.

"Medical Care for Retired Workers?" *Fortune* 62 (July 1960):211.

"Medicare Comes Back." *Business Week* (June 8, 1963):25.

"Medicare for the Aged: The Logical Solution." *Newsweek* 57 (January 23, 1961):51.

"Medicare Set for the Next Round." *Business Week* (October 31, 1964):32.

"Medicare's Expensive Companion." *Business Week* (June 25, 1966):38–39.

"Medicoup." *Newsweek* 65 (April 5, 1965):28.

Meyers, Harold B. "Medicare: The Cure That Could Cause a Setback." *Fortune* 67 (May 1963):131.

————. "Mr. Mills' Elder-Medi-Bettercare." *Fortune* 71 (June 1965):166–168.

"Mills Terms for Medicare." *U.S. News and World Report* 57 (December 21, 1964):74.

Mishell, Robert M., and Lenore A. Herzenberg. "Medicare: Second Round." *Nation* 194 (February 17, 1962):132–133.

Murphy, T.E. "Ribicoff." *Saturday Evening Post* 224 (June 21, 1952):30.

"O'Brien, Lawrence." *Current Biography* (November 1961):346.

"Old Age and Health Care." *America* 103 (June 25, 1960):87.

"Old People Will Shape U.S. Future." *Nation's Business* 50 (July 1962):34.

Paxton, Harry. "Your Prospects Under National Health Insurance." *Medical Economics* (September 29, 1975):129–152.

"Paying Health Costs of the Aged." *Business Week* (January 31, 1959):33.

Peterson, Oslo. "Financing a Medical Care Program Through Social Security." *New England Journal of Medicine* 265 (September 14, 1961):526–528.

Pollack, Jerome. "A Labor View of Health Insurance." *Monthly Labor Review* 81 (February 1958):145.

Portz, Philip, M.D. "The Elderly and Medical Care." *America* 110 (February 27, 1964):276–278.

"Rebel Without a Cause." *Nation* 194 (May 19, 1962):429.

"Resources and Health Status of OASI Beneficiaries." *Monthly Labor Review* 82 (August 1959):882.

"Ribicoff, Abraham." *Current Biography* (1952):503.

Rubinow, I. M. "Standard of Sickness Insurance." *Journal of Political Economy* 23 (March 1915):226.

"Russell Long's Capers." *New Republic* 153 (July 3, 1965):6.

"The Salami Slicer." *Time* 91 (April 5, 1968):24, 25.

Sanford, D. "Care For the Not So Poor." *New Republic* 154 (June 4, 1966):8.

Seligman, Daniel "Senator Bob Kerr—The Oklahoma Gusher." *Fortune* 59 (March 1959):136.

"Senior Citizens Organize." *America* 113 (November 6, 1965):519.

"Should Medical Aid be Added to OASDI?" *Congressional Digest* 39 (March 1960):67.

"Showdown on Medical Care Issue." *Business Week* (August 20, 1960):25.

Spock, Benjamin. "Medical Care of the Aged." *Redbook* 23 (May 1964):34.

"Wave of the Future." *Nation* 190 (April 9, 1960):306.

"Who Pays for the Care of the Aged?" *Business Week* (November 5, 1963):32.

"Who Provides Welfare?" *Newsweek* 63 (November 25, 1963):72.

"Wrapping Up the Medicare Bill." *Business Week* (March 27, 1965):132.

NEWPAPERS

New York Daily News, January 20, 1964.

New York Times, March 21, 1959 through October 10, 1984.

Wall Street Journal, December 28, 1960; March 1, May 4, 1962; February 27, May 10 1963.

Washington Post, July 15, 1962; July 23, 1980. C–3–1.

GOVERNMENT DOCUMENTS

U.S. Congress. *Congressional Record*. 85th Cong., 1st sess., 1958. Vol. 104–89th Cong., 1st sess., 1965. Vol. 111; 94th Cong., 1st sess., 1975. Vol. 121.

U.S. Congress. House, Ways and Means Committee. *Hearings on HR4700*. 86th Cong., 1st sess., 1959.

———. *Hearings on Unemployment Insurance Amendments* 85th Cong., 2d sess., 1958.

———. *Hearings on HR4222*. 87th Cong., 1st sess., 1961.

———. *Hearings on HR3920*. 88th Cong., 1st sess., 1963.

———. *Hearings on HR11865*. 88th Cong., 2st sess., 1964.

———. *Hearings on HR 1*. 89th Cong., 1st sess., 1965.

U.S. Congress. Senate, Finance Committee. *Hearings on HR12580* 86th Cong., 2d sess., 1960.

———. *Hearings on HR11865* 88th Cong., 2d sess., 1964.

———. *Hearings on S1 and other proposals* 89th Cong., 1st sess., 1965.

———. Staff Report, *Medicare and Medicaid*. 91st Cong., 1st sess., 1979.

U.S. Congress. Senate, Committee on Labor and Public Welfare. *Hearings*. 86th Cong., 1st sess., 1960.

U.S. Congress. Senate, Subcommittee on Aged and Aging. *Hearings*. 86th Cong., 2d sess., 1960.

———. *Special Report on Medical Assistance for the Aged*. 88th Cong., 1st sess., 1963.

———. *Special Report on Kerr-Mills Medical Assistance for the Aged*. 88th Cong., 2d., sess., 1964.

U.S. Congress. Senate, Special Committee on Aging. *Hearings*. 93d Cong., 1st sess. 1973.

CONGRESSIONAL QUARTERLY SERVICE PUBLICATIONS

Congress and the Nation. Vol 1. (1945–1964). Washington: Congressional Quarterly Service, 1965.

Congress and the Nation. Vol. 2 (1964–1969). Washington: Congressional Quarterly Service, 1970.

Congressional Quarterly, (1961). Washington: Congressional Quarterly Service, 1963.

Congressional Quarterly. Vol. 18 (1962). Washington: Congressional Quarterly Service, 1963.

Congressional Quarterly. Vol. 19 (1963). Washington: Congressional Quarterly Service, 1964.

PUBLICATIONS OF PRIVATE ORGANIZATIONS

Who's Who in America 34, 37th & 38th ed. Chicago: Marquis Who's Who, Inc., 1968.

Political Profiles, The Kennedy Years, The Johnson Years. New York: Facts on File, 1972–976.

Gallup Polls 2. Public opinion interview taken April 3, October 4, January 4, 1962. New York: Random House, 1972.

INTERVIEWS

Fred Arner. April 1976. Washington, D.C. Jay Constantine. April 1976. Washington, D.C. Wilbur Cohen. March 8, 1977. Fort Lauderdale, Florida. Nelson Cruikshank. May 24, 1966. Washington, D.C. Wilbur Mills. June 24, 1981. Washington, D.C. Myer Feldman. April 1976. Washington, D.C. Elizabeth Wickenden. January 13, 1982. New York City.

MANUSCRIPT COLLECTIONS

Columbia University, New York. Oral History Program on Social Security. All of the interviews were conducted by Peter Corning. Wilbur Cohen, 1966. Jacob Javits, 1966. Allen Lesser, 1966. Robert Myers, 1967. Charles Odell, 1966. Claude Pepper, 1966. William Reidy, 1966. Elizabeth Wickenden, 1966.

John F. Kennedy Library, Boston. Wilbur Cohen in a recorded interview with Charles T. Morrissey, November 11, 1964. Washington, D.C. Wilbur Cohen in a second recorded interview with William W. Moss, May 24, 1971. Ann Arbor, Michigan.

Library of Congress, Washington, D.C. Clinton P. Anderson Papers. Box 224–237 contain the material relevant to Medicare.

Lyndon Baines Johnson Library, Austin, Texas. Executive Papers. Legislative files. Mike Manatos files. Henry Hall Wilson files. White House Central files Box 1–4. Wilbur Cohen in a recorded interview with David McComb, 1968–1969. Lister Hill in a recorded interview with T.H. Baker, February 1, 1971.

University of Oklahoma, Norman, Oklahoma. Robert Kerr Papers.

Index

194   Index

Social Security Act of 1965, 130
Social Security Administration, 36
Sorensen, Theodore, 19
Spector, Sidney, 19, 21
Spock, Benjamin, 108
State 65 programs, 93
Stuart, James, 13–14
Substantial compliance, 145
Swartz, Frederick, 12
Swire, Joe, 62

Taft, Robert, 35
Ten Point Program on Old Age, 26
Thompson, Clark, 111
Townsend Movement, 22
Truman, Harry, 3, 141–142

Ullman, Al, 130
United Auto Workers (UAW), 22
Utilization committees, 145

Vendor payments, 35–36
Vladeck, Bruce, 145–146

Wagner-Murray-Dingell bills, 3, 6, 25
Ward, Donovan T., 122, 135
Watts, John, 111
Ways and Means Committee House: hearings of, 14–15, 60–61, 100; and Kennedy Administration, 55; votes of, 90, 95, 108; Medicare, 131
White House Conference on Aging, 45–48
Wickenden, Elizabeth, 50, 107, 138
Wicker, Tom, 33, 43, 85
Wilson, Henry Hall, 104, 106, 111
Wolkstein, Irwin, 133, 139

About the Author

SHERI I. DAVID is Special Assistant Professor of History at Hofstra University.